BROOKLANDS COLLEGE LIBRA
CHURCH ROAD, ASHFORD, MIDDLESE
Tel: (01784) 248666

D1139609

This item must be returned on or before the ~~last date~~
entered below. Subject to certain conditions, the loan
period may be extended upon application to the Librarian

AUTHOR .... BULL

TITLE ...... Essential guide to careers in journalism

CLASSIFICATION NO. .... ~~290 0201~~ PB

ACCESSION NO. 100335

BROOKLANDS COLLEGE LIBRARY

100335

THE NCTJ ESSENTIAL GUIDE TO CAREERS IN JOURNALISM

Andy Bull

SAGE Publications
Los Angeles ▪ London ▪ New Delhi ▪ Singapore

ACKNOWLEDGEMENTS

I am enormously grateful to Joanne Butcher, chief executive of the National Council for the Training of Journalists, for entrusting me with this project, and to NCTJ staff, including Laura Garbas, Stephen Chambers, Jan Alder, Lyn Jones and others for their help, encouragement and advice.

Finally, thanks are due to Katy Fitzgerald and Beatrice Bull for tackling the mammoth task of compiling the employer listings in Section 4.

ABOUT THE AUTHOR

Andy Bull is the NCTJ's careers and qualifications consultant. He has been a journalist for 30 years, starting on the *Hastings Observer* and working on national newspapers, magazines and websites. He has been weekend editor and picture editor of *The Independent*, features editor at the *Mail on Sunday*, online editor of *The Times*, editorial director of AOL UK and deputy editor of the *Sunday Express*. He is now a freelance writer, editor, journalism tutor and author.

INTRODUCTION:
THE NEW JOURNALIST

Journalism is changing – and so are journalists. As someone considering entering the trade, or just taking your first steps in it, you are in an enviable position. Enviable, certainly, to those who have spent some time in the job and are struggling to keep up with the speed at which things are now moving. Enviable because you will take for granted the new realities of journalism. Realities such as that, where once journalists tended to consider themselves as newspaper journalists, or magazine journalists, or broadcasters, the new journalist is likely to work in several media instead of just one.

What has brought about this change? In a word, or rather two: the internet. Because of the internet, the way news is obtained is undergoing a transformation which is nothing short of revolutionary. Increasingly, the internet is the news medium of choice for many people – particularly young people.

Don't give up. I didn't even get an interview at the BBC after university. MARTHA KEARNEY, PRESENTER, WORLD AT ONE, BBC RADIO 4

Almost all publishers of newspapers and magazines, and broadcasters of radio and television programmes, now have a web version of their product. And those websites, increasingly, use elements from all the traditional media in order to tell their stories: text and still pictures from the newspapers and magazines, audio and moving images from broadcasting.

So, whereas the old journalist only learned the specific skills required to tell a story in one medium, the new journalist is likely to learn techniques from various media. And, crucially, whereas the traditional journalist is used to simply telling the reader, listener or viewer what the news is, the new journalist understands how the internet has changed all that. The new journalist understands that the audience wants to be part of a dialogue. It wants to take part by posting its comments on a news item, by casting a vote on a burning issue or by posting views on a bulletin board. (For more on this subject, turn to Section 1, Chapter 4.)

Don't [choose journalism] because you are 'good at English', or if you baulk at the thought of knocking on the door of bereaved families or asking awkward questions of people who don't want you there, or if you don't like standing out in the cold for long hours. DAVID WOODING, WHITEHALL EDITOR, THE SUN

But, amid all this change, one key thing remains constant, and that is the need for journalists to obtain the fundamental skills of good reporting. Without the ability to compile an accurate, balanced, unbiased report, no one can prosper as a journalist – whether they are trying to make their mark in newspapers, magazines, television, radio or on the internet.

This means that the training a journalist undertakes remains every bit as important as it ever was. Arguably, in the age of the amateur **citizen journalist** who is strong on opinion but weak on objectivity, it is even more important. And this is where the National Council for the Training of Journalists (NCTJ) comes in.

The NCTJ is second-to-none in its expertise in teaching journalism. Through its examinations, and the university and other courses that carry its accreditation, it equips would-be journalists to find their first job in the profession.

Be absolutely certain you really want to do it. If you are half-hearted about it, you will fail. NEIL DARBYSHIRE, SENIOR NEWS EXECUTIVE, DAILY MAIL

An NCTJ qualification shows that you have the skills you need to be an effective news reporter. NCTJ training equips you for whatever medium you want to work in – newspapers, magazines, TV and radio, and the internet. Many successful journalists, in all media, are thankful for their NCTJ training. And many others, who didn't have that advantage, recognise that it would have been a huge help if they had.

But what is journalism exactly?

If you are to consider becoming a journalist, you first need to know what journalism is, so let's go through the basics.

Maybe you find the words 'journalist' and 'journalism' off-putting. You may actually be thinking: 'I'd like to be reporting on Premiership football matches for Sky Sports', or editing *Marie Claire*, or interviewing movie stars for *Empire*, producing documentaries for Radio 4, reviewing bands for the *NME*, running a channel on the AOL web site, or writing about politics for *The Times*. All of these tasks are branches of journalism. 'Journalist' is a blanket term, encompassing reporters, photographers, editors and a wide range of people with particular skills and specialisms.

It's the most fun you can have with your clothes on. SIMON BUCKS, ASSOCIATE EDITOR, SKY NEWS

This book is designed to help you decide whether journalism is the career for you and, if you decide that it is, to work out which branch of the media might suit you best. The term 'media', by the way, is the plural of medium. Newspapers are one medium, magazines are another, and television and radio are two more. Online journalism makes up the fifth main medium.

This book explores how the media differ and what they have in common. Today, the traditional distinctions between media are blurring. Once, a media company tended to concentrate on one or two of the media – a newspaper or magazine group stuck to print, a TV network stuck to broadcasting. Today, most media companies operate in several media. Almost all have websites, and many are involved in the other electronic means of disseminating news and entertainment, such as to mobile phones or other electronic devices.

Becoming a bad journalist is easy, becoming a good one is very hard work indeed. BILL MANN, WEEK-END EDITOR, THE GUARDIAN

This has led people in the media to talk of convergence, by which they mean that the barriers between the various media are falling, and the age of multimedia journalism is dawning. Media companies are beginning to want their journalists to be comfortable working in several media. The journalist of the future may well be writing a text report for a print publication, adapting it for a website, doing a voice piece for radio and a piece-to-camera for television.

We will look in some detail at this many-skilled creature later in the book, but for now it is worth mentioning that this convergence is only in its early stages. Currently, the media are still, largely, distinct. Publishers are strong in one or two media, but not in all of them.

The current training and employment structure reflects these traditional divisions. It is still the case that most journalists start on either local newspapers or small specialist magazines, although we shall look at all the entry points to journalism across the rest of the media as well.

We will also look at what academic qualifications you will need, and whether you should take a formal training course before applying for jobs or seek out a position in which you will be trained while being paid to work.

I'm most proud of getting my 100 words per minute shorthand – the toughest exam I've ever done.
ANDREW PORTER, DEPUTY POLITICAL EDITOR, THE SUNDAY TIMES

There are many other questions that need to be answered. For instance: Do national newspapers take trainees, and if so where do they recruit them from? Do the BBC, ITN and Sky train people? Do local radio stations have schemes? What about websites? This book will answer these questions, and help you decide what training is right for you. It will explain in detail who runs training schemes, and what they are looking for in recruits. It will tell you where, if they don't train young journalists, they recruit newly-qualified people, and what qualifications they expect recruits to have.

It offers a comprehensive guide to good training courses – everything from fast-track courses lasting a few months to undergraduate and postgraduate degrees. Everything listed is accredited by the National Council for the Training of Journalists, which is your guarantee that the course you choose is a practical one that will equip you for the trade, and provide you with the best possible grounding for getting that all-important first job.

I trained on the job, and for many years I felt inferior to trained journalists. BETTY LONG, EDITOR, STAR SERIES OF FREE NEWSPAPERS, SUNDERLAND

The book also contains an extensive listing of the main newspapers, magazines, news agencies, TV and radio stations, and websites where you might gain work experience, seek a training place, or hope to find your first job. In addition we will run through the different jobs, and career paths, that will be opened up to you once you are a qualified and experienced journalist. In short, this book is designed to tell you everything you need to know about a career in journalism.

Dispelling the myths

If you have mentioned to anyone that you think journalism might be for you, you've probably been told by now how tough you will find it to get in, how much competition you will face just to get on a decent journalism course, and then how much demand there will be for the few jobs that are available to new recruits. You may worry that you don't have the temperament for journalism – that it is only for the hard-nosed and the thick-skinned. You may simply be completely confused about what branch of journalism is right for you.

It is certainly true that journalism is a competitive business – to get in to, to progress in and simply to do every day. But, that said, there are many myths about journalism, and we can start dispelling those myths right now.

> *My father was editor of the Evening Standard so newspapers were in the blood. Despite that I have never had any formal training and it shows since I have zero shorthand and have to rely on time-consuming tape recorders or PA.* PATRICK WINTOUR, CHIEF POLITICAL CORRESPONDENT, THE GUARDIAN

First, although you will need commitment, perseverance and doggedness to get your first job as a journalist, it can be done. Accurate figures are hard to find because no one compiles them but, each year, something like 1,500 new recruits are taken on by (mainly local) newspapers, perhaps 3,000 by (mainly **business-to-business**) magazines, and around 600 by broadcasters.* These recruits get their jobs because they show a number of things. They show that:

- they are really keen to become journalists;
- they have pursued this ambition by gaining relevant work experience;
- often, they have pursued their goal by getting the necessary training before applying for jobs; and that
- they are determined to succeed, whatever it takes.

By no means all of them are ruthless. Not all journalists are hard-bitten, just as not all London cabbies are right-wing blabbermouths who won't go south of the river. Because there are so many publications, and so many different jobs calling for different skills, there is a huge variance in journalists' character. In some journalistic environments, the pace is frenetic. If you are preparing

---

*Estimate from the Broadcast Journalism Training Council (hereafter BJTC).

half-hourly news bulletins on a TV or radio station, you will have to work fast. On a daily newspaper you work pretty fast too. On a weekly, or a monthly, the pace is slower.

Temperamentally, you may be better suited for either a fast or a slower pace, but one thing you can be sure of: however fast or slow the pace, however large or small the newspaper, magazine, website or whatever you are working on, it will have a staff and a system of working that fits what has to be done, and when.

> *Anyone considering a career in journalism should seriously examine the career paths, the financial rewards at each level, how they can combine it with other skills or interests to give themselves a secondary career option. They should also be absolutely honest with themselves about the person-ality strengths needed to do the job, do they have them?* SIMON PIZZEY, SENIOR PHOTOGRAPHER, GLOUCESTER CITIZEN

It is understandable if you have no idea which medium would suit you best. Should you try to join a local newspaper, or a magazine? Should you go for a national newspaper, a radio station, a sports news agency or work on a web-site? This book will help you decide, by showing you – with the help of quotes, comments, experiences and advice from over 100 journalists – what working in each medium entails, and the skills and abilities you will need to succeed. You will see their thoughts dotted throughout the text.

Given the differences between the five media, and all the very different journalists undertaking such a wide range of tasks within them, you may think that it is impossible to generalise about what a journalist is, and what they need to know to do their job. Well, let's have a go.

One thing all successful journalists have in common is a well-developed under-standing of who their reader, listener or viewer is, what they are interested in and how to talk to them. But if that is so, how did all those very different jour-nalists learn to talk to all those very different consumers of news, information and entertainment? That is where formal training comes in.

> *The one piece of advice I would give to anyone considering journalism is this: Do it!* – ANDREW SMITH, EDITOR IN CHIEF, NORTHEAST PRESS WEEKLIES

Who can become a journalist?

There are no longer any bars to entry to journalism that have anything to do with your sex, your race or anything other than whether you've got what it takes. That's not to say that ethnic minorities have not, historically, been generally under-represented in the media. This is changing. Many media organisations are striving to make their workforces more diverse. The Journalism Diversity Fund, of which the NCTJ is a supporter, has done much to encourage this. It offers bursaries to a number of student journalists from the ethnic minorities each year. You can find out more at www.journalismdiversityfund.co.uk

The one thing I wish someone had told me when I was younger was your degree does not need to be linked to journalism. The people I work with have studied everything from Chinese and Economics to English. If I could turn back time I would do my degree in something completely unrelated, and I don't think it would change where I'm working now. ASTRA MORTON, REPORTER, NORTH SOMERSET TIMES

Where once journalism was male-dominated, today many women are making successful careers in it, are in senior positions and a significant number are editors. On some publications, and in some broadcast newsrooms, women are now in the majority. Those who have rights under disability discrimination legislation will also find employers receptive to their applications.

Those who appoint and manage journalists generally realise that a diverse workforce is a more effective workforce.

Why the right training is so important

Some journalists pick up their skills along the way. They learn on the job. But these days most journalists undergo some kind of formal training. They may have done so as undergraduates or postgraduates on a full-time course, or as trainees on **block release** at a college. They may have studied via **distance learning,** doing another job at the same time.

Not everyone who has undergone formal training is brilliant at their job, and not everyone who picked things up as they went along is a bad journalist. But what training does is give able people a short-cut. It saves them time by teaching them the basics of journalism quickly, accurately and effectively. It means they don't need to learn by trial and error. They can get it right first time. It also demonstrates to a potential employer that you are serious about becoming a journalist – serious enough to have done all you can to equip yourself for the job.

An NCTJ qualification equips you with the skills you need to be an effective news reporter. It gives you a solid grounding in shorthand, law and how government works, plus enabling you to build up a substantial portfolio of work that shows you can really do the job. With an NCTJ certificate on your CV, a prospective employer knows you have grasped the basics.

The courses at universities and other institutions that the NCTJ accredits are all highly practical. It is vital, if you want to ensure that you do not waste your time studying a course that does not give you the skills you will need to get a job, to make sure your course is accredited.

> *Behind my mother's back, [aged 16] I sent a speculative letter to the editor-in-chief of the local newspaper group, talked myself into an interview and got a job. She was furious!* MARY-ANN BLOOM-FIELD, EDITOR, MID-DEVON GAZETTE SERIES

There are many courses with 'media' or 'media studies' in their titles that are not suitable if you wish to become a journalist, and are not accredited by the NCTJ. Such courses may do a very good job at teaching you the history of the media, they may be hugely illuminating if you wish to study the sociology of mass communications or the political implications of press ownership by multinationals, but they won't teach you how to write a news story. Very few, if any, editors will be impressed by an applicant who is a media studies graduate. By all means read media studies if it interests you, but don't expect this to help you get a job as a journalist, any more than a degree in hotel management would.

One key question for you to consider when thinking about training is whether to study journalism at undergraduate or postgraduate level. That really is up to you. It depends in part on the age at which you become convinced that journalism is for you. If you know at 16 to 18, great, you are probably ready to choose an undergraduate course. If you aren't sure, then it's best to get a good, academic first degree in another subject. Even if you are certain, pre-university, that journalism is for you, there is no harm in reading something else. For one thing, having an academic specialism, say, in economics or politics, may help when you become a journalist. For another, you'll have three years during which you can pursue journalism as a hobby, just to make sure you like it.

A postgraduate journalism qualification can complement a first degree.

You may decide that you don't want to study journalism in an academic environment at all. If so, that is not a problem. You can take what is known as a pre-entry qualification – a fast-track course – and look for your first job. You may even be lucky enough to find an employer who will take you on without any journalistic qualification – on the strength of your practical experience and aptitude – and pay you and train you at the same time.

We will examine the different types of training available in more detail in the following chapters.

As you will see, the media are dealt with individually. If TV appeals to you more than newspapers, you are likely to go straight to that chapter. There is nothing wrong with that, but don't dismiss newspapers or magazines out of hand. There are sound reasons for making your start in one of those media, so do at least take a look at those chapters. After all, if you don't, you may not find out what you are missing until it is too late.

Section 1

THE MEDIA

1

NEWSPAPERS

Are newspapers for you?

The chances are, you don't read your local newspaper. Young people tend not to. It's usually only once you have a house or flat, pay Council Tax, send your kids to local schools and have a vested interest in what goes on in your area that the information local papers contain is of value to you.

If you don't read a local paper, you may not think immediately of the provincial press as being a good place to start in journalism. In fact, it is – for two very good reasons.

For one thing, a local paper offers an excellent training ground. While local news is often of less than life-or-death importance, a local paper is a good place to cut your teeth, and every big story happens somewhere, so there will be major events on your horizon at least occasionally. There is a strong culture of training cub (trainee) reporters on local rags, and trainees often make an extremely important contribution to the newspaper. There is time to teach you – rather than leave you to learn simply by trial and error – and you can make your mistakes in an environment that will be supportive of you as you learn the ropes.

> *If you seriously want a job on a paper, do some basic research before writing. Every week we receive letters from highly-qualified graduates asking for jobs addressed to 'Dear Sir'. Such letters go in the bin. You must be willing to go the extra mile – otherwise don't bother.* FERGUS SHANAHAN, DEPUTY EDITOR, THE SUN

For another thing, there are a lot of local papers – around 1,300 paid-for and free titles in the UK – and most of them have one, two or sometimes more trainees. Best estimates are that there are between 3,000 and 4,000 newspaper trainees. But unless you see the point of local newspapers, and can appreciate the opportunity they offer young journalists, they are not for you.

What about national newspapers? Some people are lucky enough to win a traineeship on a national newspaper, but there are probably no more than a couple of dozen in such positions at any one time, and they will probably have completed a postgraduate course in journalism.

If you are not an avid reader of newspapers, if you can't really see the point of them when you can get news from the TV, radio, online and on your mobile phone, then national newspapers are not for you either. But if you love newspapers, miss them when you are on holiday abroad, can't wait to read your favourite – or most hated – columnists, to enjoy the buzz of debate about big issues and gossip about the utterly trivial but irresistible ones, then a career in national newspapers could be for you.

I joined the FT's graduate training scheme, applying through the careers centre at university. But before that I had worked during university holidays on the Peterborough [diary] column of the Daily Telegraph and had had various freelance articles accepted for publication elsewhere. ANDREW HILL, COMMENT AND ANALYSIS EDITOR, FINANCIAL TIMES

And, while newspapers face great and increasing competition from other media, they are still hugely important. British people are among the most avid newspaper readers in the world. No less than 83.6 per cent of all British adults (40 million people) read a regional newspaper, and 69.6 per cent read a national newspaper (*Source:* the Newspaper Society). Many major stories that are picked up by the other media originate in newspapers and, increasingly, media companies use newspapers as the information-creating machine that drives websites and other electronic media. So it is wrong to think of newspapers as an old-fashioned medium that is in decline. Newspapers are undergoing a period of transition, but they are still central to journalism, and will remain so.

What do newspaper journalists do?

The term 'newspaper journalist' is a generic one covering reporters, sub-editors, editors, and specialist writers on education, politics, sport, features, finance and a good deal more. During training, the emphasis is on gaining the basic ability to report news – a skill that underlies almost everything else journalists do, and will be of huge value in whatever specialisms they acquire. During their career, newspaper journalists may cover a wide range of specialisms (see Section 2 for more on this).

Newspaper journalists work on a range of titles, from free or paid-for local weekly papers to daily local or regional titles and national or international ones. The jobs that newspaper journalists do can be split broadly into two categories: information gathering, or the input phase; and information processing, the output phase.

The input phase involves researching and writing a news story or feature and delivering the copy to a deadline. This process will involve developing contacts who will give you the information you need, conducting interviews, taking shorthand notes, attending a wide range of events from court cases and council meetings to sports matches, conducting research and writing copy.

The output phase involves ensuring the copy is fit to print. It must be free of errors, from basic spelling and grammar to legal pitfalls that could lead to a newspaper being sued. The copy must be laid out on a page, and cut to fit the allotted space. Headlines must be written.

> *I was never given basic training as a reporter. I missed that in later years. If I could have done formal training such as NCTJ, I would have jumped at the chance.* BEVERLEY GLICK, PAGE EDITOR, SUNDAY EXPRESS

Training concentrates on the input side of things, although trainees with an aptitude for output tasks may find they are encouraged to pursue them – it can be hard to find staff who are prepared to undertake sub-editing, when reporting is seen as much more glamorous. In recognition of this, and the fact that sub-editing provides a less overcrowded way in to journalism, NCTJ sub-editing qualifications are also available.

Do you have what it takes?

This is what employers say they are looking for in trainees:

- an interest in current affairs at all levels;
- sound news judgement;
- a lively interest in people, places and events;
- an ability to write in a style which is easy to understand;
- good spelling, grammar and punctuation;
- an understanding of the audience;

- a willingness to accept irregular hours;
- an ability to work under pressure to meet deadlines; and
- determination and persistence.

On local newspapers, they would add to this list an appreciation of the part a local newspaper plays in the community

Sixteen weeks [on the postgraduate course at Cardiff] was perfect – long enough to really learn the basics and short enough not to get bored with play acting. SUE RYAN, FORMER MANAGING EDITOR, DAILY TELEGRAPH

Trinity Mirror, one of the leading British newspaper groups, has a handy online quiz for would-be applicants. It's at http://www.trinitymirror.com/careers/journalists/ and asks you if you have experience of working on newspapers and gives you tests in spelling, grammar, punctuation and general knowledge. There is also a tricky question about which of three named newspapers is not owned by Trinity Mirror, which is a timely reminder that you must have done your homework about the owners of the newspaper you are applying to if you are to have any hope of getting the job. On completion, the quiz will tell you whether you have what it takes to become a journalist and, if you do, take you to an application form.

I first thought of becoming a journalist aged eight. We were council house readers of the Express and it went from there. NEIL WALLIS, DEPUTY EDITOR, NEWS OF THE WORLD

How do you get a job on a newspaper?

Trainees come in by a variety of routes. Some are lucky enough to be hired by regional or local newspapers and carry out their basic training and gain their Preliminary Certificate under the terms of a training contract. This is known as **direct entry**. However, most trainees get jobs after attending full-time vocational training courses for post-A level students or graduates. This route is known as **pre-entry**. Courses are held at universities and colleges accredited by the National Council for the Training of Journalists (NCTJ). Some courses are for graduates only. All NCTJ-accredited courses, whether at undergraduate or postgraduate level, lead to an NCTJ-approved qualification.

Regional newspaper groups, and individual local papers, take on trainees with various academic backgrounds. Some will be school leavers with A levels; others will have achieved a pre-entry qualification, or have graduated with a journalism degree. Some will have completed a postgraduate course in journalism. Others will be graduates whose degrees are not in journalism and who will be taken on as direct-entry trainees. They will undergo a combination of formal training, leading to examinations and on-the-job experience. Most national newspapers take on **postgraduates**, but often just one, two or three a year.

> *The best thing about my training was working with a group of similar-minded trainees. On the Tavistock Times there were four of us, plus the editor and one senior journalist, so we had the whole paper pretty much to ourselves.* SARAH BOSELEY, HEALTH EDITOR, THE GUARDIAN

Who takes trainees?

To give a flavour of the range of training opportunities available, here are some of the key newspaper groups, both national and regional, that take on trainees. You can find a full list of all potential employers in Section 4. This is also a good section to refer to if you are looking for work experience. Full details of courses mentioned can be found in Section 3.

Archant

Archant has around 40 paid-for weeklies and 50 free newspapers in Scotland, East Anglia and the South West and South East of England, and has around 120 websites to support its publications. Papers in the group take on trainees and offer work experience placements. You should apply to the editor of the title you are interested in.

Daily Express

The Express Newspapers Graduate Trainee scheme lasts two years. Trainees often have a journalistic or media-based degree as well as a postgraduate diploma in newspaper journalism. They spend three-month periods in various departments, and are either offered a full-time position or released. They say: 'We have many graduates now on full-time staff who have managed to establish reputations throughout the national newspaper industry.'

Daily Mail

Alex Bannister, managing editor, says:

> We have a trainee scheme run jointly with the Press Association for sub-editors. We take on average six people a year. It has been running four years, and successful candidates have normally completed a pre-entry course. Most end up with a job on the *Daily Mail*, though it is not guaranteed. The course lasts one year, though the majority of that is work experience at PA.'

Financial Times

Dan Bogler, managing editor, says:

> We take two or three trainees a year. They are all graduates, and usually have a degree or postgraduate qualification in journalism. The applicants are very international; one was previously an intern on the *Far Eastern Economic Review*, another edited her school newspaper at Berkeley. We look for a desire to work internationally, intellectual capacity, demonstration of an interest in journalism and experience, such as editing or writing for a school newspaper.
>
> We send them on a three-month course that Reuters has designed for us and then they will get several six-month placements, one of which will be abroad. They will get experience in print and on the web and across the newspaper.
>
> Trainees are a brilliant source for us. Traineeships last 18 months to two years but realistically by 18 months they have been snaffled and have a job. I can think of only one who didn't go on to a job with us.

The Guardian

The *Guardian* has a scheme that runs for one year. Managing editor, Chris Elliott, says:

> We have two places which are primarily aimed at increasing diversity. These last for a year. As the primary aim is diversity, candidates should have a degree, but need not have either a pre-entry or postgraduate qualification. We also look for energy, commitment, enthusiasm and a demonstrable ability to write good English. The traineeship scheme has only been running a couple of years and we have taken no one on permanent staff yet.
>
> We also have a work experience scheme specifically designed to take on 12 members of ethnic minorities for two-week placements each year.

The Independent

Managing editor, Charlie Burgess, says:

> We occasionally hire trainees, but we don't have a formal scheme. We have two at present, but didn't take on any this year. They are graduates; one a postgrad, the other we took on as an editorial assistant.

We look for people who are bright, have the ability to write, have self-belief and are ambitious. They will get a six months trial first and then we'll see how they do. They occasionally get permanent jobs with us.

Johnston Press

Johnston Press publishes *The Scotsman* and *Scotland on Sunday*, and local newspapers in 200 markets across the country.

David Rowell, group editorial development executive, said:

You should apply to the editor of the local paper you are interested in. We favour those from an area, partly because it means they already have local knowledge, also because it is our way of providing employment in that community.

We recruit mainly those who have taken the NCTJ pre-entry course. While they are with us they work towards the NCTJ's National Certificate Examination (NCE), and we have a two-year programme with internal training to support them.

We are the biggest employer of trainee journalists in the provincial press. I wouldn't like to give a total, but there are one or two trainees on each of our titles and each year 40 per cent of those taking the NCE are from our group. We have no preference for either school leavers or graduates; we have a diverse employment policy.

The News of the World

The *News of the World* runs a two-year scholarship, open to one graduate a year and run in conjunction with the Journalism Centre at Harlow College. They say they expect candidates to be able to demonstrate a passion for the *News of the World*.

The attribute a journalist most needs is a hunger to tell wonderful new human stories in an appealing way. ANDREW PEARSON, EDITOR, LLANELLI STAR

Training includes completing Harlow's 19-week postgraduate course, and working at the *News of the World* in a wide range of departments, from sport to politics to showbiz. Unusually, this course also takes in working in non-journalistic departments: circulation, marketing, production and advertising. Trainees also work on a sister paper in either Australia or the United States.

Newsquest

Newsquest has 300 titles, with 18 regional dailies. It also has 90 websites to support its titles.

Margaret Strayton, group editorial manager, says:

We don't have an annual quota, we take trainees as we require them from all walks of life and from all cultural backgrounds. At any given time we can have up to 100 trainee reporters out of 1,300 journalists employed by the company. We take them at various stages from raw trainees to those with pre-entry qualifications.

Applications are dealt with paper by paper, but the training is controlled centrally, e.g. 'raw' trainees [direct entrants] train at Darlington College, and all trainees attend workshops and pre-NCE refresher courses, all paid for by Newsquest and all conducted by trainers from Darlington College.

We are looking for someone who is interested in people and events, who can get people to talk to them. They in turn have to be good listeners, and hear the whole story, not just the bits they want to hear. Everything else they can learn, even spelling!

When we take someone on and train them we hope they will remain with us, most of our trainees do.

Northcliffe

Northcliffe Newspapers owns 18 daily titles, 29 paid-for weeklies and 62 free titles. Colin Davison, group editorial director, says:

Most titles in the group take on a couple of trainees a year. There is no central policy on recruitment and individual editors decide.

Among the factors in hiring someone are local knowledge and having a pre-entry qualification from the NCTJ. Most trainees are graduates. There are a few direct entrants who come straight from school, but they will be exceptional people who have impressed an editor by being extremely adept at picking up a story.

I'd recommend you start on a local paper, and remember – you can't run before you can walk. ANDY HOBAN, NIGHT EDITOR, SUNDAY EXPRESS

The Sun

Like the *Daily Mail*, *The Sun* runs a training scheme for sub-editors that is administered by the Press Association. Competition is fierce – 1,000 applicants for six places, on average. Following four weeks training at the PA, successful candidates spend several months on regional newspapers before moving to the subs' desk at *The Sun*. The paper does also take trainee reporters, but not regularly, and advertises posts in *UK Press Gazette*.

Trinity Mirror

Trinity Mirror has five national newspapers and around 240 regional ones. Its national newspapers are the *Daily Mirror* and *Sunday Mirror*, the *People* and, in Scotland, the *Daily Record* and *Sunday Mail*.

You can apply for a traineeship with Mirror Group Newspapers (MGN) or Trinity Mirror. The key difference is that, if accepted by MGN, you are attached to a national newspaper for the practical part of your training, if to Trinity Mirror, to a regional one. Either way, you will normally do a 16-week foundation course in the Press Association's training facility at Newcastle, followed by on-the-job training at either a national or regional newspaper, which takes three years.

The worst thing that happened during my training was coming off the high of my first splash [front page lead story] to do the chemists' rota – and making a hash of it. CHARLES HYMAS, NEWS EDITOR, THE SUNDAY TIMES

What they want from you

A keen, hard-working, flexible, inquisitive, inexpensive dogsbody.

On a provincial paper, they'll send you to all the places bread-and-butter stories are found – courts, councils, talent contests and flower shows. They may give you a geographic patch to cover.

On a national, you'll do plenty of graveyard shifts – Sundays, lates and earlies. You'll be there to man the phones and to react should a crisis happen. It can. Both the Asian Tsunami and the IRA's Brighton bomb, which almost killed the then prime minister Margaret Thatcher and her Cabinet, broke when news desks were manned by skeleton staffs.

What qualifications will I need?

Most journalists have at least five GCSEs (grades A–C), including English, and two A levels or vocational A levels. Over 70 per cent have a degree – not necessarily in journalism. To get on a degree course you need at least two A levels or vocational A levels and five GCSEs (grades A–C), or equivalent qualifications. GCSE English is essential.

Most newspapers in the UK recognise qualifications awarded, and courses accredited, by the NCTJ.

I chose to go to my local newspaper, the Surrey Advertiser, on work experience after taking my O levels and I joined as a trainee after taking my A levels. MARY GAHAN, NEWS EDITOR, BBC WORLD SERVICE

What will I have to study?

There is a wide range of different types of course you can study. Here is a brief run-down:

- BA (Hons) degree. A course which offers the opportunity to gain the NCTJ quali-fication while studying for a degree at university.
- Foundation degree. A two-year course of study during which time students sit their NCTJ exams. The option of topping up the foundation degree with an additional year of study to gain a BA is sometimes available.
- One-year postgraduate qualification. Usually an MA or postgraduate diploma, this type of course would suit a graduate who is looking to gain the NCTJ qualification.
- Fast-track. Ideal for those who want to study intensively for 18–20 weeks to gain the NCTJ pre-entry qualification.
- Pre-entry academic year. Offered through further education centres, a one-year course to study for the NCTJ pre-entry qualification.
- Two-year HND. An opportunity to gain the NCTJ pre-entry qualification while study-ing for a Higher National Diploma.

For a comprehensive list of the courses available, go to Section 3 or to the NCTJ website at www.nctj.com.

NCTJ-accredited reporting courses cover shorthand, and those aspects of law, public affairs and newspaper journalism necessary to enable a journalist to perform competently by the end of the training period. As well as demon-strating competence in these and other practical areas, trainees are expected to achieve 100 words per minute in Teeline shorthand.

The NCTJ also awards sub-editing qualifications, which cover everything on the reporter syllabus, except shorthand.

Your ultimate aim is the NCTJ's National Certificate Examination (NCE), the qualification most editors in Britain agree is the best proof a journalist has been properly trained. To get it, you have to:

- have the minimum academic qualifications (see above);
- pass the NCTJ Preliminary Certificate in journalism, law and public affairs;
- pass an NCTJ shorthand examination at a speed of at least 100 words per minute;
- do at least 18 months' paid work as a trainee journalist on a newspaper;
- compile an NCTJ portfolio of story cuttings (examples of things you have written during your training on a newspaper); and
- pass the final NCTJ National Certificate Examination (NCE).

The full programme normally takes about two years, which includes between six and nine months studying for the preliminary exams at a university, college or by distance learning, and 18 months working on a newspaper or other publication. You can do the college course first and then get a job, or find yourself a job first and do your studying while already employed.

[I'm most proud of] naming the first National Lottery jackpot winner. MIKE GLOVER, EDITOR/PUBLISHER, WESTMORELAND GAZETTE

Postgraduate fast-track courses lasting between 18 and 20 weeks are available at some colleges.

What else will I learn as a trainee?

Your on-the-job training will give you enormous practical experience, and enable you to apply what you learn at college. You will learn:

- what news is;
- to recognise the news that your audience is interested in;
- to write concise, bright, accurate copy to a tight deadline;
- to find stories, to research stories comprehensively, to interview;
- to develop a thick skin and to recognise when sensitivity is called for;
- the vital importance of a contacts book; and
- to trawl competitors and other media for stories you can develop for your own publication.

What will I earn?

Pay for local newspaper trainees generally falls in the range £12,000–£15,000, rising by around £3,000 once qualified. On national newspapers, trainees' pay is between £17,000 and £20,000.

How to improve your chances of getting a job

You should be able to demonstrate that you have a real interest in newspapers, and that you have taken every opportunity to learn about them and work on them. Editing or contributing to school or university magazines is a good start and having work-experience placements is another. And if you can show cuttings of stories you got into the paper – ideally with **by-lines** – so much the better.

> You will need a critical and analytical mind, a reverence for the English language, a strong sense of fairness and an overriding desire to   discover the bare facts of every story. NEIL DARBYSHIRE, SENIOR NEWS EXECUTIVE, DAILY MAIL

Make sure that you know about the newspaper to which you are applying for a traineeship. It is no use sending copies of a generic application letter. If you haven't done your homework, and can't demonstrate that you have taken the trouble to find out about the paper, why should an editor bother with you?

If you have any local connections, outline them. Local knowledge and connections will make you more useful more swiftly.

> The best thing about my training was being dumped in Great Yarmouth, where I had never been before, and told to come back with a story. PETER DARLING, JOURNALISM LECTURER

Life as a trainee

Whether you start on a weekly free-sheet or paid-for title, an evening paper or a national, you will be doing the basics. First and foremost, you'll be learning how to be a news reporter.

On a local paper you might start the day at the magistrates' court. On an evening newspaper you will have to file fast – either by computer or by telephone to a **copytaker**. On a weekly, you will have a little more time, and may write up the stories at your desk over lunch. You might spend the afternoon with a mix of golden weddings, retirements, and a vox pop in the high street and finish the day at a council committee meeting.

I was transferred to the Ripley and Heanor News, which incidentally was the newspaper I had been brought up with. My immediate local knowledge allowed me to progress very quickly. I was writing about people I knew, schools I had attended and companies I had dealt with. STEPHEN SINFIELD, REPORTER, RIPLEY AND HEANOR NEWS

In the first few weeks you may shadow a more experienced reporter, writing up your own version of the stories you cover alongside him or her, and then comparing your version with what the reporter has written.

Then there are the unexpected events, from a house fire to a fatal car crash. Sooner or later you will have to go on a 'death knock', where you are called upon to visit the home of someone who has died to talk to their spouse or family.

You may be given a patch to cover. This is great training; it gets you into the habit of bringing in your own stories; forces you to meet and talk to a wide range of people, and underlines the importance of contacts.

Some reporters make a note of everyone they ever speak to in a **contacts book**, cross-indexing their names with the roads on which they live, so that when anything happens in an area, they have someone they know whom they can call.

There will also be less routine stories. News happens in even the quietest places.

You need integrity, confidence, persistence, a belief in truth and the right to know. Moral courage. Tireless energy and a strong stomach. PETER DARLING, JOURNALISM LECTURER

If you are lucky enough to be a trainee on a national newspaper, your training may take you into various specialisms after you have had a good solid stint on news. While on news, you are likely to do your share of late and early shifts, bank holidays and Sundays. The advantage of these is that, if something major does break, you stand a good chance of covering it. Reputations can begin to be made on such occasions.

You may have periods on city and business, sport, features or the diary, depending on your interests and aptitudes. You may be able to shadow one or more specialists for a time. This can give you an insight into which specialism you might like to pursue later. You could get a chance to sample life as, for example, a political, science or health correspondent.

It's less usual to work on the subs' desk – most trainees are keen to write as much as they can, at least for the time being – but if you are interested, subbing can also be an option.

I am proud of – occasionally – managing to help downtrodden victims of injustice. PETER DARLING, JOURNALISM LECTURER

Whatever you do, you'll be learning about deadlines and how to handle them. You'll be learning to work as part of a team, how to cope when you find yourself part of a press pack, all chasing the same story and trying to do their rivals down. You'll learn about door-stepping, where you wait ages for someone to come home and then (often) get the door slammed unceremoniously in your face. You'll learn how tact and persistence can open doors that others have failed to unlock.

And, one day, you'll get your first story to carry an 'exclusive' tag. And when that happens, you'll know you are on your way.

DAY IN THE LIFE

Young journalist on a local newspaper

Andy Crick, chief reporter at the *Slough and Windsor Observer*, Berkshire

The one thing about a career in journalism is there is no such thing as a typical day. Every day is different. As well as my devotion to current affairs, I was also drawn into working in newspapers because I did not want to get stuck in a monotonous nine to five where every new day was like the previous one.

At my newspaper we are encouraged to go out-and-about as much as possible because the news is not happening in your office. From arriving shortly before 9am every morning I could be sent to follow a murder case at Case Crown Court, or I could be interviewing big names from the worlds of politics, entertainment or sport, or I could be throwing myself off a crane as part of a charity bungee jump or taking a new BMW for a test drive.

I have had the chance to do all these in the last two years. Yes, I admit there are the fair share of late-night council meetings and frantic moments before deadlines, but for the majority of the time I am kept on my toes and never know what my next day will entail. No one is in it for the long hours and the low pay; we are in it because we love it.

I did a joint-honours degree in History and Media Studies at the University of the West of England, Bristol, then started a four-month fast-track NCTJ

(Continued)

course at Lambeth College, London. I got a job as a junior at the *Slough and Windsor Observer* and have been here ever since.

I have now passed three-quarters of my NCE. These days everyone is going to uni so I would advise everyone to do it as much for academic reasons as for the life experience. Do not worry though about studying journalism at degree level. If you can get on an NCTJ-accredited course, go for it. Like me, you can always pick up the shorthand and media law doing a short course at a later date.

Do get as much experience as you can along the way. Do local papers, magazines, and nationals if you can. It will probably be unpaid but it will give you an insight into what journalism is like, give you cuttings to keep and working for nothing shows you are keen. I was always told getting your first job is the hardest thing. So do not give up, don't get worried if you get knocked back because it's competitive out there.

 **DAY IN THE LIFE**

Young journalist on a national newspaper

Oliver Duff, *The Independent*

I was lucky: as a student journalist I met *The Independent*'s editor-in-chief, Simon Kelner, at a newspaper debate, and he offered me work experience. Once in the office, enthusiastic tea-making and factbox-writing led to a full-time job as an editorial assistant. It was an unglamorous role, sitting on the news desk with four busy editors, ordering stationery, fixing reporters' rotas, and taking phone calls from journalists, readers and Diana conspiracy theorists. But, importantly, it gave me the chance to build up a portfolio during quiet moments, writing articles on everything from Holocaust deniers and rollercoasters to tube bombings and celebrity coke fiends. After working hard for 18 months I somehow persuaded the editor to give me a reporting contract.

A typical day begins in the office about 10am and ends somewhere between 7 and 8.30pm. Any story ideas, gleaned from contacts or future events diaries, have been emailed to the news editor the night before so he can present them in his morning conference with senior executives and get the thumbs-up or thumbs-down. Once the page-by-page news list is drawn up, by about 12.30pm, the reporters know how many words they should write, on what, by when.

Ideas often get passed down from higher up the editorial ladder, which you then have to flesh out and make work, searching for the human detail that turns the mundane into the unusual.

An afternoon editorial conference (3.30pm), updating the team on the day's events, can kibosh well-prepared plans. But by then, with early deadlines just two hours away, there is little time to reflect on what has slipped off the agenda. Just write! The first edition goes to press at 8.30pm. Most of the reporters have left the office long ago, leaving the crucial final stages to production.

But work is frequently untypical, involving unpredictable assignments and hours. I work some night shifts, where you watch the wires and wait for action. When it arrives, you have 90 minutes to construct 500 knowledgeable-sounding words on Himalayan politics or the latest killing in Iraq.

Even working daytimes, you frequently don't have time to hang up your jacket before being despatched to some corner of the capital or country, later filing your story through a long-distance call. One recent example was a group effort to find a flag-wielding fan from each World Cup country – all within five hours. It was tough, it was fun, and it made the front page the following morning.

If you think this might be for you...

If it sounds good so far, you can find out more about NCTJ qualifications at www.nctj.com.

Contact details:
NCTJ Training Limited,
The New Granary,
Station Road,
Newport,
Saffron Walden,
Essex CB11 3PL
01799 544014
Fax: 01799 544015
info@nctj.com

2
MAGAZINES

Are magazines for you?

Take a look along the racks in a larger newsagent and you'll see an enormous range of magazines for sale. In a really big store there are probably a couple of hundred titles, covering every subject you can think of, and some you probably can't. In fact, even such as array is just the tip of the iceberg. There are 9,000-odd magazines published in the UK, and most of them never see the inside of a WH Smith or a Borders. Because, while there are certainly plenty of what are called **consumer magazines** – magazines published for the general public and sold in newsagents – there are far more **trade magazines** and business and specialist consumer titles which are designed for specific, narrowly-defined audiences. These are the magazine world's equivalent to the local newspaper, and are distributed in various ways.

> *My first job was on the New Statesman. They were seeking a single graduate from university and I was the lucky one. It was a superb education working with James Fenton, Julian Barnes, Martin Amis, Clare Tomalin, Christopher Hitchens and the incomparable Anthony Howard. He was kind enough to let me run a page of university-based writing so I became a small talent spotter of my own.* PATRICK WINTOUR, CHIEF POLITICAL CORRESPONDENT, THE GUARDIAN

You don't see them in WH Smith because some are only available via subscription – a reader buys the magazine for a year at a time, paid in advance. Others will be what are called controlled circulation magazines that are sent free to the members of a particular profession, such as general practitioners, and are financed by advertising. Others may go to the members of a professional body or other organisation as a benefit of membership, and are paid for through subscription to that body.

So, the magazine industry is a far larger and more complex and diverse than most people realise. That's one reason why it can be a good place for starting your career as a journalist.

However, just having a general interest in working on magazines won't be enough to convince an editor that you should be employed on theirs. You need to know what magazine you want to work on, why you want to work on it, and how you will be an asset to the editorial team.

> *It's a buyer's market, so get as much high-quality work experience as you can, to help you stand out from the crowd.* NEIL BENSON, EDITORIAL DIRECTOR, TRINITY MIRROR

Being a magazine journalist is, in many ways, very like being a newspaper journalist, and much of what was covered in Chapter 1 is relevant here. NCTJ-accredited training covers many of the same skills, and will have at its heart learning to be a good news reporter. Where working on a magazine differs from a newspaper is that, while journalists on newspapers are often generalists – they cover all sorts of subjects – magazine journalists tend to specialise, because very often their magazine covers a narrowly-defined subject area, but in great depth.

This means that, in looking for a magazine to get work experience on, or win a job on, you should be guided by your interests, experience and academic qualifications. Some specialist magazines may want you to have a particular degree, such as in engineering, science or computing, which gives you expertise in the area the magazine covers. Others may be impressed by, for example, your encyclopedic knowledge of cats, soap operas, computer software or jet-skiing.

In some cases, young journalists are hired as much for their specialist knowledge as for their experience of, or aptitude for, journalism. Yet it's foolhardy to think you can make it as a magazine journalist on the strength of your specialist knowledge alone. As the Association of British Science Writers says in its advice to science graduates with an interest in writing:

> Science journalism is just journalism with a particularly interesting inclination. If you are keen to become a science journalist, then you would do well to cast your net wide and consult other people who offer good advice on how to become a journalist.

That advice goes for any ambition to write in a particular niche. If your interest in, and knowledge of, a particular subject are not matched by a burning desire to learn to become a first-rate news reporter, then magazine journalism is not for you, however much you may know about cars, practical physics, wedding planning or anything else.

What do magazine journalists do?

Just as with newspapers, the term 'magazine journalist' is a generic one covering a wide range of functions. What all magazine journalists have in common is that they will be researching, writing, sub-editing and editing material news stories and feature articles – that is designed to cater for the magazine's reader profile. The jobs that magazine journalists do can be split broadly into two categories: information gathering, or the input phase; and information processing, or the output phase.

The input phase involves researching and writing a news story or feature and delivering the copy to a deadline. This process will involve developing contacts who will give you the information you need, conducting interviews, taking shorthand notes, attending a wide range of events, conducting research and writing copy.

> My first job in journalism was staff writer on Sounds *[a music magazine]* in 1980. I got it because I had an incredibly supportive editor who fought for me, a mere secretary, to be given an editorial job. It took a while to convince the management, and I had to take a pay cut to start as a trainee journalist, on 75 per cent of the basic minimum. BEVERLEY GLICK, PAGE EDITOR, SUNDAY EXPRESS

The output phase involves ensuring the copy is fit to print. It must be free of errors, from basic spelling and grammar to legal pitfalls that could lead to a magazine being sued. The copy must be laid out on a page, and cut to fit the allotted space. Headlines must be written.

Whereas newspapers tend to cover everything important that happens for a diverse group of people living in a particular area – from a village to a country – the readership of magazines is often defined by a core common interest or need for information of a particular type. Magazines can be divided into four broad categories: business (e.g. *Management Today*), professional (e.g. *Professional Photographer*), consumer (e.g. *Vogue*), and specialist consumer (e.g. *Your Cat*).

One other difference for magazine journalists is that they tend to have longer deadlines than on newspapers. That means they do not have to work as fast, although companion websites mean that many magazines now put up news items daily, or several times a day, while the print publication may only appear weekly or monthly. And whereas newspapers tend to take quick bites at a story, magazines may need to offer very detailed, in-depth coverage that its audience can't get in more general-interest publications.

On a large magazine with a substantial staff, there will be a good deal of specialisation among journalists; on a smaller title each journalist will have to cover more roles. At the extreme, there are one-man or one-woman titles where the editor does absolutely everything, from coming up with the ideas, writing the copy, taking or sourcing the photographs, designing the pages, and sub-editing and proof-reading the copy.

The quality a journalist most needs is accuracy, and the best thing about the job is variety. JULIE MCCLAY, EDITOR, *BELFAST NEWS*

Do you have what it takes?

This is what employers say they are looking for in trainees:

- a passion for magazines backed up by basic skills so you will be useful from day one;
- a keen interest in the subject matter of the magazine;
- an ability to write in a style that is easy to understand;
- good spelling, grammar and punctuation;
- an ability to work under pressure to meet deadlines;
- determination, persistence and resilience;
- a proactive approach to finding things out; and
- strong interpersonal skills.

How do you get a job on a magazine?

Around 70 per cent of journalists on magazines are graduates, and many will have undertaken postgraduate pre-entry courses approved by the National Council for the Training of Journalists (NCTJ). Having completed such a course, it is often possible for young journalists to obtain jobs that do not involve any further training. This differs from the regional newspaper industry, where the training process often involves an initial period of training at a university or commercial training establishment, followed by on-the-job training of 18 months to two years on a newspaper and a final examination.

Trainees on magazine postgraduate courses often apply for jobs while completing the course, and employers often have links with a particular course that they feel produces high-quality graduates. They are usually keen to recruit from their ranks.

It is almost impossible to get a job without having completed a good deal of work experience on magazines. Committed would-be magazine journalists will begin building up a portfolio of pieces they have written during work experience, or while still at school, and will continue to do so through university. Often they have a degree in a subject other than journalism, followed by a journalistic postgraduate course. Taking a degree in a different subject can help build up your area of expertise, and could stand you in good stead if you plan a career in magazines in an area relevant to the course you studied.

Work experience is often used by magazines as a recruiting process. Rather than advertising a job, they will bring in a number of people on work experience and, if they find someone suitable, offer that person the post.

The worst thing about becoming a journalist was having no one to give feedback and no structured training. Not knowing if what I was doing was right and not having anyone to iron out any mistakes or bad habits that I was getting into. Any training I have had has been formal and external and it has been very useful to get an independent perspective from professionals. KATHARINE SANDERSON, SCIENCE CORRESPONDENT, CHEMISTRY WORLD MAGAZINE

If you have a journalism qualification, you should be able to start as a reporter or **sub-editor**. If you don't, you may have to begin with the lowlier position of editorial assistant, becoming a reporter or sub after a year or two.

National Magazines, one of the major UK publishers, offers this advice:

Be realistic about what you can expect from your first job. It's true that journalism offers the chance of a stimulating and varied working life. It's also true that it's often hard work and sometimes poorly paid – don't imagine that it's an instant passport to a jet-setting lifestyle. And the chances of you becoming editor of *Cosmopolitan* or *The Times* before you're 21? They're low – but in the unpredictable world of journalism many things are possible. That's one of the reasons it's such fun.

Who takes trainees?

Generally on magazines, unlike newspapers, all your training takes place before you get your first job. You need to concentrate on building up a substantial portfolio of work experience before, during and sometimes after gaining your qualification. With sufficient practical experience and an NCTJ-accredited qualification you can apply for jobs.

Almost all magazine groups run work placements. To give a flavour of the range of training opportunities available, here are what some of the key magazine groups offer, and what they are looking for in applicants. I have chosen to feature them at this point because the advice they give, and the requirements they have, are typical across the industry.

You can find an extensive list of employers in the magazine industry, in Section 4. This is also a good section to refer to if you are looking for work experience. Full details of courses mentioned, at both academic intuitions and commercial concerns, can be found in Section 3.

> *I trained on a rock magazine. I would have preferred some sustained period away from the gruelling routine to hone my skills (I never did become a very good reporter).* BILL MANN, WEEKEND EDITOR, THE GUARDIAN

Centaur

Centaur is one of the UK's largest independent business publishing and information companies. It has a range of magazines tailored to particular businesses. These include *Marketing Week*, *Money Marketing*, *The Lawyer*, *Design Week*, *New Media Age*, *Creative Review*, *Televisual*, and *Employee Benefits*.

Michael Nutley, editor of the Centaur magazine *New Media Age*, a business publication for those working in the online medium, says:

> It's really important to have a journalistic qualification when you apply for a job. Having that gets you through the first sweep, when we do the initial sift of applicants. So it gets you considered. Then I'll be looking for relevant experience, including work experience.

Condé Nast

Condé Nast has some of the most glamorous titles, including *Vogue*, *Condé Nast Traveller*, *GQ*, and *Glamour*. Their personnel department has this advice:

> Apply for work placements to the editor of the magazine you are interested in. We would not hire a young journalist on the strength of academic achievement alone. They will need to show a solid amount of work-relevant experience.
>
> Work placements here last two to three weeks. Only very occasionally do job offers come directly out of a placement, but they are a good way to get your face known. A young journalist applying for a job with us will need a good journalistic qualification, aptitude, and relevant experience.

If you are in the offices of a publisher such as Condé Nast, you'll find vacancies advertised internally. Just because you are not on staff does not mean you cannot apply for them, but only by being on the premises are you likely to hear of them.

> *The achievement I'm most proud of is being given the go ahead to write my first article.* DAWN CRAN, EDITORIAL ASSISTANT, *WINE INTERNATIONAL*

Daily Mail and General Trust (DMGT)

DMGT, part of the group that owns the *Daily Mail* and a string of regional newspapers, also owns specialist magazines, including *Antiques Trade Gazette*. Editor Ivan Macquisten says:

I limit work experience numbers to about half a dozen people a year – I never have more than one person in at a time. I want to make sure that whoever comes in gets real value from their time here. There are too many firms who put work-experience people In corners and get them to do the filing or make the coffee or, even worse, just ignore them.

When considering someone for work experience, the first thing I do is get a copy of their CV and have a chat on the phone with them. This is to establish what they are looking to get out of being here and whether we are, indeed, a suitable place for them to come to. I will initially book them in for a week to see how they get on. If all goes well I might book them for a second week and then more.

Candidates for work experience don't have to be interested in art and antiques, just journalism, but they do have to be self-starters and keen. Work experience can take the form of me setting them projects to follow up that have nothing to do with the paper, but might help them establish contacts in local newspapers or magazines, as well as learning how to put together freelance feature proposals.

As for job applicants, they need to be able to show that they can source stories, can write well, can spell and are reasonably numerate. Most can do this, but what sets the best apart from the rest will be their cuttings and CV of work experience. Cuttings should include raw as well as subbed and published copy and should include a broad range of stories, not just impressive-looking big features. I also want to see that they have gone out on their own account from as early an age as possible to get work experience in as many different places as possible that are relevant to their ambitions. This sort of initiative often proves to be the deal breaker between job candidates. If they can touch type and already have 100wpm shorthand, all the better. The rest will come out at interview.

Haymarket

Haymarket publishes over 100 titles, and is the largest private magazine publisher in the UK. Its titles cover professional, business and customer sectors. Consumer magazines, many with editions around the globe, range from modern and classic motoring and motor sport to classical music, consumer electronics (including hi-fi and home cinema) and football. Business and professional interest magazines range from medical reference data to news coverage of marketing, advertising, public relations and charity professionals, management and human resources, computer security, the print industry, horticulture, planning and development, as well as youth workers.

It's better than working for a living but don't expect to make your fortune. BOB SATCHWELL, EXECUTIVE DIRECTOR, SOCIETY OF EDITORS

Like most magazine groups, it is working hard on its websites, some of which are online versions of a print magazine. Others are portals, such as brand-republic.com, which combine material from its advertising, public relations and marketing titles.

Ranita Patel, one of Haymarket's human resources managers says:

> We used to have an arrangement where we would have trainees who we'd finance through training but we haven't done that for a number of years now. We'd expect them to have a postgrad qualification. We'd also expect them to have solid work experience.
>
> People in editorial start with us either as editorial assistants or as reporters or sub-editors. To come in as an assistant, you don't need too much experience and will work closely with the team – that's a very junior way to come in. For reporters, good work experience is essential.
>
> Work placements usually last two weeks but if they go very well they might be extended. occasionally job offers come from them. For work experience we have a website on which all vacancies should be posted, but sometimes a person with a real passion will contact an editor of a particular title direct.

Bronagh Miskelly, editor of the Haymarket magazine *GP*, says:

> For work experience you should definitely contact the magazine you are interested in working on. Placements last two weeks and they have led to jobs, I can think of two cases. One of those had a background in health care as well as a postgraduate qualification.
>
> What do I look for in a young journalist? I want them to demonstrate an interest in the subject we cover – have they gone into the subject, have they found out about us and our market?

The National Magazine Company

Natmags, as the company is known, publishes 17 consumer titles, including *Company*, *Cosmopolitan*, *Country Living*, *Good Housekeeping*, *Harpers & Queen*,

House Beautiful, She, Esquire and *Zest*. You should apply in writing to the personal assistant (PA) to the editor of the magazine you are interested in. You can also tell them what journalistic area you are interested in and have experience of, for example fashion, health, beauty or whatever.

They say:

> There's no substitute for first-hand experience. If you have a local paper in your area, find out whether they take on unpaid help. If you want to work in magazines, contact all your favourite magazines to see whether they have work experience opportunities. Find out whether your school or college produces a newspaper or magazine – if not, start one.

> *My first experience was in student journalism at Manchester University – walked in through the door and asked the editor for some work. I ended up being elected editor.* IAN KING, BUSINESS EDITOR, *THE SUN*

Reed Business Publications

Reed has magazines in 18 fields, including aerospace, agriculture, banking, catering, chemicals, construction, healthcare, personnel, property, recruitment, social services and transport. Again, identify the magazine you are interested in and apply direct to the editor.

They ask these questions of potential recruits:

> Are you someone who ... thrives on challenging opportunities? Loves to stretch your abilities? Is a team player who has the initiative to work autonomously as well? Possesses a willingness to handle demanding projects? Do you have high personal standards, excellent interpersonal effectiveness and enjoy delivering results with creativity and innovation?

John Baker, editor of the Reed magazine *European Chemical News,* says:

> For work experience I'd want someone who had a relevant academic background, and who was either on or had completed a postgraduate course in journalism. I have recruited people who I've first met through work experience with us, but we would tend to advertise vacancies through our own totaljobs.com website and internally. We always have applicants in for a day before we make a job offer – so we can see them in action and they can see us.

Don't overlook websites when seeking work experience. For instance, Haymarket's Brand Republic is the home of *Campaign* and *Marketing* magazines on the web, and serves the world of advertising, marketing, public relations and new media. Editor Gordon MacMillan says:

You should contact editors directly if you are interested in work experience, but you must have more than a vague idea of who you are applying to. It's always nice to have a pre-entry qualification, but we take people who don't have them. When hiring, however, we would only hire someone without experience if they did have a pre-entry qualification (as we did this year, from Cardiff). We're unlikely to hire graduates with no pre-entry or experience. We are looking for enthusiasm, some knowledge and writing skills. We always put people through a writing test.

The length of placements varies; we have had people for a week or for several months. If we have the free space, we're happy to have people in. Working online at a rolling news website means that someone doing work experience will get to write a lot and so, hopefully, in turn will learn something and walk away with useful hands-on experience.

A placement hasn't led to a job so far, but it's a definite possibility.

Wardour

Wardour Publishing is one of the many groups that specialise in customer magazines. Its clients include banks and other financial institutions, such as Lloyds TSB, Standard Life, Alliance and Leicester, Bradford and Bingley and the Mortgage Express.

Sharon Gethings, their editorial director, says:

For work experience you should write or e-mail me directly, specifying how you want your career to progress and where and on what kind of publication you would ideally like to work eventually. Look at our website carefully to learn about the type of publishing we do.

The more qualifications the better – preferably NCTJ. Cuts of published work and excellent references from tutors or previous employers can help. We always give interviewees subbing and grammar tests at interview; our journalists need to be good all-rounders, whatever they choose to specialise in.

If you have the relevant practical skills, then enthusiasm, humility (ready to turn their hand to anything that needs doing, however menial), passion, curiosity and ambition go a long way. And a sense of humour is always a plus.

Someone who has demonstrated their skills during work placement is much more likely to be considered for a job interview.

What they want from you

Someone who is useful from day one. That means successful applicants will usually have a postgraduate qualification in journalism and substantial work experience. A qualification in journalism may not be essential, but if you have one it will show that you have sufficient training to be able to research and write. You'll have an advantage over other applicants if your course has taught you a bit about **subbing** and if you are familiar with word-processing and design packages.

What qualifications will I need?

Most journalists have at least five GCSEs (grades A–C), including English, and two A levels or vocational A levels. Over 70 per cent have a degree – not necessarily in journalism. To get on a degree course you need at least two A levels or vocational A levels and five GCSEs (grades A–C), or equivalent qualifications. GCSE English is essential.

Requirements for a postgraduate course will vary (see Section 3).

What will I have to study?

NCTJ-accredited courses in magazine journalism cover media law, ethics, government, shorthand at between 60 and 120 words per minute, news and feature writing, production and design, subbing and background to the magazine industry.

Nothing beats breaking a story. I'm particularly proud of being the first journalist to reveal the story that Wembley's Twin Towers were going to be demolished, JAMES TONEY, SPORTSBEAT/NEWS ASSOCIATES

There is also a period of work experience on a magazine. NCTJ preliminary examinations will be undertaken, together with the assessment of a portfolio of work produced on the course. The portfolio will contain evidence of knowledge and competence in feature writing, production and design, background to the magazine industry, and a report on work experience from the relevant employer.

There is currently no equivalent qualification to the National Certificate Examination in Newspaper Journalism (see Chapter 1), which means that once you have passed your prelims you will be free to find a job and learn from then on in a less formal way.

What else will I learn as a trainee?

If you are one of the majority of new entrants to magazines who gain pre-entry qualifications and then find a job, it is the work experience element of your training that will give you substantial experience of what life on a magazine is like. You are likely to write a lot of news reports, particularly if the magazine has a companion website where news is updated daily or several times a day. Magazine teams tend to be small, and you'll often find yourself doing a bit of everything from research to subbing to sourcing photographs, even laying out pages. If you go in, as an editorial assistant, perhaps without a pre-entry qualification, you will probably find you are doing a good deal of administration, sending bikes and calling in products for review and so on, and working under the guidance of reporters and other members of staff.

> *Make sure you start at the bottom and learn the ropes thoroughly before trying to break into the big time.* JOHN KAY, CHIEF REPORTER, *THE SUN*

What will I earn?

Joining a magazine after a pre-entry course, your salary as a reporter or sub-editor is likely to be in the range of £18,000–£20,000. Salaries for editorial assistants range widely, and can be very low. Anything from £12,000 to £15,000 is good.

How to improve your chances of getting a job

You should be able to demonstrate that you have taken every opportunity to learn about magazines and work on them. Editing or contributing to school or university magazines is a good start. Having work-experience placements is essential, so contact all your favourite magazines (i.e. the ones that you know well as a reader) and see if they have work-placement schemes. You will need to be able to show a portfolio of cuttings – ideally with by-lines – to prove that you have done something concrete to pursue your desire to be a journalist.

Don't turn down any opportunity that might lead to a job. Even if you have a pre-entry qualification, a job may not come easily. It is important that you grasp any opportunity to keep your hand in – even if the work is unpaid. The more you work in magazines, the more experience you have, the better your portfolio, and the more opportunities there are to be in the right place at the right time.

Concentrate on getting the right work-experience placements. Use placements to find out which type of magazine you like best – perhaps consumer magazines will prove less attractive than the specialist magazine where you can indulge your interest in potholing. Perhaps you will find you like being part of a small team doing a bit of everything, or perhaps you will find that specialising is more your style.

My NCTJ course was harder than my degree and A levels, but the skills I learnt are useful in everyday life (law and politics). Obtaining 100wpm shorthand is a challenge but the skill is really useful, I use it all the time, even for writing notes to myself at home. STEPHEN SINFIELD, REPORTER, *RIPLEY AND HEANOR NEWS*

Identify what you hope to learn on the placements and make it clear to the employer that you have goals and expect something concrete in return for your free labour. Tell them what you can offer and what you hope to get out of it. Do your homework. Read the magazine thoroughly for several issues before arriving on work placement. Aim to show them you are a highly useful and effective person, who is a potential recruit once a vacancy arises. At the end of the placement, ask for feedback – 'how did I do?'

Use your placement to network, and observe possible openings. If you hear talk of the health editor, for example, going on maternity leave, ask if a stand-in has been identified. If not, tell them why you'd be perfect for the slot. Watch out for vacancies advertised internally on the staff notice boards. Just because you are not on the staff doesn't mean you can't apply.

Life as a trainee

Experiences can vary widely. Some trainees or raw recruits find themselves being something of a dogsbody, even though they probably have a degree and perhaps a postgraduate qualification in journalism. Others find they swiftly move up the ranks, becoming news editor within months and editor within a year. Many are in the middle, working hard as a news reporter, learning about the magazine, the business it covers and the needs and interests of the readers.

Magazines vary widely in how well-resourced they are, but a raw recruit, particularly if he or she comes in as an editorial assistant, is often seen as a fixer. If a writer or one of the editors needs a hand organising a feature, or some other project, you will be the one to do it. You'll jump in the taxi to take the clothes to the fashion shoot; you'll go through the cuttings to check background information for the writer of an article. You'll assist writers by making some of their calls, and contribute a few paragraphs to pieces they are writing. If a time-consuming ring-round of celebrities is needed to accompany a main feature, you'll hit the phones. If your star interviewer wants to line up another batch of interviewees, you'll be the one to contact their agents, send the cuttings and start negotiations. In short, you will help out anywhere and everywhere.

You'll quickly gain a clear picture of how the magazine works and what everyone does on it. Little by little, you'll be given responsibility for projects. You might begin by running a small features item – perhaps finding the subjects and briefing the writers for the 'What's in my fridge?' column, or some such. Do that well and you'll be allowed to write your own pieces. If you are coming up with a stream of ideas, and selling them well to the relevant editor, they will eventually reward you by allowing you to research and write one of them unaided. You may help out on the editing side, giving copy an initial fact-check and subbing it for **style**.

Within a year you'll be an effective all-rounder, able to help anyone with anything, and solve any problem. At this time you'll be asking for a step up and a title such as feature writer. If there are clearly no openings on your magazine, you'll be sniffing around other titles in the group, or your rivals, to see if they can give you your next challenge.

DAY IN THE LIFE

Young journalist on a business-to-business magazine

Sally Percy, reporter at *Accountancy* magazine

I work for *Accountancy* magazine, a glossy monthly magazine for – yup, you've guessed it – accountants. After graduating from Oxford University, I worked as a management consultant for Accenture for a few years. Then I married a New Zealander and my husband and I decided we should try out life Down Under in the town where he was brought up. I wanted to make a career change from consultancy and was lucky enough to find a job as a rural reporter on the local newspaper (which was a bit ironic considering I was a semi-vegetarian, ex-city-dwelling Pom!). That sparked my enthusiasm for journalism as a career and I haven't looked back since.

Although I enjoyed my job, I found life in New Zealand too quiet so my husband and I moved back to the UK and I enrolled for a postgraduate diploma in periodical publishing.

My day starts with a general perusal of the daily papers (focusing on the business pages obviously, but occasionally the eye does wonder into other sections) and I check the e-mail for press releases. The morning is spent writing stories for the internet (we're supposed to put up five stories a day) and doing any research I may need to do for my features. Generally I interview people by telephone, but I also go to press conferences and to meetings at accountancy firms.

Accountancy has a small and friendly editorial team and we go out for lunch together most days. Our favourite place is a café called Jaxx in Kingston, which is close to our office.

Afternoons always seem to pass in a flash. I often write my features during this time. Everyone in the team is very hands-on and we all do a bit of everything as part of our work – news and feature writing, subbing, proof-reading, etc. That suits me as it means no two days are ever the same. I really enjoy my job as I find it mentally stimulating having to get my head around new – and often complex – ideas very quickly.

If you think this might be for you...

If it sounds good so far, you can find out more about NCTJ-accredited courses in magazine journalism at www.nctj.com.

Contact details:
NCTJ Training Limited,
The New Granary,
Station Road,
Newport,
Saffron Walden,
Essex CB11 3PL
01799 544014
Fax: 01799 544015
info@nctj.com

3

TELEVISION AND RADIO

Is broadcast journalism for you?

Good reporting skills underpin TV and radio journalism, just as they do newspapers and magazines. Yet reporting skills and good story-telling are not all you need to make it as a broadcast journalist. You also need to be a natural performer, and comfortable in front of the camera or microphone. Not many people excel at all of that.

In TV, pictures matter as much as words. It's not enough to have the right script; you need the right pictures to go with it if you are to craft a successful television news story. On radio, sounds can be as important as language if you are to communicate the sense of being where you say you are, in the situation you describe.

I first thought of becoming a journalist as a child in Scotland watching TV news reports about the civil rights protests and riots in the United States. I didn't understand why black people were treated so badly and I wanted to find out. GAVIN ESLER, PRESENTER, BBC2 NEWSNIGHT

Your voice and, on TV, your looks are also important. While these days you don't have to use Received Pronunciation (a posh accent), the quality of your speaking voice is still a key factor in your success as a broadcast journalist. And, to appear on camera, you generally need to be relatively young and relatively attractive.

In terms of pressure, TV and radio news are unremitting. Deadlines are often hourly or half-hourly, which means you have to be able to work fast and accurately against the clock. With the advent of rolling TV and radio news channels, the pressure is even greater – you must get things to air as they happen. While speed and immediacy are plus-points in broadcast journalism, lack of depth can be a minus. When time is limited, and minutes on air rationed, reports may need to be much simpler than the equivalent report in a newspaper or specialist magazine. If you enjoy really getting into an issue and analysing it, you may find broadcast journalism frustrating.

> *The best thing [about my training on the BBC's journalist training scheme] were the excellent lectures and hands-on experience; the worst was persuading a traditional northern news editor that a southern graduate with no newspaper experience was any use to him.* JOSHUA ROSENBERG, LEGAL EDITOR, DAILY TELEGRAPH, WHO WAS ON THE BBC'S JOURNALISTS' TRAINING SCHEME

Training opportunities are severely rationed. While there are thousands of trainees in newspapers and magazines, there are merely hundreds in TV and radio. Industry estimates are that around 600 trainees enter broadcast journalism each year (*Source*: BJTC). Nevertheless, TV and radio are expanding media. The development of digital broadcasting has led to plans for more TV channels and national and regional radio stations. It may well be that the number of graduates finding jobs in TV and radio will increase in the near future.

What do TV and radio journalists do?

News comes from current events, and from follow-ups and developments of stories that have broken elsewhere, on rival channels or in other media. Despite their slower pace, national newspapers are still a great source of news for TV and radio. Broadcast journalists need to be able to pick up on stories and develop them for their own medium, and also generate original story ideas.

> *I trained at LBC Radio in London. The training was very practical, learning on the job which was good. But there was not enough formal training – no law, no shorthand etc.* MARTHA KEARNEY, PRESENTER, WORLD AT ONE, BBC RADIO 4

Of course, not all broadcast journalists appear on air. As with the other media, in addition to reporters there are many who work on the news agenda, compiling and editing news bulletins, determining running orders, checking timings and briefing presenters.

A TV or radio reporter will generally be assigned one or more subjects for each shift they work, researching the items, gathering the interviews and other material they need, and preparing the **package** to go on air. TV journalists need to be good at working with a team – camera and sound will be with you, and will want the item to work in their terms as well as yours. But there are many other journalistic tasks, including presenting story ideas, monitoring news wire services for breaking stories and updates to items already on the schedule, supervising the editing of reports, preparing scripts for presenters, deciding on the best order for stories in a bulletin, and presenting itself.

It is often said you are only as good as your last story, in fact you are only as good as your next story. EDWARD STOURTON, PRESENTER, RADIO 4 TODAY PROGRAMME

Broadcast journalists work shifts and are used to unsocial hours. They are often employed on short contracts, and can find it necessary to move around to secure a new contract. Permanent contracts are rare, and there is great competition to win them.

Do you have what it takes?

This is what employers say they are looking for:

- an understanding of the audience;
- dedication and commitment;
- an insatiable interest in the world;
- a clear, authoritative broadcasting voice and manner;
- a natural story-teller;
- calmness when things go wrong on air;
- the ability to present information with clarity when under pressure; and
- an exceptional interest in, and grasp, of current affairs.

I was given a place on the BBC's General Trainee Scheme. The worst thing about it was the absence of any training at all. I wished I had gone into newspapers. ROGER BOLTON, PROGRAMME MAKER AND RADIO PRESENTER

How do you get a job in broadcast journalism?

Many journalists who work in TV and radio started on newspapers and switched media later, once they had mastered basic reporting skills. One reason for this is that the number of trainee places is greater in local newspapers; another is that many broadcasting employers seek a high level of skills, knowledge and judgement, and prefer to take on staff at the ages of 23–25. A few trainees go straight into TV on an in-house journalist training scheme, but these places are hugely over-subscribed. More manage to win a traineeship in local radio.

A degree in politics, government, public administration or economics may help your chances, and a postgraduate qualification in print journalism that is recognised by the National Council for the Training of Journalists is becoming increasingly important. But academic qualifications are of little use without extensive evidence that you are truly committed to a career in TV or radio. So work experience – ideally stretching back to school – is very important. You need to have taken placements during your vacations, on hospital radio or other outlets. There is no better evidence that you are a suitable candidate for a vacancy at, say, the BBC, than having actually worked successfully somewhere in the Beeb on a placement. There are more opportunities in regional stations, particularly radio, for work placements than on the national networks.

> *Ignore the rejections. I kept a very big and fat rejection file for a long while and would show it to young hopefuls. Landing a job involves an element of being in the right place at the right time.*
> SURREY BEDDOWS, EDITOR, ANGLIA NEWS

Placements are of great use to you, too. If you get a range of them, in different areas, you will gain an insight into what is a very diverse and complex industry, and decide what area would suit you best. They also help you build up your contacts, which can be a means to gaining extra work. In an industry where taking on someone who cannot perform well is a disaster, editors tend to hire people with a proven track record, whom they have seen in action themselves, or who are vouched for by people whose judgement they trust. So, the more unpaid placements you get, the closer you are likely to move towards a paid contract – as long as you really do have what it takes.

Who takes trainees?

To give a flavour of the range of training opportunities available, here are some of the key broadcasting groups that take on trainees. For an extensive listing of sources of work experience, training and jobs, go to Section 4. For details of academic study, go to Section 3.

BBC

The BBC has a Broadcast Journalist Trainee Scheme, with a handful of spaces. It says:

> The BBC looks for exceptional individuals to join this scheme, which offers both on- and off-the-job training in broadcast news and current affairs. Initially [trainees will be] working from a purpose-built centre in Bristol and later from one of the 14 regional news rooms.
>
> All traineeships are advertised according to operational needs and although they don't guarantee a job upon completion, they have a great track record for launching many successful careers.

Inevitably, the BBC's scheme is massively over-subscribed.

The corporation also runs a News Sponsorship scheme. Sponsored trainees get a four-week paid work placement in one of the BBC's newsrooms in London, Scotland, Wales and Northern Ireland. They say of it: 'As well as a dedicated mentor and plenty of training, you'll get a contribution of £3,500 towards your living expenses and your course fees paid.'

You can learn what a story is from training, but you need tenacity to take a tiny lead and turn it into something worth having. DAVID PEEL, MEDIA CONSULTANT, AND FORMER LOCAL RADIO JOURNALIST

Work experience is available in all sorts of news areas from local radio to the World Service. Opportunities are listed on the BBC's website, and although they are extensive – scores are listed at any one time – demand is strong, so the advice is to check regularly and apply as soon as something suitable is posted.

ITN and IRN

ITN, which provides the news service on ITV, Channel 4 and, via its IRN arm to 270 UK radio stations, sponsors 11 trainees a year. Course fees are paid plus a living allowance. The company says of successful candidates: 'Most will then be taken on by ITN itself so the prospects of obtaining work on completion of the course look very good. Details will be advertised when the scheme is announced each year.' For work experience placements, once again, look to the website.

> *I got onto the LBC/IRN trainee scheme by happy accident: I had been rejected by a number of other more classic schemes, and only applied to this one because a friend of my parents thought I had 'a good voice' and took the trouble to send me the advert. Not wanting to be rude, I applied, and was chosen despite there being 800 applicants for four places.* EMMA UDWIN, FORMER BBC POLITICAL CORRESPONDENT

The Local Radio Company

The Local Radio Company owns and operates 30 stations across the UK, from Falkirk in Scotland to the Isle of Wight and from Hastings to Yeovil. Andrew Carpenter, head of news, says:

Each of our stations has its own newsroom (we have no central news hub), and anyone looking for work experience, a training place or a job should contact their local station direct. All our news is local, and we take the provision of that news very seriously. We focus on family, health and wealth, and will concentrate on items that relate to these things rather than the world stage of politics.

We don't take 16-year-old GCSE students on work experience; we concentrate on those on a relevant degree or postgraduate course. We hire young reporters who have completed degree or postgraduate courses, and will give them additional training while they are working with us as reporters. There are probably around ten in this category at any one time; all appointed by their local news editor. Those who join us fresh from college courses can expect to cover six subjects on our internal training courses. These are: news writing, both basic and advanced; law, which is increasingly important and is also studied at basic and advanced levels; live radio, which covers interviewing skills, asking the right questions and so on; sport; voice training and news presentation.

Our other training scheme is in conjunction with Cleland Thom Journalism Training Services. [They train people to sit NCTJ exams as external candidates] and the practical element is carried out on work placement at one of our radio stations.

Sky News

Sky's editorial training scheme is announced on its website. The company says this about it:

Over 12 months you will work with/learn from top journalists in our television and radio news-rooms, from our political unit at Westminster, from correspondents at home and abroad, and from the leading sports reporters in the country.

In order to be considered for this opportunity you must be able to demonstrate a commitment to journalism, a keen knowledge of world events and current affairs and the creativity to be able to take an original angle on a story.

It asks applicants to send a 500-word critique of *Sky News*, and details of relevant work placements. For work experience placements, look for contact details on the website.

What they want from you

To consider hiring you, a TV or radio station will expect you to have a wealth of relevant work experience to show you really are determined to break into news broadcasting. As in any branch of journalism, you must show that you understand the needs of the audience. They'll expect you to be steeped in media – to know what story will appeal to which radio or TV news pro-gramme, why, and how it should be handled to make it absolutely right for that outlet. You'll need to come up with good ideas and know how to research and execute them. You'll need to be able to conduct an interview.

> *Don't – really don't – [become a journalist] if you just want to be famous or on the telly. Do something else. Journalism is absolutely not for you. But if you want to find out things, have an inexhaustible curiosity about the world, want to examine conventional wisdom and overturn stereotypes, plus can communicate what you have found, you might be a journalist.* GAVIN ELSER, PRESENTER, BBC2 NEWSNIGHT

Shorthand is extremely useful, particularly if you have to rush out of a court hearing and deliver two minutes live coverage, and straight from your notebook. Last but by no means least, you'll also need a good broadcasting voice.

What qualifications will I need?

Over 70 per cent of entrants are graduates, though occasionally there are opportunities for non-graduates with specialist knowledge or substantial relevant experience. A degree is required for entry to the BBC and ITN training schemes.

Most employers will want you to have an undergraduate degree and a postgraduate diploma or MA in broadcast, bi-media (TV and radio), multimedia, TV or online journalism.

What will I have to study?

Course content is likely to include:

- spoken-word communication skills;
- the role and responsibilities of the reporter, professional conduct and the place of personal values;
- how a newsroom works;
- the importance of teamwork;
- what news is, news values and the editorial requirements of different organisations;
- target audiences;
- how the legal system and government operate;
- codes of journalistic practice;
- developing ideas for news stories;
- identifying, assessing and using sources;
- how to research stories; and
- developing interviewing skills.

I'm most proud of curbing the National Front in Bradford in the 1970s and 80s. ARNOLD HADWIN, RETIRED EDITOR, BRADFORD TELEGRAPH AND ARGUS

What else will I learn as a trainee?

How to be a better reporter, so you get the story. How to be a better storyteller, so you tell it well. How to be a better editor, so you draw your words, those of the interviewees, and the evocative sounds or telling pictures into a really effective whole or, to use the jargon, a good package.

While in a newsroom you will learn about the dynamics of the news team, what the producers are looking for, and how the news should be set out. You may start by doing basic tasks, such as working an autocue or fetching tapes, before moving on to interviewing, initially off-camera and then on-camera. You may also be trained in the use of specialist software or technical equipment.

What will I earn?

Typical starting salaries for trainees and newcomers to the industry are between £12,000 and £20,000, with local radio at the lower end and television at the upper end.

How to improve your chances of getting a job

Start small, in hospital, student or community radio. At university, work on student newspapers, magazines, TV and radio stations and websites. Tape an entire day's news bulletins and analyse them to see how stories fit into the whole and how they are developed. Be full of ideas about fresh ways to handle stories that come round regularly. Freelance for local newspapers, news agencies or any other outlet you can find – you might be able to cover local sports fixtures or review plays or other performances. It will help you develop your news sense, ideas, style and contacts.

> At the end of my BBC traineeship I had to apply for the job of researcher. The Religious department turned me down for The Question Why with Malcolm Muggeridge but The Money Programme took me on. It can't have been for my financial skills. ROGER BOLTON, INDEPENDENT PROGRAMME MAKER AND RADIO PRESENTER

If after completing your course you can't find paid work, do any unpaid work you can. Not only does this increase your experience, it means you may just be in the right place when a vacancy comes up. And if you have impressed staff with your determination, tenacity and willingness to do menial tasks, you might also impress then as the person they are looking for. Many jobs are never advertised, so be prepared to write on spec and ask to meet key potential employers – producers, editors, heads of news – for an informal chat about you, your ambitions, and what openings they might possibly have in the future.

When you approach possible employers, send them evidence that you have a good broadcasting voice and, if television is your goal, presentation skills. Take any opportunity to put together a show reel, and if you can't go that far, at least tape yourself reading a news item.

If you are on a work placement, push yourself forward. Don't hold back, waiting to be given things to do. Make suggestions, come up with ideas and, keep asking for projects.

Life as a trainee

You will find yourself doing a wide range of tasks as a trainee, from answering the phones during a phone-in and monitoring e-mail messages to a programme to assisting senior reporters on stories. They might have you fixing interviews for them, or conducting short interviews which they do not have time for, and which they will feed into their package.

> *The best thing about being a journalist is covering a story and observing how the quality of the public discussion thereafter was affected by it.* KIERAN FAGAN, FREELANCE WRITER

You will often shadow a range of more senior journalists, from general reporters to specialists. You will see how they go about their work, how they conduct interviews, how they use charm, tenacity or sheer bloody-mindedness to get to the people they need to interview, and to get them to address the questions that need answers. From them, and from the assignments you undertake on your own, you'll learn how to report, interview and structure a piece. You'll also learn how (in radio) to get the sound effects you need to bring a package to life and (on TV) how to write to the best-available pictures, so your words and the pictures combine to tell the story really effectively. You will also be trained in presentation and in making the best of your voice.

--- DAY IN THE LIFE ---

Young journalist working in television

Rachel Gaunt, researcher at an independent TV company in Manchester

I am a researcher for an independent TV company in Manchester. My role is to provide support to the producer and that really can mean absolutely anything! The only thing that is typical about my typical day is that it will be totally different from any other.

I did a postgraduate diploma in Bimedia journalism, but decided pretty early on that off-camera TV work was what I wanted to do. The first day we made our TV news programme as part of the course at Trinity and All Saints in Leeds (TASC), I volunteered to be producer (no, I don't know why either!). It was stressful, tiring and I made loads of mistakes, but I loved it!

(Continued)

Before I went to TASC I did a month's work experience on documentaries at the BBC in Manchester, and that was where I got a taste for documentaries – the extra detail compared to news and the ability to be creative and artistic in filming. I want to produce and direct my own films, so I am working my way up.

I start at about 10am. The series I am working on is about the history of forensics and each programme is about a different part of forensics. I go through the script and highlight all points where there might be archive footage available (newspaper headlines, photographs, television news reports), where there might be scope for reconstructions – not complete re-enactments of the crime, but creating a *mise-en-scène*! What GVs [general views] do we need of country lanes, villages, prisons, graveyards? I am trying to think of what pictures are going to be there for the audience.

I make lists of what I need, based on the script – I love lists. Journalism training taught me to document and keep thorough notes, and when working for a longer period of time on things this is really important. Archive photographs and footage all have to be cleared for use so all my correspondence and efforts have to be documented. The legal training at college gave me the ability to notice a potential legal trap, such as copyright. This is important in all broadcasting, not only in news.

I am chasing expert interviewees for the series as well, so I have a conversation with the media department at the Forensic Science Service about trying to organise when we will be able to film interviews. I also speak to the communications director of a gun club in London about filming there – the ballistics programme needs guns and lots of them.

There is a constant pressure to think of ideas, find your way around a problem, and work out how to get what the producer wants. I take notes of odd things: locations with good views and the names of interesting interviewees on programmes. You never know when you will need an expert in forensic lip-reading!

I am filming at a graveyard on Sunday, on a DV [digital video] camera, which I learned to operate at TASC. So at the end of the day I get to work on the risk assessment for that, which shouldn't be hard but takes a long time because you have to think about every possibility: How will I take steps to avoid the extreme temperatures? 'Researcher will undertake to wear sun cream and a hat!'

DAY IN THE LIFE

Young journalist working in radio

Gary Andrews, acting head of news, Ivel FM, Yeovil

An assault on a man in Yeovil town centre, leaving him fighting for his life. Cigarette smuggling in sleepy Somerset villages. A local farmer who's created a new variety of shallot. Martock's Maria battling for her place in Andrew Lloyd Webber's production of *The Sound of Music*. Bar the morning cup of tea, the only thing that can be said about a day working for The Local Radio Company [owners of 30 radio stations including Ivel FM] is it's typically atypical.

The exciting thing about working as part of a small team of two in the news-room is you're never bored and cover everything from charity fundraising events to campaigns to save historic buildings – giving you a chance to become a semi-expert on a wide variety of topics.

A lot of the time I'm manning the newsroom alone. There are two shifts, each with their own challenges. Early mornings, starting at 6am, give me the chance to set the agenda for the day's news and to co-ordinate our strategy for any ongoing or breaking stories. I also produce and present our 15-minute bulletin at one o'clock.

The 11am–7pm shift may mean more of a lie-in, but is no less challenging, as it's your responsibility to chase next day's stories. Often, in a matter of min-utes, you're shifting between interviewing two completely different people about stories that couldn't be more diametrically opposed if they tried. There's usually a package to put together for the lunchtime bulletin, giving you a chance to get your creative juices going. With stories to gather and bulletins to read it's a challenge, but I've created some truly innovative and entertaining pieces of radio working to tight deadlines.

If this sounds like hard work, it is, but it's also immensely enjoyable and rewarding – especially when you hear your story reach the airwaves before any of your local rivals. And I can't say I didn't know what I was letting myself in for. Over the past five years I've spent time at broadcasters around the country doing work experience, freelance shifts and tea-making duties (caf-feine is an important part of journalism. Without it, news as we know it might cease to exist), with the goal of working towards a career in broadcast journalism.

It started at Cardiff University where a friend dragged me along to a welcome party for the student radio station, Xpress Radio. I soon found myself volun-teering for late-night producing shifts and early-morning newsreading slots and it didn't take long to convince me this was where I wanted to be. Towards the end of my time at university, I took a quick detour into print media and ended up taking a sabbatical year to edit the student newspaper, gair rhydd, crown-ing a successful year by taking both Guardian Student Newspaper of the Year and Guardian Student Magazine of the Year.

But it still didn't diminish my desire to enter radio, and I continued to free-lance with local radio stations (something I'd done since securing work expe-rience at Gemini FM in Exeter during my first year of university) and undertaking work experience at places I wasn't yet qualified to freelance at. Towards the

(Continued)

end of my time at university, I decided I needed to hone my broadcasting skills further, as well as get NJTC-accredited law and public administration qualifications, so I re-enrolled at Cardiff University on a Postgraduate Diploma in Broadcast Journalism. This gave me a chance to iron out bad habits, and mock production days prepared me for a full-time job in broadcasting. So, when I applied for a job with Ivel FM I could hit the ground running – and I don't think I've stopped since.

If you think this might be for you...

If it sounds good so far, find out more at www.nctj.com.

Contact details:
NCTJ Training Limited,
The New Granary,
Station Road,
Newport,
Saffron Walden,
Essex CB11 3PL
01799 544014
Fax: 01799 544015
info@nctj.com

4

ONLINE JOURNALISM

Is online journalism for you?

Online, or multimedia, journalism is the future. Increasingly, journalists working online will use the latest technology to produce stories for websites, mobile phones and other portable devices, plus interactive television. They will be able to draw on story-telling methods from all the other media – the written word, audio, still photography and video.

That is not to say the other media are doomed – far from it. Cinema didn't kill theatre, TV didn't kill cinema. Newspapers, magazines, TV and radio will survive, with increasingly discerning consumers of information and entertainment choosing the medium that best suits them, depending on where they are, what they are doing, and what they need to know.

Online is undoubtedly the future, and online journalists will shape it. RICHARD ABBOTT, FREELANCE WRITER

At present, the traditional media are going through a rather painful process of adjustment as they learn how to harness the opportunities of multimedia and reinvent their brands as sources of information that are successful in several formats. So, almost all newspapers and magazines have a companion website. Many are experimenting with audio and video on their websites, and with **podcasts** and **vodcasts**. TV and radio stations also have websites. Increasingly, the traditional media are employing journalists with multimedia skills, even if that move is as simple as a magazine hiring an online reporter who puts up several news stories a day on the website, while the rest of the team works on items for the print edition.

Despite all this, news reporting skills are still the absolute key to making it as a journalist in the online medium, just as they are in every other. However, there are many online journalists who are not reporters – all those opportunities to use video, audio and so on require a good deal of manpower, and of technical expertise. Having a whole toolbox to play with means you need a substantial number of mechanics doing just that, and these are production or desk jobs, they are not at the sharp end of news gathering.

If you go into online journalism, you need to decide which area appeals to you, and make sure the work experience you get, the qualifications you obtain, the training you receive and the jobs you apply for will allow you to pursue your particular interests. Increasingly, the media will converge, with any publisher using all the media, and publishers will therefore want to employ journalistic staff who are comfortable working with any of them.

The other key difference between online and the traditional media is that there is a high degree of feedback from the audience. Traditionally, newspaper and magazine journalists wrote the news, TV and radio journalists announced it, and that was pretty much that, apart from the odd readers' letter page or phone-in. With online journalism, the audience has its say as well. They want to vote on it, chat about it, post messages on a bulletin board, take part in a debate and write their own versions of events. The old media are adapting, with some reluctance: viewers' and listeners' e-mails are read out at the end of television and radio news bulletins; newspaper websites allow readers to blog alongside the professionals. Successful online journalists need to embrace the idea that they are in a dialogue with their audience.

Love it or leave it. NEIL WALLIS, DEPUTY EDITOR, *NEWS OF THE WORLD*

Online journalism is now a viable alternative starting point to newspapers, magazines, TV and radio. In the words of Liisa Rohumaa, assistant news editor at FT.com: An online journalist, 'can be a writer, editor, columnist, podcaster, blogger, broadcaster and publisher. In one day.'

What you can achieve online is really only limited by your inventiveness and your imagination, and the training opportunities are increasing. The Association of Online Publishers (AOP), which represents many traditional media companies that are expanding their online operations, has identified a serious skills shortage and the need to encourage more recruits to the industry. For example, in a survey, it discovered that 31 per cent of respondents had unfilled vacancies for editorial staff.

Bill Murray, AOP chairman and managing director of group business information strategy for Haymarket Publishing, said:

> We shouldn't be surprised that as our industry develops at such a pace there is something of a lag in the arrival of talented, skilled people to help us take advantage. The great news is that there can't be a more challenging, rewarding and dynamic area for people either considering or already developing a career in media than in online publishing. In many respects, our challenge is to make sure we are properly publicising and explaining to the broader employment market just how exciting these opportunities are.

What do online journalists do?

What online journalists do varies enormously. Some are straight reporters, the only difference being that they post their stories online as soon as they are written – in 'real time', to use the jargon. Such people tend to be employed by companies that have their roots in traditional media. Online journalists who are employed on websites that have no corresponding enterprise in print or broadcasting tend to have a much stronger technical background. Indeed, in the early days of online publishing, they probably had no journalistic qualifications and little experience. Increasingly, online journalists combine traditional journalistic and new-technology skills, but the proportions of those skills that each online journalist possesses vary hugely.

I got my first job by offering to do work experience for free. This turned into paid employment after just two weeks. HELEN PREEN, ASSISTANT EDITOR, *DAILY EXPRESS*

Many online journalists need to be familiar with the **content management systems** that are used to direct material to a number of different destinations – to update a website, feed a newspaper or magazine edition, and broadcast SMS messages to mobile phone subscribers. So, a real-time feed of information from a reporter at a football game could be directed to a website for a move-by-move commentary on the game, selectively to SMS for scores and texts at key points in the game, and someone may be re-editing it for a print publication. The same reporter might also be sending voice reports to a web or radio outlet, although they'll be a little busy if they are!

The journalist who takes advantage of all that can be done online will be a real one-man band. There aren't many at present, but this could change in a few years. They will carry a video camera as well as a reporter's notebook, and their reports will mix moving and still images with audio clips and text. They will be able to knock up simple graphics, use Flash, Dreamweaver and **Photoshop**, voice-up their report for audio outlets and talk to camera and create a package for streaming video channels. Depending on the nature of the organisation they work for, they might also have the skills of the foot-in-the-door reporter and the paparazzi photographer.

Such hydra-like journalists will need a converged newsroom in which to function. But not all journalists in that newsroom will be such adept multi-taskers. In large newsrooms, journalists will still specialise in one medium or another, but the demands of the story that presents itself will determine how the news is delivered, and what skills are needed.

This is not a profession for the shy and retiring. Be confident but not arrogant when you are starting out. Listen and watch others. A sense of humour and quick wit also help. JAMES TONEY, SPORTSBEAT/NEWS ASSOCIATES

To sound one cautionary note: by no means all of the material on content-heavy websites was created in-house. Very often, particularly with **ISP** (Internet Service Providers) content areas, that material is bought in. Many of the breaking-news services, for example, are supplied by an agency such as the Press Association (**PA**) or Reuters. Often, an ISP has a range of contracts with partners to provide content. So, if you want to be an online journalist who creates content, you need to be sure that the places where you look for work experience, and perhaps a job, will actually let you do that.

Do you have what it takes?

In such a diverse medium, not all recruits will have all the skills listed below. You will notice, if you have read the preceding chapters, that some of the qualities online employers look for also occur in newspapers, others in broadcasting, which makes sense because online journalism is an amalgam of those media. If you are employed in the online offshoot of a newspaper or magazine, your employer will be looking for the skills they expect their offline (or 'dead-tree edition') staff to have, plus aptitude with the technology of online publishing.

Here's what online employers say they are looking for in new recruits:

- an interest in current affairs at all levels;
- sound news judgement;
- an ability to write in a style that is easy to understand;
- a willingness to accept irregular hours;
- an understanding of the online audience;
- an affinity with the medium;
- the ability to present information with clarity when under pressure;
- an understanding of the unique attributes of online technology as it relates to journalism; and
- competence with the key technology used in online journalism.

How do you get a job in online journalism?

Most new recruits to online journalism will have journalism degrees or postgraduate qualifications. (The days of hiring geeks who can't write are over.) Those qualifications will not necessarily be solely in online journalism. In fact, if you can demonstrate competence across several media, you will be seen as highly useful. Many will have NCTJ qualifications.

Michael Nutley, editor of *New Media Age*, a business magazine that serves those who work in online publishing, counsels against choosing a training course that concentrates too closely on online journalism. 'You are cutting off your options if you do that,' he says. 'I'd say get training that exposes you to a range of media.'

I'm most proud of organising a text message poetry competition that attracted thousands of entries mainly from people who had never written a poem in their lives. VIC KEEGAN, ONLINE EDITOR, *THE GUARDIAN*

At least a basic understanding of html, or the ability to use a package such as Dreamweaver, will stand you in good stead. Some employers may be looking for a high level of competence in technical skills, such as JavaScript or Java. If you want to be involved in site design, or are a photographer working online, you will need to know Photoshop, Illustrator, Fireworks or Flash. Not every online journalist is competent in these things, just as not all drivers know what happens under the bonnet of their car. But be clear whether you are keen to learn these skills or not, and if not, avoid jobs where they are needed, or there will be disappointment all round.

Not all recruits to online journalism came straight into that medium. Many started out on newspapers and magazines and moved across. For example,

Emily Bell, editor-in-chief of *Guardian Unlimited*, studied law at Oxford, then joined *Big Farm Weekly*, and spent five years as media business editor of *The Observer* before taking her online chief's job in 2000.

Who takes trainees?

Many ISPs plus newspaper, magazine and broadcaster-linked sites have dedicated teams of online journalists. With budgets tight, there are often greater opportunities for work experience than in traditional media, but don't expect too many formal traineeships. Even with a degree or postgraduate qualification in journalism, you are likely to start with unpaid work experience, which you have won because of your computer skills and your awareness of the potential and practices of online journalism. That work experience can be very rewarding, both in terms of the experience gained and the amount of material you amass for your cuttings book. You could easily find yourself being asked to put up several stories a day online.

Cunning is the attribute a journalist most needs. JOHN WELLINGTON, *MAIL ON SUNDAY*

The Association of Online Publishers, which represents many of the major UK online publishers, says that, with an increasing skills shortage, there are growing opportunities for young journalists and would-be journalists seeking work experience, trainee places and jobs in the medium. However, with a medium that is still relatively young, many companies are still addressing the question of what qualifications they expect their journalists to have, and what training they feel they can offer.

Alexandra White, director of the AOP, says:

> Our organisation was only formed in 2002 and we are now, in the light of a growing skills shortage, working with our members to identify the essential skills needs for journalists in online companies and have a committee looking at the whole question of what training and which courses are best suited to the medium.

If an online publisher has its roots in another medium, it is likely to look for the same qualities, experience and qualifications in its online recruits as in its old media ones.

It is fair to say that many predominantly online publishers have no formal structure for offering work experience, or training places, and no clear criteria by which they judge would-be recruits. No doubt that will change rapidly over the next few years but, for now, here is a representative survey of the scene. For a full listing of contacts for work experience, training and jobs, go to Section 4. NCTJ-accredited journalism courses are listed in Section 3.

AOL

Vicky Prior, senior communications manager for AOL (UK) says:

> Members of our editorial team have a variety of experience and qualifications. As a general rule, experience and attitude are as important as specific educational or professional qualifications.
> We tend to look for journalistic experience gained in either traditional or new media. Depending on the job, we look for people with writing or sub-editing skills and, crucially, the ability and understanding to adapt those skills to a web audience. As the industry matures, we increasingly expect people to have some experience of working online.

AOL does not offer a graduate training programme. It had, at the time of writing, just offered its first extended summer work placement and was considering developing the scheme in the future.

Associated New Media

The owners of the *Daily Mail*, *Mail on Sunday* and *Evening Standard* also have a clutch of websites, including thisislondon.co.uk, femail.co.uk, thisismoney.co.uk and thisistravel.co.uk. All draw heavily on material **re-purposed** from newspapers, but also contain web-exclusive material. For work experience, contact the sites directly via e-mail.

BBC

The BBC offers a bursary to one online journalist a year, with a six-month placement on its news website, bbc.co.uk. You need either to have recently completed a journalism course or have less than two years journalism experience, and a passion for science and technology.

The best thing about being a journalist is getting paid for something you'd do for nothing if you had to. JOHN SMITH, SENIOR LECTURER, DARLINGTON COLLEGE

There are substantial opportunities for work experience across the corporation's online enterprises. As with TV and radio, all vacancies are advertised on the BBC's website, and although they are extensive (scores are listed at any one time) demand is strong, so check regularly and apply as soon as something suitable is posted.

Brand Republic

When you are looking for work experience, don't forget the web versions of magazines and newspapers. Haymarket's Brand Republic, for example, is the home of *Campaign* and *Marketing* magazines on the web, and serves the world of advertising, marketing, public relations and new media. Editor Gordon MacMillan's advice, if you want to work on his own or any other magazine-related website, is this:

> You should contact web-editors directly if you are interested in work experience, but you must have more than a vague idea of who you are applying to. It's always nice to have a pre-entry qualification, but we take people for work experience who don't have them. When hiring, however, we would only hire someone young without experience if they had a pre-entry qualification (as we did this year, from Cardiff). We're unlikely to hire graduates with no pre-entry or experience. We are looking for enthusiasm, some knowledge and writing skills. We always put people through a writing test.
>
> The length of placements varies; we have had people for a week or for several months. If we have the free space, we're happy to have people in. Working online at a rolling news website means that someone doing work experience will get to write a lot and so, hopefully, in turn will learn something and walk away with useful hands-on experience. A placement hasn't led to a job so far, but it's a definite possibility.

Stick with it, and be prepared to do some crappy jobs before you get to do the better ones. Don't get sucked into the glamour that surrounds media, it can be hard work. JUSTIN LAMBERT, BBC GARDENER'S WORLD MAGAZINE

Financial Times

The *FT*'s graduate training scheme covers a stint at ft.com, but will also take you right around the newspaper. Dan Bogler, managing editor, says: 'We take two or three trainees a year. They are all graduates, and usually have a degree or postgraduate qualification in journalism.' You get an initial three months on a Reuters-designed journalism course, followed by a series of six-month attachments, one of which will be to the website.

Guardian Unlimited

Guardian Unlimited, the online edition of the *Guardian* newspaper, offers a small number of one- or two-week work placements (or internships as they prefer to call them). They are open to student journalists and recent graduates who can demonstrate a commitment to journalism and an enthusiasm for the possibilities of the internet. Successful applicants will be placed on one of the *Guardian Unlimited*'s network of websites (media, politics, society, arts, news, books, film, sport, education, money and travel).

The best thing about being a journalist is being a journalist. KENNY CAMPBELL, EDITOR, METRO

The Press Association

The Press Association (PA) runs a three-year multimedia journalist traineeship designed to equip the successful candidate with news-reporting skills across the media. It combines 18 months' formal classroom tuition with on-the-job training at one of its news centres, focusing on video gathering and news reporting, followed by a similar period working as part of its multimedia reporting team. A permanent job with PA is likely to follow. There is also a one-year production journalist training programme, for journalists who want a career in editing, design, new media and production.

They say:

> The course will comprise intensive classroom tuition in all aspects of the modern sub-editor's role, including story construction, style, grammar, headline writing, design, Quark and Photoshop skills and newspaper law. This will be followed by attachments to all the production desks within the PA, including the main news wire (serving national and regional newspapers, broadcasters and online publishers), Teletext, digital, video and page-ready news, features and sport. Subject to satisfactory completion of the programme, the trainee will be awarded the PA Diploma in Sub-editing and the trainee position is likely to lead to a permanent position with the Press Association.

TEAMtalk

TEAMtalk, based in Leeds, runs sports websites, including sportinglife.com, the companion site to the *Sporting Life* newspaper, as well as teamtalk.com, sportal.com, bettingzone.co.uk, football365.com, and golf365.com. It has opportunities for work experience, and expects you to directly contact the website that interests you.

What they want from you

Someone who is hugely flexible and multi-talented. You'll need to be even more flexible than a trainee on one of the more traditional media, because 24-hour working is common. They'll expect you to understand the web and its audience. They'll want you to turn your hand to a very wide range of skills, some of them traditionally associated with reporting, some with sub-editing and production.

What qualifications will I need?

Most journalists have at least five GCSEs (grades A–C), including English, and two A levels or vocational A levels. Over 70 per cent have a degree – not necessarily in journalism. To get on a degree course you need at least two A levels or vocational A levels and five GCSEs (grades A–C), or equivalent qualifications. GCSE English is essential. Most employers will be looking for an undergraduate degree, plus a postgraduate diploma in journalism.

> *The one piece of advice I would give to anyone considering a career in journalism is: read the papers – a tabloid, a broadsheet, and a regional – every day! And make lots of contacts early on.*
> LAURA NAYLOR, MA STUDENT, NOTTINGHAM TRENT UNIVERSITY

It is worth pointing out that, while the online medium may look a good deal different from print, the training required to be a good online journalist is, at heart, exactly the same as for a print journalist. This means that NCTJ-accredited courses will equip you extremely well for a career in online journalism. As the technical know-how necessary to publish online reduces, most online journalists find that they need to master very little that is technical. Modern content management systems make putting a story online as easy as writing an e-mail, and the reporting skills required in online are exactly the same as those for the print media.

What will I have to study?

As will have become clear to you from the earlier sections of this chapter, many online publishers are still uncertain about exactly what training they would like their journalists to have. Where web publishers have their roots in traditional media, they tend to fall back on the training requirements they have in their core newspaper, magazine or broadcasting businesses. Stand-alone web businesses tend to be uncertain what training they require.

So, when in doubt, you could do a lot worse than follow an NCTJ course. As has been mentioned by more than one of those quoted above, a qualification and experience in traditional media stand online journalists in good stead. As mentioned in Chapter 1, there is a wide range of different types of course you can study. Here is a brief run-down:

- BA (Hons) degree. A course which offers the opportunity to gain the NCTJ qualification while studying for a degree at university.
- Foundation degree. A two-year course of study during which time students sit their NCTJ exams. The option of topping up the foundation degree with an additional year of study to gain a BA is sometimes available.
- One-year postgraduate qualification. Usually an MA or postgraduate diploma, this type of course would suit a graduate who is looking to gain the NCTJ qualification.
- Fast-track. Ideal for those who want to study intensively for 18–20 weeks to gain the NCTJ pre-entry qualification.
- Pre-entry academic year. Offered through further education centres, a one-year course to study for the NCTJ pre-entry qualification.
- Two-year HND. An opportunity to gain the NCTJ pre-entry qualification while studying for a Higher National Diploma.

For a comprehensive list of the courses available, go to Section 3 or to the NCTJ website at www.nctj.com.

NCTJ-accredited reporting courses cover shorthand, and those aspects of law, public affairs and newspaper journalism necessary to enable a journalist to perform competently by the end of the training period. As well as demonstrating competence in these and other practical areas, trainees are expected to achieve 100 words per minute in Teeline shorthand.

The NCTJ also awards sub-editing qualifications, which cover everything on the reporter syllabus, except shorthand.

Your ultimate aim is the NCTJ's National Certificate Examination (NCE), the qualification most editors in Britain agree is the best proof a journalist has been properly trained. To get it, you have to:

- have the minimum academic qualifications (see above);
- pass the NCTJ preliminary examinations in journalism, law and public affairs;
- pass an NCTJ shorthand examination at a speed of at least 100 words per minute;
- do at least 18 months' paid work as a trainee journalist on a newspaper;

- compile an NCTJ portfolio of story cuttings (examples of things you have written during your training on a newspaper); and
- pass the final NCTJ National Certificate Examination (NCE).

The full programme normally takes about two years, which includes between six and nine months studying for the preliminary exams at a university, college or by distance learning, and 18 months working on a newspaper or other publication. You can do the college course first and then get a job, or find yourself a job first and do your studying while already employed.

Postgraduate fast-track courses lasting between 18 and 20 weeks are available at some colleges.

Anyone wanting a well-paid job should definitely not go into journalism. LENA DAVIES, TRAINEE REPORTER, SLOUGH OBSERVER

What else will I learn as a trainee?

Again, a mix of what you'll learn in other media. Depending on whether you are focused on reporting or production during your work experience attachments, you will learn a range of the following:

- How to be a better reporter, so you get the story.
- How to be a better story-teller, so you tell it well.
- How to be a better editor, so you use text, audio, stills and video where they will help tell a story and not simply for the sake of using them.
- How to recognise the news that will interest your audience.
- How to write concise, bright, accurate copy to a tight deadline.
- How to find stories, how to research stories comprehensively and how to interview.
- How to develop a thick skin and to recognise when sensitivity is called for.
- The vital importance of a contacts book.
- How to trawl competitors and other media for stories you can develop for your own publication.

What will I earn?

Trainee and raw-recruit salaries vary enormously in the range from £12,000 to £17,000.

How to improve your chances of getting a job

You will need to show that you are steeped in the online ethos, can demonstrate a wide knowledge of online news and entertainment sites, and possess a clear understanding of how news can best be presented online. Know that interaction with the user is a vital ingredient of a website's offering. In online journalism you don't just tell readers the news; you interact with them, enabling them to express their opinions about it and discuss its implications.

Edit or work on your school or university magazine. Work for free on a website to get experience. Write a **blog** – it can be about your travels, a hobby or anything that lends itself to regular updating. Write it as a reporter would, focusing on what has happened; don't just give your views on events, like a columnist. And remember, your blog should be a demonstration of what a great employee you would be, so don't present an image on it that would damage your chances with an employer.

Design a website as an illustration of what you can do – it will become a highly effective CV. Show that you understand offline media and that you will be able to help reporters steeped in the traditions of newspapers and magazines or TV and radio to adapt the ways that they work for online journalism.

Life as a trainee

If you are on a website allied to a newspaper or magazine, you may find you are filling a very traditional role, as either a reporter or a sub-editor. On a stand-alone website, because online staffs are small and the medium requires a good deal of technical input and mastery of a wide range of skills that stem from both print media and broadcasting, your training will inevitably cover a wide range of tasks. Employers are often looking for technical skills far more than journalistic ones. If you do start out in online journalism, expect to begin as a general dogsbody, doing basic html, sourcing photographs, liaising with content providers and generally helping out.

On sites where original news material is generated, you can find yourself checking the wires, chasing up press releases, tracking down spokespeople for comment and writing a stream of news that will have to be produced swiftly and accurately. This is the sort of training that would stand any reporter in good stead – even if they ended up on a newspaper.

On sites where only minimal copy is originated by the online team, the opportunities to write stories or create other original editorial content will be very limited. If a major media company has a website, it may take content from its other arms – its movie company, record company and TV news channel, for example.

The material that is generated by the online team will be in a form appropriate to the web. So, for instance, you might spend a day building up a **slide show** of celebrities on a particular theme, such as 'Bad hair day' or 'Awful Oscar frocks', and writing a witty caption to accompany each.

Your name soon gets known by readers and people will speak to you in shops and in the street because they know you as the voice of their local paper. STEPHEN SINFIELD, REPORTER, RIPLEY AND HEANOR NEWS

Such a website – and most ISPs fall into this category – is likely to have commercial partners. The deal with them is likely to be that they provide content in some form, and you place **banner ads** or links on the relevant pages, encouraging readers either to go to the partner's own website or to enter into e-commerce with them.

This blurring of the line that exists in traditional media between editorial and advertising is something you need to be comfortable with if you are to be happy in this sort of online environment. Such relationships need a lot of managing, and as a raw recruit you may find that it is this that fills up your day. You may be building pages on which partner copy appears, and ensuring the links they require are as they want them.

DAY IN THE LIFE

A young journalist working for a business magazine's web edition

Iain O'Neil, online reporter, themorningadvertiser.co.uk

When someone of the stature of Rupert Murdoch says the internet is an 'opportunity to improve our journalism and expand our reach' you know it's time to take online publishing very seriously. My switch from regional newspapers to a news website was the best career move I've made.

I've always been interested in the internet and the possibilities it offers but I've never known anything about how it all works. However, since I've been at the *Morning Advertiser* all that has changed. In the past nine months I've learnt to use Photoshop, **RSS feeds** and even some html.

My route into journalism was fairly traditional. I went to university then signed up for an NCTJ postgraduate course at Harlow. While there I was sent to the *Brentwood Gazette* in Essex for work experience on Fridays and luckily for me a position became available exactly as I completed my course. I spent three invaluable years covering regional news in West Essex and the training I received is just as important to my online work.

The basic principles of cultivating contacts and how to spot and write a good story are exactly the same, but obviously the production side is very different.

My work for morningadvertiser.co.uk [the web edition of the *Morning Advertiser*, a weekly magazine serving the pub trade] involves as much design, production and re-sizing pictures as it does writing copy. I get much more input in how the final product looks and works than is possible in a printed newspaper.

We get instant feedback on our stories from our readers and we offer them **forums** and access to archive stories – things they cannot get from our highly successful magazine.

The website is also much more about breaking news. If a story changes throughout the day I follow it and update our copy, which is something I love because I hate sitting on stories waiting for press day and watching the opposition to see if they've got it first.

The internet is all about speed. To get people to visit our site we aim to get the news first. Internet users have unlimited options in front of them and if we offer them something they've already seen they will go elsewhere. We also package our news differently. We cut the number of words and use as many images as we can to make the copy pleasing to the eye.

Because of the need to get things first, my day starts early. Every morning I turn on my laptop at 7.30am. I work from home in the mornings – because I can update the site from anywhere there is mobile phone coverage – but I drive into the office most days to keep up-to-date with the stories the magazine journalists are working on.

I scour the newswires for stories and I prepare and send our daily e-mail news alerts, which go to thousands of readers all across the world. I also take my laptop 'on the road' to industry meetings and Commons debates in an effort to stay ahead of the competition. I would hate to have to wait for press day to publish some of the stories we get.

At the newspaper we would go out, gather the news, follow up leads and come back to the office to write it up. Then it would be out of our hands. Now I take my printing press with me everywhere I go. If something happens I can write it up instantly and get it on our site – that is the main difference for me.

Online publishing is relatively new but, like everything on the internet, it is moving at an incredible pace and by getting in now I hope to be ahead of the game.

If you think this might be for you...

If it sounds good so far, you can find out more about NCTJ qualifications at www.nctj.com.

Contact details:
NCTJ Training Limited,
The New Granary,
Station Road,
Newport,
Saffron Walden,
Essex CB11 3PL
01799 544014
Fax: 01799 544015
info@nctj.com

5

NEWS AGENCIES

Are news agencies for you?

News agencies come in all shapes and sizes. Perhaps the most famous is Reuters, which covers the world with 2,300 journalists in 190 bureaux. It competes in the UK with the Press Association, and several other major agencies, which supply national and international news.

As media converge, the news agencies are coming into their own. From their roots in print, supplying text stories to newspapers, the major agencies have become multimedia giants, tailoring material for each and every one of the media. This means that a news agency will need all the skills that are present in newspapers and magazines, TV, radio and online. They also offer completed pages for newspapers, covering areas such as sports results, so also employ production journalists.

At college you really don't learn much about the practicalities of the job. Working on an agency [in Bristol] taught me a lot about 'selling a story'. If you can get a news editor interested, you can get a reader interested. SIMON BUCKS, ASSOCIATE EDITOR, SKY NEWS

But there are also many smaller agencies. They include well-resourced regional agencies that supply all categories of news and pictures from a city or other substantial geographic area; specialist agencies which cover a particular field, such as sport, health or showbiz; and one-man local outfits that might concentrate on a particular Crown Court.

The National Association of Press Agencies (NAPA), which represents many of the smaller UK agencies, says working for an agency:

is one of the best opportunities for young reporters and photographers – and more experienced ones – to begin a career in national newspapers. Most NAPA agencies employ a staff of reporters and photographers. Some also employ feature writers. Journalism is a challenging profession and successful agency reporters use their enthusiasm for the job to meet exacting standards. The hours can be long, the work sometimes frustrating and the rewards are not always immediate.

News agencies differ from other media organisations in that, by and large, their role is not to publish in their own branded newspapers, TV news programmes or other outlets. Rather, they are suppliers of information to other news organisations which either publish it as supplied to them, with or without a **credit**, or use it as raw material to inform its own reporting. Reports in newspapers will often contain agency copy in addition to that created by its by-lined reporter.

I started out as a freelance shift journalist at a London news agency. [I succeeded] by getting some good news stories that started earning the agency money. I was actually at university in London but I didn't tell anyone and skipped lectures for shifts. I got a few exclusives that caught the News of the World's attention and that set me up. JAMES TONEY, MANAGING EDITOR, NEWS ASSOCIATES/SPORTSBEAT AGENCY

Increasingly, major news agencies supply breaking news headlines and other material to websites and for distribution via other electronic media such as mobile phones. Sport is an area in which agencies dominate.

The best thing about being a journalist is you can say what you like and get away with it most of the time. MARK HOULDEY, EDITOR AND OWNER, KNS NEWS AGENCY, NORWICH

What do news agency journalists do?

Given the very wide range of material that news agencies cover, the range of jobs journalists do at them is enormous – just as wide as that in online journalism, and then some. In a major agency, there will be plenty of reporters covering, as Reuters puts it in describing its functions, 'everything from corporate takeovers to market crises and wars to political turmoil', and specialist **correspondents** covering education, politics, sport, features, financial news and other areas. By no means all agency journalists are reporters. Just as with a newspaper, there will be sub-editors, editors and other production journalists.

During training in an agency, the emphasis will be on gaining the basic ability to report news – a skill that underlies almost everything else a journalist does. In a small, local agency, you will work in a similar way to a local newspaper reporter, covering the patch and tackling anything that comes up on it. You will also respond to assignments from national newspapers and others to investigate stories. This might be something as simple as knocking on the door of a person who is involved in some way in a major story the paper is investigating. Nationals also use local agencies for their contacts – they know agencies will often know how to find someone on their patch more easily than a national reporter who has just stepped off a train.

Many routine news events are only attended by the agency reporter, with all other outlets relying on them, so a news agency reporter's material could go to dozens of outlets. So, if you are a reporter who likes to be out of the office, agency reporting could be for you. However, if you live for by-lines, then you are likely to suffer constant disappointment – you don't get the glory of having your name on a story all that often when you work for an agency. You may even suffer the ignominy of seeing someone else's name on your work, as some newspapers still prefer to by-line their own correspondent, even when they had nothing to do with the material.

> *If you're considering doing a course, make sure it's one that offers you practical experience in professional newsrooms that you can boast about to potential employers.* ANDREW HILL, COMMENT AND ANALYSIS EDITOR, *FINANCIAL TIMES*

Do you have what it takes?

This is what employers say they are looking for in trainees, although not all aptitudes will apply to every agency:

- a keen interest in current affairs at all levels;
- an enquiring mind;
- sound news judgement;
- a lively interest in people, places and events;
- a talent for communicating;
- good spelling, grammar and punctuation;
- an ability to express complex issues in simple, direct language;
- a willingness to accept irregular hours (and, for some, foreign postings);
- an ability to work under pressure to meet deadlines; and
- determination and persistence.

How do you get a job in a news agency?

The major agencies have well-established training schemes and a substantial number of opportunities for internships and work experience placements. Check their websites and advertisements in the *Media Guardian* and other outlets. The National Association of Press Agencies, which represents many of the smaller agencies in the UK, has this to say about finding a job:

> Like many industries some openings are never advertised – being filled internally, or through personal contacts. The most common vehicle used for advertising vacancies is the situations vacant column of UK *Press Gazette*. However, it can be worth putting in a speculative letter. Lots of NAPA members have a healthy turnover of staff and application letters 'kept on file' are often used to help draw up shortlists for interviews. Some agencies prefer to receive job applications in writing, but you may also e-mail principals. In either case you should include a concise CV.

A list of agencies is included in Section 3.

Who takes trainees?

Local news agencies

Many local agencies take work experience, and have trainees, although not all their trainees work towards an NCTJ or other qualification. Their strength is the strong practical experience they offer.

> *In what other profession could I meet the King of Jordan, Angelina Jolie, Kelly Holmes, Mark E. Smith, Jacques Chirac, Bill Clinton, Iain Paisley, various terrorists and their acolytes, Mrs Thatcher, and the leaders of the Sandinistas – plus get paid for doing so?* GAVIN ESLER, PRESENTER, BBC2 NEWSNIGHT

One, KNS news in Norwich, provides news and features to national newspapers and magazines and is run by Mark Houldey. The agency takes people on work experience and also has trainees. Mark is less interested in what experience and qualification a person has than in how they come across. He says:

> I prefer them to give me a phone call and then a meeting to have a chat. You can't beat on-the-job training from experienced journalists and learning as you go along. I went on a year's

pre-entry course at Highbury College, Portsmouth, which I found useful, but I prefer to recruit through recommendations and people who telephone me. Enthusiasm and intelligence count more than qualifications. The best way to get a job is to phone up the person who hands out the jobs and arrange to meet them.

The Press Association

The Press Association offers a range of traineeships that reflect the multimedia nature of its operations, and the fact it produces finished material that is ready for print. It says that most of its trainees already have journalistic qualifications and experience through graduate or postgraduate courses, but that it values talent, enthusiasm and 'a real drive to succeed' over academic achievements.

If you're not sure it's what you want to do, don't do it. JOHN SMITH, SENIOR LECTURER, DARLINGTON COLLEGE

Among the courses the PA runs is a three-year multimedia journalist traineeship designed to equip the successful candidate with news-reporting skills across the media. It combines 18 months' formal classroom tuition with on-the-job training at one of its news centres, focusing on video gathering and news reporting, followed by a similar period working as part of its multimedia reporting team. A permanent job with the PA is likely to follow. There is also a one-year production journalist training programme for journalists who want a career in editing, design, new media and production.

They say:

> The course will comprise intensive classroom tuition in all aspects of the modern sub-editor's role, including story construction, style, grammar, headline writing, design, Quark and Photoshop skills and newspaper law. This will be followed by attachments to all the production desks within the PA, including the main news wire (serving national and regional newspapers, broadcasters and online publishers), Teletext, digital, video and page-ready news, features and sport. Subject to satisfactory completion of the programme, the trainee will be awarded the PA Diploma in Sub-editing and the trainee position is likely to lead to a permanent position with the Press Association.

The PA also runs a two-year Sport Editorial Traineeship that covers every aspect of sports reporting and production. Trainees learn how to write for national and regional newspapers, for international clients, and for Teletext, digital, and new media. There is tuition in sub-editing, in page design for those with an aptitude for it, and the training 'could lead to a permanent position'.

When I was a trainee, senior journalists expected trainees to pick everything up by osmosis. CATHY DUNCAN, ASSISTANT EDITOR, SOUTH WALES EVENING POST

Reuters

Reuters has its own in-house training scheme for graduates, plus internships and placements. The graduate training scheme is primarily focused on financial and business journalism, so applicants will be expected to demonstrate an interest in this area. You'll need to be fluent in English plus either Arabic, Chinese, Russian or German.

Reuters' three-month internships and 12-month placements are designed to appeal to gap-year students. They offer around 60 attachments in total, but don't invite speculative applications. You need to monitor Reuters' website, and look out for advertisements.

They say:

> Reuters looks for bright, motivated self-starters for our internships. In return for their enthusiasm and hard work, we aim to provide them with exposure to varied and interesting projects which are often high-profile within the organisation. In previous years, Reuters has employed some outstanding interns who gained invaluable experience, greatly assisting them in their future careers.

What they want from you

The national and international agencies often require fluency in a second language and expect a deep interest in and knowledge of international business and current affairs. This comes in addition to the universal requirement that you are a keen, hard-working, flexible, inquisitive, inexpensive dogsbody, and that you have a ready acceptance of long days and unsocial hours.

The best thing about my training was being treated as a grown-up and being encouraged to act independently while adhering to general policy and rules of engagement. Both inside and outside the office I was treated as an equal . . . age, gender and background were not issues. MARY-ANN BLOOMFIELD, EDITOR, MID-DEVON GAZETTE SERIES

As a reporter in a small agency you will find yourself in a very tough environment. Often, when a big story breaks, the **Fleet Street** pack descends on an area. The local agency only makes money if its reporter gets facts or an angle everyone else has missed. Knowing your patch inside out and having brilliant contacts is the only way to succeed.

What qualifications will I need?

Depending on the agency, trainees are accepted with any qualification from GCSE to postgraduate level. Although there are some A-level entrants, the majority are graduates or postgraduates, and many have an NCTJ journalism qualification. Make sure you know what experience and qualifications the agency expects applicants to have. If a traineeship anticipates that you already have shorthand, there is no point applying if you don't.

What will I have to study?

If the agency's training courses are accredited by the National Council for the Training of Journalists, they will cover the core requirements outlined in Chapter 1. If you are not being offered NCTJ-approved training, you need to consider whether the agency is giving you the professional support that you need. You may decide that the benefit of the practical experience gained outweighs the lack of formal training, but think carefully whether this will hold you back in your career should you wish to leave the agency and join, for example, a regional newspaper.

> *The best thing about being a journalist is reading a first-rate newspaper that you have helped to produce.* NEIL DARBYSHIRE, EXECUTIVE, DAILY MAIL

What else will I learn as a trainee?

You will also learn the following:

- What news is.
- How to tailor what you write to a specific audience and medium.
- How to write concise, bright, accurate copy to a tight deadline.
- How to find stories, how to research stories comprehensively and how to interview.
- How to develop a thick skin and to recognise when sensitivity is called for.

- The vital importance of a contacts book.
- How to trawl competitors and other media for stories you can develop for your own clients.

In a major agency you will undergo an intense rotation around the key desks, and learn everything from financial reporting to sport and politics. In a small agency you'll be learning how to survive in the most competitive newsgathering environment imaginable.

What will I earn?

Trainee salaries can be anything from £12,000 to £18,000, depending on the stature of the agency.

I moved from a north London weekly, to the Press Association before moving into Fleet Street at the age of 22. HEATHER PREEN, ASSISTANT EDITOR, DAILY EXPRESS

How to improve your chances of getting a job

You should be able to demonstrate that you have a real interest in news, and that you have taken every opportunity to gain work experience on newspapers, magazines, on television or radio, or at press agencies. Editing or contributing to school or university magazines is a good start and having work-experience placements is another. And if you can show **cuttings** – ideally with by-lines – so much the better.

Life as a trainee

In a major agency with a graduate recruitment programme, you will probably begin with a couple of months induction, where they make sure you know the basics: that you can write a good news story and that your law, shorthand and general knowledge are up to scratch. The PA says its scheme offers 'a mix of formal classroom training, the environment of a modern multimedia news-room, professional tutors and working with talented and experienced people'.

Following induction, you will probably start a string of attachments to the main reporting desks – general news, financial, political and so on. You will be overseen by a senior person on the desk, and perhaps mentored by a more experienced reporter. Within a few months you will be covering major stories unaided, interviewing senior figures in business, politics and other fields, and seeing your stories printed prominently in a wide range of newspapers, on websites and used as the basis for radio and television reports.

> I went to [a free paper] for work experience because a friend of mine worked there, and while I was there, he handed his notice in. They took me on as a temporary stop gap, and I brought in a front-page story. They asked me to apply for his job, which I got, and I stayed there for two years. WENNA COOMBS, CHIEF REPORTER, WESTON AND SOMERSET MERCURY

The aim is to create a structured environment in which you can broaden your experience, hone your skills and build up that all-essential network of contacts. If all goes well, and the agency is international, you can expect to be assigned to an overseas bureau after a year or so. If the agency is purely domestic, you'll move into a permanent position on the desk for which you showed the greatest aptitude.

Reuters says this about its scheme:

> In the graduate programme, you begin with an intensive six-week induction and writing course, then move straight to the newsroom for hands-on reporting. After just a few months, you could be interviewing the CEO of a major company. The next day, you could be questioning a politician during an election race or reporting from the scene of a coup. Your reports could make headlines in the world's top dailies, pop up on websites around the globe or be read out on radio and television bulletins. Guided by experienced professionals, you will hone your skills, broaden your knowledge and develop your all-important contact network. Subject to satisfactory progress, you can expect to be assigned to a news bureau overseas after a year or so.

If the agency you are on is a small one, things may be much less structured. Often there is no formal training leading to an NCTJ qualification, which means that while your practical experience may be excellent, you will not have paper qualifications. Once again, the emphasis will be on training you to be a good reporter. If the agency covers a geographic patch, developing a comprehensive network of contacts will be even more important than for your rivals on the local newspaper or radio station. In almost everything you do you will be competing with those rivals. They only need you if you have knowledge or information that they do not have. If the Fleet Street pack descends to cover a big story in your area, you will probably file your copy to all the nationals, but they will only use the information their own reporter has not been able to glean. You might get one paragraph in a long report, but you'll have the satisfaction of knowing that it is there because your reporting skills outshone those of the staffer – at least in some detail or angle.

You will often be asked to do things on behalf of a national newspaper or magazine. For instance, a national may get a local agency to call round to a person whom they wish to interview, or to find someone whom they believe lives on your patch but they can't easily trace themselves.

Although we have a reputation for being a bit manic, I think the best quality a journalist can possess is organisation. Organised journalists are the best journalists, especially if managing other people. ROBIN SLINGSBY, ASSISTANT EDITOR, NORTH SHROPSHIRE CHRONICLE

Your value to your agency depends entirely on you getting results. To outwit all the opposition, you need to know everything there is to know about your patch.

DAY IN THE LIFE

Young journalist working for a regional news agency

Andrea Daniel, trainee reporter, KNS News/cash4yourstory agency in Norwich, Norfolk

I got the job with the agency because I used to work as a researcher for a TV company which shared an office with KNS News. I approached Mark and Jonathan, who run the agency, and asked whether there were any opportunities. As it happened, the girl who worked for them was leaving at the end of her six-month contract and they agreed to give me a month's trial.

After the month was up they took me out for a meal and I was delighted when they told me that they were very pleased with what I had done. I was offered a six-month contract and now I have been working for KNS News for nearly a year. It is the best job I have ever had and I look forward to going to work every day with excitement. I know that sounds corny, but it's true. Every day is different. I work mainly on stories for women's magazines such as *That's Life*, *Take A Break*, *Real People*, *Love It*, etc., while Mark and Jonathan work mainly for the national newspapers and handle the administration of the business.

An average day would go something like this: I arrive at 8.30am and check e-mails from overnight to see if there are any new stories to chase up. We operate

---

a system whereby people contact us with stories and we sell them to magazines, getting them a fee at the same time. From the overnight e-mails there are probably several that need chasing up. I will then contact the person who has e-mailed us and talk to them at some length to find out whether they have a story which is worth pursuing. If it is, I check with either Jonathan or Mark to make sure the story is saleable. Then, if they agree, I will pitch it to our contacts on the magazines. Invariably we find our instincts about stories are right and we are able to sell it. It is then a case of getting contracts out to the people concerned, interviewing them at greater length, organising for a photographer to take pictures, then writing the story.

I find the job interesting and challenging. Some of the people I speak to have extraordinary stories and it really is no holds barred. For instance, one of the first stories I worked on was about a woman who had done a giant poo! I am now 11 months into my job and I have never looked back. In the short term I am planning to study for my full NCTJ proficiency certificate via a correspondence course. It is hard work, but rewarding, and I would thoroughly recommend the career path to other young people.

DAY IN THE LIFE

Young journalist working for a major news agency

Catherine Hornby is a trainee journalist at the Reuters news agency

As a graduate trainee at Reuters, there are no typical days. The programme is so varied that every day you can be doing something new and exciting. If I am on a financial desk, such as equities or foreign exchange, I tend to arrive quite early in the morning, at around 7am. This is when the markets open and I often have to write an opening report, which could be for the sterling currency market, the coffee commodities market, or the FTSE stock market.

I normally check which key events are coming up during that day, and mention anything that is likely to have an impact on trade in my report. Then I call an analyst or a trader and speak to him/her about the market and what he or she thinks will be the main driving force on that day. Once I have a good quote to back up my story, I write up the report, usually in about half an hour, and include the current price levels in the market.

After that is out on the wire, I start to chase up developments in the market. For example, if one company's stock starts to surge when I am working on the

(Continued)

equities desk, then I will phone around traders and find out if there is a rumour in the market or any new information about that company which is circulating. If I get the same story from two or three traders, I can send out an alert followed by a more in-depth story explaining the increase in that particular stock and the main reason for the rise.

Sometimes I go to news conferences or briefings, which are often held by companies who want to present new products, or a bank which invites several investors and clients to talk about topics such as investing in China. I go along and listen out for an interesting angle that I could use in a story, which I write up on the same day. I have to make sure I get back to the office in time for my shorthand lesson at around midday.

During the afternoon I may also make some calls for a more long-term feature or analysis that I'm working on about market trends or new developments. Towards the end of the day I will also be preparing to write the closing report for the market and put in a last call to a trader.

At any time, if a major story breaks, such as a police raid or a train crash, I can expect to be sent out to the scene to gather quotes and background from people who are caught up in the event. This adds a lot of excitement to the job as you often get sent to cover really big stories.

I wanted to get into journalism from quite a young age because I have always enjoyed writing as well as talking to others about their experiences and feelings, and relaying that back to other people. I had fun writing and editing school newspapers and I went on to get involved with various student and street papers at university in Edinburgh. The fact that I lived abroad when I was younger gave me an advantage for being taken on by Reuters because I managed to pick up quite a few languages, which is really valued here, because Reuters is such a global company.

If you think this might be for you...

If it sounds good so far, you can find out more about NCTJ qualifications at www.nctj.com.

Contact details:
NCTJ Training Limited,
The New Granary,
Station Road,
Newport,
Saffron Walden,

Essex CB11 3PL
01799 544014
Fax: 01799 544015
info@nctj.com

You can find out more about the training courses on offer by visiting the agencies' own websites at www.reuters.com.uk, www.thepagroup.com and, for local agencies, via www.napa.org.uk.

6

SPORT

Is sports journalism for you?

You might think this is a simple question to answer. If you like sport, then obviously sports journalism is for you. Certainly, if you don't like sport, you should do something else. But there is much more to being a sports journalist than being a sports fan.

The first question is – is *journalism* for you? If you have read through this book reasonably systematically up to this point, you will probably have a clear answer to that question by now. If you haven't, you might just skim back through the preceding chapters. But if you can't face that right now, here are some key points to bear in mind.

> *If you want to be a sports journalist, have an interest in more than just football. And don't say: 'I just want to watch sport and get paid'.* JAMES TONEY, MANAGING EDITOR, SPORTSBEAT/NEWS ASSOCIATES

First, sports journalism is more than just writing. While there are sports reporters and sports features writers, there are also sports production journalists – sub-editors and editors. So if you don't see yourself as a writer, but still see yourself working in sports, there are a number of other jobs you might consider.

Secondly, sport coverage appears in all media – newspapers, magazines, on radio and TV, on websites, mobile phones and all sorts of other electronic devices. Also, sports copy is provided by news and specialist sports agencies to a number of outlets across a range of media. So you will need to consider which of these media appeal to you, or whether you would like to work for an agency and contribute to a range of media.

Some sports journalists enjoy specialising in the printed word, and will be happiest on newspapers or magazines. Others are happier with the spoken word, and so will be more at home on radio or television. And some love being jacks of all trade – writing a news report on a major football transfer row, interviewing a golfer, compiling a TV or radio package about the Winter Olympics and hosting a chat on a sports website. If you suspect that sport on a particular medium will suit you best, then the appropriate preceding chapter will give you a lot more help in deciding whether that medium really is for you.

> *While I was working [as sports editor] at the Barnet Press I did shifts for a number of national papers and was eventually offered a job as a sub on the sports desk at The Times.* PAUL NEWMAN, CHIEF SPORTS FEATURE WRITER, THE INDEPENDENT

All that said, there are many big stories in sport, and being a specialist sports reporter means you could be the one to break them.

What do sports journalists do?

The jobs a sports journalist does can be split broadly into two categories: information gathering, the input phase (reporting); and information processing, the output phase (editing). That is true of whatever media you are working in.

> *The best thing about being a journalist is interviewing people you have a lot of respect for – for me, various members of the World Cup-winning England rugby team, FA director of football development Trevor Brooking and Sir Steve Redgrave.* ANDY MOORHOUSE, NEWS EDITOR, SPORTSBEAT/NEWS ASSOCIATES

The input phase involves researching and writing a sports news story or feature and delivering the copy, voice report or TV package to a deadline. This process will involve developing contacts who will give you the information you need, conducting interviews, taking shorthand notes, attending a wide range of events (from games to press conferences), conducting research and writing copy.

The output phase involves ensuring the copy is fit to print, or the TV or radio package is fit to air. For print, it must be free of errors, from basic spelling and grammar to legal pitfalls, that could lead to a newspaper or broadcaster being sued. In the print media, the copy must be laid out on a page, and cut to fit the allotted space. Headlines must be written. For TV and radio, the package must be perfect, the presenter or news reader may need to have a link written, and a decision will have to be taken on where in a programme the item should be slotted. On a website, the raw text will have to be loaded into a template and **html**-coded. Still pictures may have to be sourced, and there may also be an audio or video element.

> *Work for free to start if you need to – and act on all the advice you are given.* PHILIP BRADFIELD, REPORTER, BELFAST NEWSLETTER

Do you have what it takes?

This is what employers say they are looking for in trainees. Not all criteria apply to sport in every medium:

- a wide knowledge of a substantial range of sports;
- sound news judgement;
- an ability to write in a style which is easy to understand;
- good spelling, grammar and punctuation;
- a willingness to accept irregular hours;
- an ability to work under pressure to meet deadlines;
- determination and persistence;
- an understanding of the audience and the medium/media you work in;
- a clear, authoritative broadcasting voice and manner;
- calmness when things go wrong on air; and
- the ability to present information with clarity when under pressure.

> *Which attribute does a journalist most need? A partner with a reasonable income!* RICHARD SHIMELL, NEWS EDITOR, DEVON GAZETTE

How do you get a job as a sports journalist?

It can be difficult to break straight into sports journalism. Some trainees manage to get taken on by broadcasters, sport and news agencies or sports websites, but it is widely considered that a basic grounding in news reporting is a valuable prerequisite for an aspiring sports journalist. And it isn't just non-sports journalists who believe that.

James Toney is managing editor of Sportsbeat, a major sports news agency that manages a 300-strong network of football match correspondents, and covers the World Cup, the Olympics and other major sporting events. He says:

I believe that before you can be a sports journalist, you first have to learn to be a journalist. There is nothing wrong with specialising in sport but it's important that you develop a strong news sense, even when working for the back pages.

Sport is increasingly taking a role at the front of papers, with most nationals now employing a sports news correspondent, usually directly responsible to the news, rather than sports, editor.

Sports journalism isn't about getting paid to sit in the best seats at the best sports event. The best sports reporters are those that use their news skill, often developed while starting their careers as news reporters, to develop contacts and break stories.

However, if you do want to try your luck going straight into sports journalism, the National Council for the Training of Journalists (NCTJ) accredits a (currently small) number of sport courses. As the number of courses rises it may well be that more people will find it possible to go straight in as sports journalists, but at present it is tough.

I first thought of becoming a journalist aged 15, as a Saturday copy boy at The Star, Sheffield. NEIL BENSON, EDITORIAL DIRECTOR, TRINITY MIRROR

Many sports journalists began in local newspapers or local radio, and gained a general qualification from the NCTJ before specialising in sport. A few trainees go straight into TV on an in-house journalist trainee scheme, but these are hugely over-subscribed. More manage to win a traineeship in local radio, but many journalists who work in TV and radio started on newspapers and moved medium later, once they had mastered basic reporting skills.

One reason for this is that the number of trainee places is greater in local newspapers. Another is that many broadcasting employers seek a high level of skills, knowledge and judgement, and prefer to take on staff at the ages of 23–25.

It is rare for newspapers and magazines to take trainees in sport; they are much more likely to take general journalism trainees and allow them to develop sport as a specialism if they have a particular aptitude for it, and then move them into a sports job once their training is complete.

Less formally, there are opportunities for freelance match reporters to file to the major – and local – sports agencies, which supply a wide range of newspapers, websites and other outlets, but to win such work you will need to demonstrate a good portfolio of published material.

Who takes trainees?

BBC

Work experience is available across the BBC's sports output, including, to take just a few examples, a 10-week sports internship on BBC Radio 4, a placement with the Radio Football department, which works mainly with Radio Five Live providing match coverage of over 1,000 games a season, and another with the Sport Interactive team, which provides up-to-the-minute sports news, and live text commentary to numerous sporting events. Opportunities are listed on the BBC's website (http://www.bbc.co.uk/jobs/workexperience), and although they are extensive (scores are listed at any one time) demand is strong, so check regularly and apply as soon as something suitable is posted.

Young journalists get noticed by breaking stories, not writing 400 words on a football match. JAMES TONEY, MANAGING EDITOR, SPORTSBEAT/NEWS ASSOCIATES

The Guardian

The *Guardian* offers a 12-month placement for a trainee sports journalist on its sports desk. It advertises the scheme in the paper. It accepts applications from both undergraduates and postgraduates, and expects you to have demonstrated your commitment to sports journalism either through experience on a university publication or through work experience. The scheme covers a comprehensive grounding in all aspects of sports journalism, including news, features, commentary and analysis.

The talent a journalist needs most is the ability to listen. MARK BRADLEY, GROUP EDITOR, WAKEFIELD EXPRESS

The Press Association

The Press Association runs a two-year Sport Editorial Traineeship that covers every aspect of sports reporting and production. Trainees learn how to write for national and regional newspapers, for international clients, and for Teletext, digital and new media. There is tuition in sub-editing, in page design for those with an aptitude for it, and the training 'could lead to a permanent position'.

Sky

Sky's editorial training scheme includes sport training. The company says this about it:

> Over 12 months you will work with/learn from top journalists in our television and radio newsrooms, from our political unit at Westminster, from correspondents at home and abroad, and from the leading sports reporters in the country.
>
> In order to be considered for this opportunity, you must be able to demonstrate a commitment to journalism, a keen knowledge of world events and current affairs and the creativity to be able to take an original angle on a story.

It asks applicants to send a 500-word critique of *Sky News*, and details of relevant work placements. For work-experience placements, look for contact details on the website.

Sportsbeat

Sportsbeat is pioneering the training of sports journalists, with NCTJ-accredited commercial training courses run within its own newsroom. There are also opportunities for work experience and some traineeships.

Think about how you would feel as a trainee journalist covering register office weddings, magistrates' courts, council meetings and Sunday League football matches. If the thought of that bores you, forget it. If you're excited by the idea of the sort of stories those situations might throw up, give it a go. PAUL NEWMAN, CHIEF SPORTS FEATURE WRITER, THE INDEPENDENT

TEAMtalk

TEAMtalk, based in Leeds, runs sports websites, including sportinglife.com, the companion site to the *Sporting Life* newspaper, as well as teamtalk.com, sportal.com, bettingzone.co.uk, football365.com, and golf365.com. It has opportunities for work experience.

What they want from you

Whatever the medium, your employer will want you to have all the attributes they would expect in a general trainee, plus a passion for sport and an encyclopaedic knowledge of any particular sport you are to cover.

What qualifications will I need?

Most journalists have at least five GCSEs (grades A–C), including English, and two A levels or vocational A levels. Over 70 per cent have a degree – not necessarily in journalism. To get on a degree course you need at least two A levels or vocational A levels and five GCSEs (grades A–C), or equivalent qualifications. GCSE English is essential.

Most newspapers in the UK recognise qualifications awarded, and courses accredited, by the NCTJ.

What will I have to study?

An NCTJ sports qualification includes study of law and shorthand, plus sub-editing, and shows not just that you are a competent sports journalist, but that you are a competent journalist – full stop. To take one example of an NCTJ-accredited sports course, the BA Sport Journalism degree at the University of Brighton combines journalistic training with a study of the sociology of sport.

> Became a sports editor, then a sub-editor, assistant editor and might have made it up to editor at an early age had I not deviated away from newspapers for three years and gone into PR with British Gas. When I eventually returned, I had to make my way up from sub-editor again. RICHARD PARSONS, PARTNER, SPORTSBEAT NEWS AGENCY

The NCTJ is currently developing its sports journalism courses.

What else will I learn as a trainee?

You will learn what sport news is and how to report it. You will learn to sum up the main moves in a game with brevity and precision, in either a voice or word report, depending on the medium. Often newspaper and website reports are filed in sections during the match, with a couple of paras at the start, some more during the first half, at half time, during the second half and with the intro being tacked on the minute the game ends. For radio and TV, you may be given a minute or perhaps two to sum up a game.

Training on print media concentrates on the input side of things, although trainees with an aptitude for output tasks may find they are encouraged to pursue them. It can be hard for publishers to find staff who are prepared to undertake sub-editing, when reporting is seen as much more glamorous.

> *I first thought of becoming a journalist in my last year at Liverpool University when I realised you could get paid for asking questions.* ROGER BOLTON, INDEPENDENT PROGRAMME MAKER, RADIO PRESENTER

Some traineeships in the broadcast media and in online publishing have a high production content. You need to be aware of what the balance will be before you accept a place, or you may find the course frustrating. Depending on how multimedia-oriented your course is, you can expect your college to have a newsroom with sports wire feed, and TV and radio studios.

What will I earn?

Pay scales for sports trainees vary widely – anything from £12,000 to £20,000, depending on the medium you are working in, and the size and status of your employer.

How to improve your chances of getting a job

You will need to have a clear, demonstrable interest in sports journalism supported with a string of successful work placements in a variety of media.

Life as a trainee

Even if you are lucky enough to be taken on specifically as a trainee sports journalist, you will still need to master the principles of good reporting. As in any other field, you need to learn to write a story effectively, to interview and quote accurately – so shorthand is very useful – and to know about the law.

You will learn how essential it is to have a comprehensive network of contacts. Because so many of the stories you will cover in sport are **off diary**, you will only get them if key players, managers and support staff are prepared to talk to you. If you lack contacts, you won't get the stories your rivals are running. A passion for sport will probably be taken for granted, but you will need to spend every spare moment watching and reading about the sports you cover, so that you are up to speed.

The best thing about journalism is making a difference. MALCOLM WARNE, EDITOR, *DARLINGTON AND STOCKTON TIMES*

If you are taken on by a large sports agency, you can expect, after proving yourself, to be part of the team attending major events such as the Olympics, tennis, football tournaments and so on. There will also be much routine match-reporting. Many games have to be covered, even if very few outlets will run much more than the result.

If you are working on a sports website, you will be doing a great deal of routine desk work. As websites generally originate much less material than newspapers or sports broadcasters, you will mainly be taking submitted material and putting it online. To do this you will need to know basic html, and perhaps also video-editing. You might find yourself writing a minute-by-minute commentary on a game, typing a sentence about almost every move so that the online reader gets a steadily updated account of the flow of the game.

DAY IN THE LIFE

Young journalist working for a national sports agency

Craig Chisnall took his pre-entry NCTJ Preliminary Certificate at the University of Central Lancashire before becoming a trainee reporter with Sportsbeat, in London.

One of the things that I enjoy the most about journalism is that no one day is ever the same. You can plan and prepare but one phone call or event can put you back to square one in a second.

My job at Sportsbeat involves me in our major event coverage, working as a reporter on our newsdesk and occasionally deputising for our news editor. If working on the newsdesk, my day would normally start at 9.30am with an informal meeting with our managing editor or executive editor about what lies ahead.

I try to read a couple of papers on the way to work or listen to Five Live if I'm driving in, so I've got some idea of what's happening before this meeting. Usually there are three or four reporters on the newsdesk on a weekday, working on news stories, features and interviews, in addition to our correspondents working remotely. During the football season, the day tends to be more hectic as the weekend approaches.

On a Saturday afternoon we have over 300 correspondents at football matches the length and breadth of the country, filing their match reports to us. We have to make sure each of these is briefed and knows their copy instructions. Our operation swells with sub-editors, copytakers and additional staff, many of them casual, and my job is often is act as a 'firefighter'. That means chasing up copy that's late or replacing it with an alternative if it doesn't arrive. I also get a chance to act as a 'revise sub' on our camera-ready pages before they are sent to clients for final approval.

The pace is frantic, the air can sometimes be blue but the satisfaction of hitting the deadline, despite all the obstacles that are usually placed in our way, makes up for it all.

If working out in the field, the day has been known to start at 6.30am and finish at midnight. It's often exhausting but also incredibly rewarding, especially when you see your by-line in so many publications. For example, I often work on our golf coverage, reporting on events such as the Ryder Cup or majors such as the Open Championship.

At the Open we work for approaching 20 UK regional and Scottish national newspapers titles, such as *Scotland on Sunday*, *Northern Echo*, *Edinburgh Evening News*, *Birmingham Mail*. Because we work for a mixture of morning and evening newspapers, in addition to websites, there is always a deadline. Each client has a different requirement. Some might want a 500-word story on the leaders and another a 350-word sidebar on a local golfer. Some might want an off-beat diary and colour piece on a particular golfer to sit alongside a panel on the leaders, with news of their regional golfers 'blobbed' on the bottom. Each client has different deadlines and during the morning, especially for the big city regional papers, we have to refresh copy for each new edition. That might mean a story needs to be filed at 9.30am and then updated for 10.30am and noon.

At big events, we often employ a reporter just to gather quotes from competitors as they finish. They'll then rush back and these quotes will be 'added' into the stories which myself and our chief sports writer are bashing out and sending back to the newsdesk for distribution.

The pace of working as an agency reporter is hectic but it hardens you up to working under pressure and producing large volumes of copy in a short pace of time. It also allows you to write for lots of different styles of publications – broadsheets, tabloids, magazines and websites. If you are looking for a quiet life, it isn't the place for you!

If you think this might be for you...

If it sounds good so far, you can find out more about NCTJ qualifications at www.nctj.com.

Contact details:
NCTJ Training Limited,
The New Granary,
Station Road,
Newport,
Saffron Walden,
Essex CB11 3PL
01799 544014
Fax: 01799 544015
info@nctj.com
www.nctj.com

7
PHOTOGRAPHY

Is press photography for you?

Press photography is an incredibly competitive area. There are around 25,000 professional press photographers in the UK, and most are self-employed.

On local newspapers, where most press photographers train, there is huge demand for each place that comes available. Picture editors on national newspapers are inundated with calls from very able photographers looking for day shifts, on which they will do a number of jobs for a set – and modest – fee. With money tight, the number of staff photographers is falling, and newspapers and magazines come increasingly to rely on agency photographs, from Reuters, the Press Association or from other more specialist agencies, and on picture libraries that have vast collections that can be bought off-the-shelf, saving time and money.

> *I wanted a job that was not 9 to 5 in an office that would challenge me and involve me in real life at the front line.* SIMON PIZZEY, SENIOR PHOTOGRAPHER, GLOUCESTER CITIZEN

Nevertheless, really good press photographers will find themselves in demand. Very few photographers have the journalistic ability to capture the essence of a story in a single image, whether it's a straight news report or a feature. On magazines, where very high photographic skills are also required, the really good photographer will truly shine, and will always be in demand.

The burgeoning paparazzi side of press photography has tended to give news photographers a bad name. The 'paps', who tend to work as freelances but channel their material through a particular agency which represents them and sells on their behalf to newspapers and magazines, are rarely trained photographers. Paps make their money by snapping celebrities in public places, often when they do not wish to be photographed. Their work has little to do with photographic ability; it's all about getting a snatched shot that makes a point: pop star X looking fat/pregnant; TV presenter Y looking drunk.

Even in the quality press and mainstream magazines, the space allocated to personality pictures is rising, and that given to hard news is falling, which means the qualified press photographer is competing against the pap to get their work used.

What's the best thing about being a journalist? The certainty of uncertainty. CHRIS WALKER, REGIONAL MANAGING EDITOR, FOR TRINITY MIRROR, IN THE NORTH WEST

Good news photographers have all the news sense and eye for a story of a wordsmith. Their job is harder because there is no margin for error. The photographers have to be there when news happens – they can't cover their back by picking it up later, as a reporter often can.

But being a good photographer is not merely about being in the right place at the right time. Substantial technical skills are needed too, and press photography is one of the few areas of the photographic profession where a structured training scheme is available – and essential, if you want to be able to offer employers evidence that you are a qualified press photographer.

You come into contact with people you'd never normally meet and experience things you'd never normally have a chance to experience. EMMA CLAYTON, FEATURES WRITES, BRADFORD TELEGRAPH AND ARGUS

Press photography can be lonely and exhausting. With digital cameras and laptops, a press photographer works from their car, travelling from job to job, filing their pictures as they go. On a national newspaper, they may not go into the office for weeks on end. They get their assignments, probably via e-mail, and will have occasional chats with the picture desk but, apart from that, they can be on their own. Some jobs involve a good deal of waiting around – inevitably in the rain – while others require that they spend no more than 10 minutes, get a first-class shot, and then move on to the next job.

All that said, there is a magic about the work of a really good press photographer. Just as no one can explain David Beckham's ability to curve a penalty ball over the wall and into the net – certainly not Beckham himself – a photographer cannot explain the instinct which enables them to capture a story, to punch home its emotional impact, with a shot grabbed in often frantic and confused circumstances. Pulling that off is the joy of press photography – for the photographer, the picture editor and the reader.

What do press photographers do?

Press photographers cover news stories that are worthy of a picture – and many that are not. They take pictures to illustrate features and interviews. On national newspapers they tend to split into two categories: general news, which usually includes features and portraits to accompany interviews; and sport. The big press agencies – Reuters and the Press Association, for example – also run comprehensive photo services. There are big sports picture agencies and a string of local agencies that cover a patch for whoever needs them.

Don't do it for the money! PAUL MCGINLEY, PRODUCTION EDITOR, BRADFORD TELEGRAPH AND ARGUS

With magazines, many photographers are freelance and, apart from those who take the bread-and-butter pictures (attending events, photographing subjects of interviews, winners of awards and participants at conferences and exhibitions), they tend to specialise. There are photographers who specialise in landscapes, food, fashion, portraits, war and sports, including wind surfing, mountain biking, skiing and many more. These specialist photographers will be renowned in their field, and tend to sell to a selection of established clients.

[Journalism] was always in my mind from the time of my first John Bull printing outfit, and the William books, in one of which he and his friends make a paper. PETER DARLING, JOURNALISM LECTURER

Many photographers, particularly those in local agencies, also do corporate and commercial work. Often the commercial work is used to supplement the money that the pure press photography brings in. They may also supply stock images to libraries, or perhaps run a library of their own. Really successful magazine and national newspaper photographers may find they move over into highly lucrative commercial work, taking pictures for poster or press campaigns perhaps.

A few photographers also write articles and class themselves as 'photojournalists'. They will tend to work on longer, documentary-style stories for magazines. They might follow a family of travellers through the year, for example, or document the rebuilding of Wembley Stadium.

> *There is no set career progression in press photography. It really depends on your interests, your skills, your personality, luck, and what aspects of your life you are prepared to compromise. I knew I wanted a family, and to be there for my kids, so regional press work to date has suited me.* SIMON PIZZEY, SENIOR PHOTOGRAPHER, GLOUCESTER CITIZEN

Sport has a strong appeal for many photographers because of the opportunities to capture drama and excitement. The demand for great images delivered fast puts a lot of pressure on sports photographers. At a game they may have to file from their laptop every 10 minutes, sending something after each goal, at half-time, full time and at other key moments, depending on the demands of their clients. Many sports photographs take 200 pictures during a game, and one of their key skills is being able to select the right image and move it fast. Sometimes, the agency photographer is the only one there, so if the game turns out to be an exciting one, there will be huge interest in what the photographer has produced, and plenty of customers to keep happy.

> *Progress came only with experience; you can't fudge it in this game!* PAUL MCGINLEY, PRODUCTION EDITOR, BRADFORD TELEGRAPH AND ARGUS

Most press photographers work on local newspapers, and have to provide a stream of pictures that make the most of golden weddings, flower shows, school plays and talent contests, awards ceremonies, fires and traffic accidents.

Do you have what it takes?

This is what picture editors say they are looking for in a photographer:

- a news sense as sound as any wordsmith;
- the ability to sum up a complex story in a single picture;
- the technical ability to capture the image that they need;
- energy, drive and commitment;
- single-mindedness;

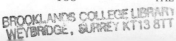
BROOKLANDS COLLEGE LIBRARY
WEYBRIDGE, SURREY KT13 8TT

- an enquiring mind;
- the personality and charm to coax subjects into the pose they want; and
- the ability to look at the obvious and see something different (or better) by way of a news line and picture.

How do you get a job as a press photographer?

Most press photographers train on local newspapers and gain formal qualifications from the National Council for the Training of Journalists, which trains photographers to the same level as it does reporters. The NCTJ endorses two main training schemes. One is by direct entry to a newspaper, involving on-the-job training supplemented by block release to Norton College, Sheffield. To enrol on this course you need to have been hired by a newspaper that has agreed to fund your training. The alternative is to complete the full-time course at Norton College, or the Digital Photo Journalism course at Darlington College of Technology, and to seek employment afterwards. If you take this route you are classed as a pre-entry student – you are training before you have found a job in the trade.

There is intense competition for places on these courses, and you will need to demonstrate the perseverance, motivation and resilience required to succeed in the job in order to win a place on them. Very occasionally a national newspaper will take a student from a college course for extended work experience, but by far the most common route is via the local press.

If you are considering any other career do that one. Candidates have to be convinced that journalism is the only thing for them. ROBIN ESSER, EXECUTIVE MANAGING EDITOR, DAILY MAIL

Who takes trainees?

Local newspapers and some photographic agencies take trainees but places are scarce. Many trainees take a pre-entry course and then seek further on-the-job training with an agency or newspaper. Some agencies, such as Newscast, which has offices in London and New York, take qualified trainees for a year.

Most press photographers can't find traineeships, so take a pre-entry course and go freelance straight after college. Many work on day shifts, doing a number of jobs for a set fee.

What they want from you

They will want you to be a journalist through and through, with all the news sense and hunger to get the story that they see in their reporters. You'll need to be self-motivated and hard-working. You'll need a fundamental understanding of digital photography, your own cameras and the computer equipment to send in pictures straight from a job. You'll also need a full driving licence. You'll need to be able to work quickly under pressure, hit deadlines, recognise an angle and, in local newspapers, make mundane picture opportunities fresh and interesting.

What qualifications will I need?

To get on an NCTJ direct entry course you will need four GCSEs (grades A–C), including English. For a pre-entry course an additional A level is required. In most companies that take direct entrants, you will work towards the NCTJ's National Certificate in Press Photography/Photojournalism. At some others you will work towards a National or Scottish Vocational Qualification (NVQ/SVQ) Level 4 in Newspaper Journalism (Press Photography).

If you don't live and breathe news, don't bother. KEVIN WARD, PUBLISHER, NEWSQUEST, SOUTH-EAST WALES

For an NVQ, the minimum requirement to take part in the one-year, full-time course at Stradbroke College is one A Level plus four GCSE passes or equivalent. Direct entrants are required to have five GCSE passes (grades A–C), including English. Alternatively, applicants with fewer than these qualifications will be eligible if they have had at least two years' relevant experience of photographic techniques, either within or outside the industry, or have undertaken an equivalent further education course in photography. A National or Scottish Vocational Qualification or National Certificate in Press Photography will be available after a successful period of work experience.

Modern apprenticeships are also available in press photography. This scheme enables employees of participating companies to undertake relevant training leading to an NVQ Level 4 in Newspaper Journalism: Writing, News & Features or in Press Photography. A number of publishers participate in the scheme with their local Training and Enterprise Councils (TECs). Entry is open to any non-graduate between the ages of 16 and 23 years, although you should have completed the programme by your 25th birthday. The more likely age range is from 18 to 19 years.

When applying for direct entry places you should ask publishers whether they participate in the scheme.

> *Door-stepping the mother of a child who has been killed in a road accident is very different from interviewing a celebrity. Many people become disillusioned.* SIMON PIZZEY, SENIOR PHOTOGRAPHER, GLOUCESTER CITIZEN

What will I have to study?

The NCTJ's Photojournalism qualification is a journalism-based course with photography as its foundation. The NCTJ says of it:

Tutors will help you develop your news sense in tune with an ability to use a camera and ancillary equipment to the best advantage. The course covers photographic knowledge, newspaper practice/public affairs, law, caption writing for press photographers and news writing for photo journalists. The Press Photography course contains all the above except the news writer's module. You'll also complete a log book of photographs taken during on-the-job training that will be a record of your abilities in photographing a wide range of stories.

Successful trainees qualify for the NCTJ's National Certificate Examination [which is] taken about 18 months after joining a newspaper.

What else will I learn as a trainee?

You will learn how to be a reporter through images rather than words, how to tell a story through your pictures, how to charm people into posing for you, how to work with reporters and to give editors what they want.

What will I earn?

You will earn between £12,000 and £15,000 on a local newspaper, rising by about £3,000 when you are qualified. Agency rates vary wildly. National agency pay rates are in the range £18,000–£20,000.

How to improve your chances of getting a job

Demonstrate that you have all the attributes of a good news reporter, that you have a comprehensive portfolio of published press work and a list of work-experience placements on local newspapers, agencies, magazines, community newsletters – anything you can find. Carry your camera everywhere and if you take a picture of anything newsworthy, offer it to local press outlets. If you come up with something useful, they'll remember you and might put some work your way.

If sport interests you, or even if it doesn't, go to games and try to get good shots. If you can gather the equipment together, try to work as a professional photographer would, editing and selecting shots as you go.

Study the photographs in the publications you admire, look at how their photographers shoot things, and compare them with photographers on other publications. Do they come in tight, for example, or shoot with a wide-angle lens? Know the different styles and how to adapt to them.

> *My single piece of advice is to be honest, and as truthful as possible. It is not only right in itself, but it will repay in the end since people will talk to you and trust you. From this, all else flows.* PATRICK WINTOUR, CHIEF POLITICAL CORRESPONDENT, THE GUARDIAN

Think of photojournalism projects that might appeal to local newspapers or magazines. If binge drinking is in the news, spend a few Saturday nights with the police or ambulance services, with the pub doormen and in the A&E unit at your local hospital. If you can't get a publication to commit themselves in advance, do the project anyway and offer it to them later – at the very least you can add it to your portfolio. In short, any practice or experience you can get is going to help you convince others – and yourself – that you have got what it takes.

Try to build up a relationship with the picture editor and editor of your local paper or photo agency. Let them know that you want to train and pray that, if they have a vacancy, they will take you on and you can study as a direct entry student.

Life as a trainee

If you are lucky enough to become a trainee photographer on a national news-paper, you will be treated just like any other casual photographer on a day shift. You will be expected to do the round of half a dozen jobs in a day, perhaps more. You'll need to drive yourself to the location, get the picture, transmit it electronically back to the office and move on swiftly to the next job.

A typical day might see you photographing a company chairman announcing his annual results, politicians on a **photo-op**, defendants arriving at or leaving court, and someone who is the subject of a feature. You might have to take by-line pictures of staffers and stock pictures for the library – everything from estate agent's boards to traffic jams. You might have to do a doorstep – waiting in the cold and rain for someone you are interested in to dash from house to car.

> *The attribute a journalist most needs is good writing ability that can be adapted for different stories and readers. After that, confidence to be polite but persistent in chasing a story.* PHILIP BRADFIELD, REPORTER, BELFAST NEWSLETTER

You will need to know as much as any news reporter about the law, and of the Press Complaints Commission's code of conduct on privacy, which sets out when and where you can and cannot photograph someone.

On a local paper you will be doing the rounds of golden weddings and flower shows, with the disadvantage that – unlike the reporter who can get what he needs on the phone – you have to turn up to each and every little job.

You will need to like people and be able to charm them into allowing you to take a good picture. And you will build up contacts in the emergency services, who will let you know what is going on and allow you good access to fires, accidents and other emergencies – as long as you print off a few shots for them.

DAY IN THE LIFE

Young photographer on a local newspaper

Jade Gardner, *Rochdale Observer*, Greater Manchester

The *Rochdale Observer* is a local newspaper in Greater Manchester and is very community-oriented. We do a lot of jobs within schools, local news as well as local sport and community events. Every day is different, and it's impossible to give an idea of a typical one, but here's what I did today.

(Continued)

I was on a late shift, which for us is 12pm–8pm. My first job was a carnival in Oldham. I went early and got a load of pictures for a spread before the carnival set off. Next I popped into the office and put these pictures on to the computer as I had an hour to spare until my next job. At 2pm I went to a church fun day where I got pictures of children on bouncy castles, face painting, 'hook a duck' and the band. This is a very typical job for the summer months.

Next, I made my way to Spotland Stadium for the Rugby: Rochdale Hornets v. Widnes. The paper wanted action shots plus a half-time presentation by the Navy to the ball boys. Then it was on to a local cricket match over in Oldham, again action shots of the match. After this I went to a church where a local drama group was doing a dress rehearsal of a play – *Who Killed Kitty O'Hara?* – and took a group shot of the cast. My last job was at 7.30pm back at a school in Rochdale. They were having a cowboy-themed party night for kids and parents. The paper wanted a couple of pictures of people dressed up.

I decided to become photographer about a year after finishing a geography degree at university. I went travelling in South America for three months with a point-and-shoot camera – I had never done any photography before and really enjoyed it. Back in the UK I did some temp work while deciding what I wanted to do.

One day I was looking on the internet at journalism courses and found information about the NCTJ course on press photography and photojournalism at Norton College, Sheffield. I applied and got an interview, but when I sat the entrance exam it was a complete disaster – I knew nothing about photography. But the college told me that if I did some work experience, and practised with my camera, I could have a place the following year.

When I started the year-long course I still felt very behind. Everyone else seemed to have been doing photography for a long time. But everyone helped me out, and I passed. My first job was as a trainee photographer with *Wales on Sunday*, but the location was wrong and I moved to the *Rochdale Observer* 18 months ago.

If you think this might be for you...

If it sounds good so far, you can find out more about NCTJ qualifications at www.nctj.com.

Contact details:
The National Council for the Training of Journalists
The New Granary,

Station Road,
Newport,
Saffron Walden,
Essex CB11 3PL
01799 544014
Fax: 01799 544015
info@nctj.com

Section 2

CAREER PATHS

INTRODUCTION

Right now, you are probably much more concerned about working towards your first job in journalism than you are in considering what career path you might follow once you do find a starting point. That's perfectly understandable. After all, having made you aware of all the many entry points that there are to the trade, it might seem a bit much to expect you to know how you want your career to develop. But, there are some sound reasons for trying to think about such things. For example, where you start often has an impact on where you can move to easily, and where it might be a little more complicated. While the key journalistic skills – news reporting being prime among them – are highly transferable across the various media, it's a good idea to try to begin your career in the medium that most interests you, and in which you hope to work for some time.

In this business, career paths have many twists and turns. I always have the feeling that the best is yet to come. ELENA CURTI, DEPUTY EDITOR, THE TABLET

Even if you are not starting in your chosen medium – perhaps you have had to settle for local newspapers when you would rather be in television, or a magazine instead of a website – this section of the book will give you some ideas on how you can get from where you are to where you want to be. In addition, a favourite question that is often asked at interview is 'Where do you see yourself working in five years' time? To answer 'I dunno' suggests that you haven't thought all that deeply about journalism. To give a coherent outline of what your ideal job would be, and to acknowledge clearly what you will need to learn along the way if you are to get it, will impress those who are interviewing you.

It is by no means a simple task to outline all the possible career paths. That is because there are almost as many journalistic career paths as there are journalists. A good reporter has the essential skills that are required to work in any medium, provided they are flexible enough.

I'd been sports editor for 13 years and said to Simon Kelner, the editor, that I fancied a change. A fortnight later he offered me the job of chief sports feature writer. PAUL NEWMAN, CHIEF SPORTS FEATURE WRITER, THE INDEPENDENT

When you do turn your mind to the career you would like to have, there are a couple of key things to consider. One fairly obvious one is the medium in which you want to progress: newspapers, magazines, television, radio or online journalism. Another is whether you want to be a reporter, a feature writer or a photographer: a news gatherer, to give the broadest definition or become a news processor (someone who works in what is generally known in all media as the production arm). Another consideration is whether you think you would like to try to move up the management chain, to become a department head (e.g. a news editor) and perhaps, eventually, an editor.

I stayed [at The Independent] nearly 10 years, becoming night editor, until David Montgomery bought the Mirror Group, gave me a big sack of money and invited me to leave. Went to Hong Kong and became ballet critic of the South China Morning Post. Returned to UK and joined the Financial Times by accident, leaving them after a few weeks to find my niche at The Guardian. DAVID MARSH, ASSISTANT EDITOR (PRODUCTION), THE GUARDIAN

By no means every journalist wants to become an editor. Many feel that the best job is a news-gathering one – as a reporter or photographer. Even if you do remain a reporter, there is still a career path you can follow, depending on the medium you have chosen. If you like newspapers, you may want to move to a daily paper from a weekly, or to a national from a provincial daily. If you are a TV reporter, you may want to move from a provincial station to a national one. As a photographer, you might want to move from a local paper to a national or international magazine.

If you choose the newspaper production path, you may decide to become a sub-editor, with the intention of moving on up the production chain and hopefully becoming an editor one day. If reporting is what you want to do, you may hope to focus on a specialism and apply it across media. For example, you might be a TV political correspondent as your main job, but also have a newspaper column and host a regular chat online.

Every job I have had, apart from the first, was offered to me by people I had worked with previously.
SUE RYAN, FORMER MANAGING EDITOR, DAILY TELEGRAPH

One thing to remember is that journalism is an unpredictable profession. Things can change fast. A new editor can radically alter a publication or a TV or radio programme, and your face may no longer fit.

Some people are focused and single-minded. They know that what they want to be is, for example, environment editor of the *Guardian* or a football correspondent on the BBC, and they pursue their goal doggedly, not being deflected by interesting and lucrative offers which would take them away from their goal. But it can be very hard to do this. Some career paths show odd turns, jumps and leaps, as you will see from the quotes from practising journalists in this section of the book.

After a spell running the BBC in Manchester I was fired over Irish coverage. I moved to Thames Television as editor of This Week and was almost fired over Death on the Rock, a programme about the shooting of IRA members in Gibraltar. I survived, but Thames did not. It lost its franchise in 1992. Nobody offered me a job, and I had young children to support, so I became an independent producer. ROGER BOLTON, INDEPENDENT PROGRAMME MAKER AND RADIO PRESENTER

If you are talented and doing a good job, editors who have vacancies to fill are likely to ask you to step into them. If you say no, it can count against you. If you turn down one offer, an editor may be reluctant to offer you another one. Perhaps the editor wants you to do something but you hate it, or are lousy at it. There is a falling out and you have to move on. Maybe, in moving on, you have to take what is the best available alternative job offer.

Some journalists get to the top in one branch and then decide they would be happier in a less pressurised job. A sports editor might want to return to sports writing. The editor of a local paper might want to become a sub-editor on a national. A news editor might decide that they have had long enough on the desk and want to get out reporting again.

I have never been promoted because I have never sought it. Promotion invariably means that writers turn into administrators. JIM GREENHALF, FEATURES WRITER, BRADFORD TELEGRAPH AND ARGUS

Journalists are very flexible – they have to be to survive. They are tolerant of change, and understanding of career patterns which may involve some unusual switches of direction. If things do not work out the way you hoped in one job, and you are respected, you should have little problem landing another one that suits you better. Equally, you may find you hit it off with an editor and he or she invites you to move with them to a new publication. This high-flyer may change jobs regularly, insisting that you accompany them each time they move, and paying you handsomely for doing so. You may find you end up doing jobs you had never considered when you mapped out your career path as a young journalist.

In the rest of this section, we shall run through a range of common career paths – ones that many journalists have followed.

Career Path 1:
Newspaper or Magazine Reporting

You may decide that reporting is what you love, and that newspapers or magazines are the place to do it. Reporting is a highly portable skill. Whether you decide to stay in the medium you began in, or move to any of the others, your reporting skills will stand you in good stead. But let's assume, for the purposes of this section, that you want to stay in the medium you are used to. One career path open to you, if you began on a regional newspaper or trade magazine, is to remain where you are, perhaps becoming chief reporter or a specialist writer of some kind.

My first job was as a reporter for the Western Morning News, Plymouth. I was made London editor of the Western Morning News (based in the House of Commons) after one year. I went to Sunday Business as political editor 18 months later. Three years later I was recruited by the Sunday Times to work on the Business section. A year later I was appointed deputy political editor. ANDREW PORTER, DEPUTY POLITICAL EDITOR, THE SUNDAY TIMES

If that is not enough, you may decide to move to a bigger outlet, either a daily or national newspaper, or a major consumer magazine. In these bigger ponds, with their substantial news operations, you will have many more opportunities to progress as a reporter.

I did a short spell as education correspondent, then crime reporter, chief reporter, deputy news editor and then news editor. Every time I wanted to join the nationals I was promoted, so I stayed [on a provincial paper]. BOB SATCHWELL, EXECUTIVE DIRECTOR, SOCIETY OF EDITORS

Most reporters decide to specialise. It means they cover a patch in depth, and that they are pulled off the main diary where they can be called upon to chase any story that presents itself. Specialist reporters are often called correspondents, and cover everything from aspects of the domestic scene, such as politics, business or the arts, to regions of the country (North of England correspondent, Northern Ireland correspondent). There will be foreign correspondents too. In key locations – New York, Washington, Brussels –special correspondents are likely to be on the staff. In less newsy places, correspondents are often freelance, and will probably combine broadcasting outlets with newspaper reporting and writing magazine articles.

I was promoted to education correspondent on the South Wales Argus, *then moved to general news reporter on the* Western Mail *in Cardiff. Became education correspondent on the* Western Mail, *then got the lobby job for the paper based in London. Moved to the* Yorkshire Post *as its political correspondent, from where, finally, at the age of 29, I got the education correspondent job on* The Sunday Times. CHARLES HYMAS, NEWS EDITOR, *THE SUNDAY TIMES*

It might sound trite but I'm just proud to have spent all my working life in regional newspapers. CHRIS WALKER, REGIONAL MANAGING EDITOR, TRINITY MIRROR IN THE NORTH WEST

You may find you are able to remain with one publication, for most of your career, moving to new reporting briefs every few years, or you may find you change broadcasters or papers several times.

Career Path 2:
Newspaper or Magazine Production

Formal training on newspapers and magazines is almost exclusively about developing your abilities as a writer. But many people find they have an aptitude for production.

Moved to Edinburgh Evening News *as assistant chief sub, then to* Daily Mail *as sub for launch of Scottish edition, progressing to deputy night editor before moving to* Scottish Express *as night editor. Then turned down chance to deputy edit* Scottish Mirror *and moved instead to London as No. 2 for launch of* Metro. *Then spent a year as deputy editor of* Scottish Mail *before returning to* Metro *as editor.* KENNY CAMPBELL, EDITOR, METRO

The first step on the production ladder is to become a **sub-editor.** That means you take a writer's copy and prepare it for publication. You check it for accuracy, grammar, spelling, legality and other questions of fact. You tighten the writing and cut it to fit the space it has been allocated on the page. You also often write the headline, and other 'sells', including **strap lines**, **stand-firsts** and picture captions.

I was crime reporter on the Reading Evening Post, *then switched to subbing, became deputy chief sub, and moved to Fleet St. I did a year's subbing on* The Times *then landed a job at the* Daily Mirror. *After two years I was made assistant chief sub, then moved to Manchester to be deputy night editor of the* Daily Star. *In 1989 I was offered a job on* The Sun *and have been here since.* FERGUS SHANAHAN, DEPUTY EDITOR, THE SUN

A sub-editor who wants to progress in production will look for an opening as a chief or deputy chief sub. In this role, you oversee the work of the subs. You assign material to them and ensure that it is handled effectively. You also liaise with the departments that originate the copy, design the pages and supply the pictures.

The next step is to become **production editor**. In this role you have overall responsibility for the creation, on time, of the newspaper or magazine. It is up to you to liaise with departments, including advertising, to oversee the collation and distribution of **flat plans** for those who need to follow them. You will liaise with the printers and the **repro house**, if your publication uses one.

I heard The Guardian *needed a foreign chief sub and applied. Didn't get that but was instead offered a job as an all-purpose backbench journalist, deputising for the night editor. After a couple of very happy years of this, I was put in charge of production for the whole paper.* DAVID MARSH, ASSISTANT EDITOR (PRODUCTION), THE GUARDIAN

On national newspapers, and big regional papers, there may be something called the **back bench**. This is the desk at which the team that oversees the production of the newspaper sits in the final hours as the pages are completed and the paper is finally, to use the jargon, put to bed (sent for printing). The production editor will probably sit here. The back bench is usually run by the **night editor**. As editors tend to go home at 7pm or 8pm, they need to hand over to someone. Usually, the editor will make sure he or she is happy with the first edition and then leave any later changes necessitated by late-breaking or developing stories to the night editor. Once the editor leaves the building, the night editor is in charge.

I have stuck with the Telegraph and Argus, *moving from reporting into sub-editing and on to design work. I was instrumental in introducing and progressing the use of colour in the T&A, when we were at the forefront of its introduction in the UK's regional newspapers.* DOUG AKROYD, DESIGN EDITOR, BRADFORD TELEGRAPH AND ARGUS

My first editor ... bullied, cajoled and encouraged me to construct good foundations on which my working life has been built. He encouraged me in every way, particularly sub-editing at a time when it was not deemed to be 'women's work', and set high standards in all facets of a journalist's life. He also taught me a lot of good swear words! MARY-ANN BLOOMFIELD, EDITOR, MID-DEVON GAZETTE SERIES

Often, night editors have come up the **subbing** route, because they need a firm grasp of production to do their jobs effectively. Because most of the paper has already been created, their job is seen as a largely administrative role. The editor creates the newspaper they want, then leaves. The night editor makes sure they get what they have asked for, and takes responsibility for any changes that it is necessary to make to bring the paper as up-to-the-minute as possible.

Night editors may become editors, but it is more likely that an editor will have come up the more creative route, running departments where a good deal of material is originated, and where key parts of editorial strategy are formulated.

> *Became* Kentish Times's *first woman sub and woman's page editor at 24, then career break for children, returning to work at* Birmingham Post and Mail, *then via deputy editor to editor on weekly titles since 1985.* LIZ GRIFFIN, EDITOR, HEREFORD TIMES

One other possible course allied to production is design. On magazines, designers will almost always have an art college background. In newspapers that was not traditionally the case, largely because newspaper design values were much lower than those of magazines. Today that is changing, and many more art college graduates are employed to lay out pages. However, plenty of journalists with an aptitude for design and layout become designers.

Career Path 3:
Features on Newspapers and in Magazines

The **feature** writer may have started as a news reporter, which is an excellent grounding because any writer will benefit from having those basic skills. They may have started as a freelance, successfully offering items to one or more paper or magazine, and find that they can make a living at it. They may also have started as a secretary on a magazine, or as a fashion assistant, and convinced their bosses that they deserved a chance to try their hand at writing – and impressed them.

> *I went straight into doing major interviews of up to 2,000 words without ever having covered a flower show ... I became features editor of* Beat Instrumental *in 1971 after having interviewed Marc Bolan and Rod Stewart.* STEVE TURNER, FREELANCE ROCK JOURNALIST AND AUTHOR

Feature writing suits those who want to focus on the how and why of things, not just the fact that they have happened. Feature writers are interested in personalities and in getting behind the news. They write creatively, adding a strong individual style to the basics of good writing that they will have learned if they started out as a news reporter.

> *After two years as a staff writer [on* Sounds *magazine], I was appointed features editor of an off-shoot magazine called* Noise!, *which sadly only lasted six months. After that I moved to another music magazine,* Record Mirror, *as assistant editor, moved my way up to deputy editor and was appointed editor in 1986.* BEVERLEY GLICK, PAGE EDITOR, SUNDAY EXPRESS

Feature writers often choose to specialise in a particular field, at which they can gain expertise and a good reputation. They might go in for travel writing, interviews, movie reviewing, writing a first-person column, or any of dozens of other specialisms.

The career path for a feature writer will be very individual, reflecting their particular skills and interests. However, successful feature writers do have some moves in common. Often they will start out at less prestigious publications and move on to better (and better-paying) ones. A good interviewer may find their talents in demand at more than one newspaper.

> *I was working part-time as assistant news editor, on the newsdesk, and part-time in features. Newsdesk was good experience but I wanted to get into features full-time. When a vacancy came up, I went for the job.* EMMA CLAYTON, FEATURES WRITER, BRADFORD TELEGRAPH AND ARGUS

Really good columnists can spur many readers into buying the magazine or newspaper regularly, and a proportion of them will follow a writer they really like if they move to a different publication.

> *My first few years were marked by feelings of shock and anxiety when the job called on me to con-front my own natural shyness and go forth to interview the relations of murder victims and later the great and the good. Over and above talent, integrity and the obvious most quoted virtues, a plain old thick skin is the best protection against ulcers, alcoholism and probably cancer.* JIM GREENHALF, FEATURES WRITER, BRADFORD TELEGRAPH AND ARGUS

A feature writer may also develop an interest in going up the management chain. The first move is likely to be becoming features editor. On a magazine particularly, they may be in line for an editorship.

Career Path 4:
TV and Radio Reporting

If you want to progress as a reporter in TV and radio, you are likely to aim to join a major broadcaster and to become a correspondent. Correspondents cover everything from aspects of the domestic scene, business, showbiz, politics, etc., to regions of the country, such as North of England correspondent or Northern Ireland correspondent. Foreign correspondents can be based in any part of the world.

> *When* Channel Four News *began no one thought it would last so those of us brave enough to join got ahead quickly – at 27 I was sent to Washington as the programme's first correspondent there.*
> EDWARD STOURTON, PRESENTER, RADIO 4 TODAY PROGRAMME

At the BBC, where many radio journalists are employed, the advent of **bi-media**, where reporters work for both TV and radio, has opened up opportunities for moving into specialisms and reporting in both media.

> *My first job was writing the early morning local news bulletins for the AM programme on LBC radio, with a daily start time of 5am five days a week. A year later I became a reporter. Another year later I joined the IRN political unit, and was recruited from there to the BBC. Five years after finishing my training, I was the first female national political correspondent the BBC had had in 20 years.* EMMA UDWIN, FORMER BBC POLITICAL CORRESPONDENT

If you do choose to remain as a TV reporter, beware of ageism. Television is a visual medium, and there are plenty of able, experienced TV reporters who find that, once over the age of 40, their faces don't fit any more. In this case, if not before, you need to go into management if you are to remain in broadcasting, or find your way into another medium.

I started at LBC as a freelance phone operator, then got a place on the in-house training scheme. I became a political specialist, joined A Week In Politics *on Channel 4, then* On The Record *at the* BBC. MARTHA KEARNEY, POLITICAL EDITOR, BBC2 *NEWSNIGHT* AND PRESENTER, RADIO 4 WOMAN'S HOUR

Often, senior on-air journalists spent a good deal of their careers in newspapers. The BBC, in particular, has in recent years hired several senior on-air journalists, who are given the title of 'editor' and who have a strong press background.

Career Path 5:
TV and Radio Production

The path up the off-air side of a broadcaster is through what is known as production. In rising seniority the titles are: researcher, assistant producer and producer. Researchers are responsible for supporting reporters, identifying and researching stories, helping pull packages together. Producers make sure a programme is complete, balanced and runs to time, and assistant producers help them do that. Depending on the programme, the producer may write the script for the presenter or news reader.

I got a job in BBC local radio and went from there to national radio. After eight years as a radio journalist I went freelance. I had a young family by then and my last radio job had been as a political correspondent for Independent Radio News *at Westminster. I found the hours punishing and was looking for a better balance between work and looking after my children. That proved difficult to achieve. I switched to production and was involved in producing television and radio news and current affairs programmes. I was a producer on* Kilroy! *for three years. Later I had a series of short-term contracts with periods of intense activity and no work at all. Most of the work was absorbing but the stop-start nature of it became wearing.* ELENA CURTI, DEPUTY EDITOR, THE TABLET

From working on a news agency, I did a brief training course on writing for radio and how to slice tape together. Joined the Birmingham commercial radio station BRMB. Then joined Anglia TV as a production journalist. SURREY BEDDOWS, EDITOR, ANGLIA NEWS

If you find that on-air reporting is not your forte, or you have had enough of it, the production career path might be for you. From producer you might become an editor of a bulletin or a programme. You'll be deciding what to cover, how, and who to assign to the story. To your reporting and broadcasting abilities you will need to add good organisational skills, leadership and a sense of how each segment or package fits into the whole of the bulletin or programme.

From here you might become a series editor or executive editor, at which point you'll be dealing with policy and budgets more than what actually appears on air.

I switched from a regional evening newspaper to BBC local radio and went through reporter, producer, programme presenter, news editor, assistant editor, managing editor. DAVID PEEL, MEDIA CONSULTANT

Many young journalists who started out on newspapers move across to TV or radio. They might do so as reporters, or may find they have to take their first job as a researcher. From this post you might become a reporter or choose the production career path.

Career Path 6:
Online Writing and Production

Online news is a young medium, without the ranks of senior journalists who, in traditional media, stand between newcomers and the top jobs. So there are plenty of opportunities to progress fast.

Most publishers and broadcasters have developed websites to accompany their newspapers, magazines, TV or radio programmes and, increasingly, original content is generated for these websites. Up until recently, many online reporters had little formal training or experience. As online journalism matures, that is changing. There are an increasing number of online reporters who moved across from newspapers, magazines and broadcasting, and who are valued because of their NCTJ or other qualifications, and their experience. Many who become online reporters find it a liberating experience. For example, if you work as a reporter on a weekly magazine or newspaper, you only get one day a week when your material is really fresh. If you are on a fortnightly or monthly publication, it's one day in 30. In online journalism, however, you will probably be expected to file and update many stores every day.

There is also the interaction you get with your readers, members or users, as some websites prefer to call them. In online journalism, a reporter does not just present the news; readers are invited to comment on it, to add their thoughts to a story, to take part in votes or chats, or to post responses on a bulletin board.

My switch from regional newspapers to a news website was the best career move I've made. The basic principles of cultivating contacts and how to spot and write a good story are exactly the same – but obviously the production side is very different. I've learnt to use Photoshop, RSS feeds and even some html. IAIN O'NEIL, ONLINE REPORTER, MORNING ADVERTISER

However, if you want to progress as a writer, opportunities are still limited in online publishing. Most writing specialisms are better catered for in traditional media so, while you may gain valuable experience as a reporter online, you may find that to progress you need to move into traditional media. Of course, as the boundaries between online and other media dissolve, that situation will change. Increasingly, reporters are expected to work on several media at the same time.

You can move forward in online production. In fact, the traditional distinction between reporting and production does not really exist in online journalism. Most reporters will need to know how to publish their story online, and that requires production skills. You might be happy with this career path if you enjoy both writing and subbing.

It is worth pointing out that while websites that are owned by traditional media companies tend to uphold principles of separating editorial content from advertising, companies that are exclusively new media often do not. At ISPS [Internet Service Providers], which are often owned by telecommunication companies, the progression up the journalistic career ladder involves taking editorial control of increasingly large areas of content. You might be called a producer rather than an editor, but your job will be to determine the content of a **channel**, or part of a channel. Often that will involve re-purposing

Nothing beats breaking a story. I'm particularly proud of being the first journalist to reveal the story that Wembley's Twin Towers were going to be demolished. And I'm also proud of a series of stories revealing the extent of sports doping in East Germany. JAMES TONEY, MANAGING EDITOR, SPORTSBEAT/NEWS ASSOCIATES AGENCY

In broadcasting, sports news is semi-detached from sports commentating. As a journalist, it is the news route that you are most likely to be interested in taking.

The second main career path is to go into production, in which case, depending on your chosen medium, you might become a newspaper sports subeditor, with the intention of becoming sports editor one day. On TV or radio you might become a sports producer, with the intention of becoming the editor of a sports programme in the future. Unless you are working on, say, a dedicated satellite sports news channel, you are likely to be moving away from news if you do this.

While I was working at the Barnet Press I did shifts for a number of national papers and was eventually offered a job as a sub on the sports desk at The Times. *I was there for nine years and was assistant sports editor when I left. I joined* The Independent *as deputy sports editor in 1990 and was made sports editor a year later. I was sports editor for 13 years.* PAUL NEWMAN, CHIEF SPORTS FEATURE WRITER, THE INDEPENDENT

Sport is a specialism that can take you across media with comparative ease. It's not a big step from writing a live match report to picking up a phone and talking about the game for 90 seconds on the radio, for example. A good knowledge of sports and sporting stars is a very portable asset, and will be equally valuable in any medium – from newspapers and magazines to TV, radio and in online journalism.

Get the right careers advice, from someone currently in the industry. You could end up taking an unnecessary course or wasting your time with hopeless applications. RICHARD PARSONS, PARTNER, SPORTSBEAT NEWS AGENCY

A TV sports commentator might also have a column in a newspaper.

What's the best thing about being a journalist? Being given a passport to look into the lives of other people. PAUL NEWMAN, CHIEF SPORTS FEATURE WRITER, THE INDEPENDENT

There are good opportunities for freelances. One major British sports news agency runs a network of 300 football correspondents and serves local and national newspapers, websites and many other outlets.

Career Path 9:
Photographers

If you want to stay taking pictures, you may want to move to a more prestigious publication. A practised route is from local newspapers to national ones. You may have impressed a national picture desk with work you have done on their behalf, or which you or your newspaper has sold to them. The reality is that to do so you will probably have to go freelance. There are very few staff jobs these days. With so many extremely good freelance photographers clamouring for shifts and assignments, there is simply no need to employee staffers.

You might develop a specialism – perhaps fashion, portraits or sport. With a specialism, you may be able to command a higher price for your work.

You may eventually be considered the best in your field, whether its golf or what is euphemistically known as 'glamour' photography. Editors who want nothing but the best will pay you handsomely. After all, you get star photographers, just as you get star interviewers or columnists.

I became a picture editor simply because the editor asked me to do it. I was quite happy as features editor, but didn't feel I could turn down this opportunity. I found photographers very different to writers. Managing them was like herding cats, and I hated having no space in the paper to call my own – I had to rely on other departments giving my pictures a good show. RICHARD ABBOTT, FREELANCE WRITER

It can be possible to get lucrative corporate work on the back of your editorial reputation. This can pay very well and sometimes subsidises the editorial assignments you need to undertake to maintain your reputation and keep your name in the public eye.

You may want to work a geographic patch but open up more outlets for your work, either by simply going freelance and working from home or by working for or setting up a local photo agency and serving a mix of newspapers and magazines.

> *As a trainee reporter I learned a lot from staff photographers and from freelances I met on assignments.* PETER DARLING, JOURNALISM LECTURER

If you want to move up the management chain, that will mean moving on to the picture desk, perhaps as deputy picture editor initially, or possibly going straight in as picture editor. On the desk you will have a mix of former photographers and picture desk assistants who have never taken pictures professionally. These assistants are often former secretaries who have taken on extra responsibility and learned about picture desk administration. You'll need to inspire, nurture and manage this team as well as your photographers.

Your abilities and experience as a photographer will recommend you for the top job, but even if the boss doesn't realise it, there is a huge amount of administration involved. Photographers are often used to working alone and pleasing themselves. As a picture editor, they have dozens of people relying on them, and editors who expect them to come up with the exact goods they want at the right time. It can be a culture shock.

Career Path 10
Freelancing

Freelancing is something many journalists turn to at some time in their lives. For some, it's the way in. For many it's a way of developing their career, of jumping to the next level at certain key points. For others, it comes about because of redundancy or a falling out with an employer. For relatively few, it's a way of life that suits them down to the ground.

Find out who commissions pieces of the sort you would like to write or produce and send a couple of pieces on spec. If they say: 'Not this time, but try again', TRY AGAIN! MARY DEJEVSKY, CHIEF LEADER WRITER AND COLUMNIST, *THE INDEPENDENT*

Some senior journalists, who have a wealth of experience behind them, find they can sell themselves as consultants, to be called in when a publication needs fundamental re-directing, or when a publisher has a project they want to develop editorially.

[I started out with] freelance writing on rock music for the NME. I sent in speculative reviews, which were published (and paid for!). BILL MANN, WEEKEND EDITOR, THE GUARDIAN

It is very hard to start your career as a freelance in any branch of journalism where you need well-developed skills, such as news reporting or sub-editing. Those who manage to start their career as freelances are much more likely to do so as feature writers of some description. They may have a knack for a certain type of article. Perhaps they send in reviews which are accepted. The section editor likes them and gives them more work. They go on from there, becoming regular, well-established contributors. Many a big-name columnist has started in this way.

For others, freelancing can be a way of developing their career. The classic route to Fleet Street for newspaper journalists is to start doing shifts at a national newspaper while still working in the provinces. There is a ready market for both reporters and sub-editors on the nationals.

Photographers may find it harder to be reference because there are so many people chasing each shift, but it can be done. If such shifts go well, they may be offered a regular contract or summer relief work. If they are really lucky, they'll be offered a staff job.

As part of my postgraduate diploma, I spent two weeks at The Bookseller, *a much-respected publishing trade title. I left with a good collection of by-lines and made it clear I was keen for paid work. Since then, I've been commissioned to work and invited in for day shifts on the news desk, which pay nicely.* HAYLEY PINKERFIELD, FREELANCE JOURNALIST

However, it's most likely that, to be taken seriously by the paper or magazine you want to work on full-time, you will need to go freelance and make yourself readily available to them. You want to be the first person they call when a shift or an assignment comes up.

Once you have the skills and experience to be able to get shifts, you may find you prefer to be freelance. Doing shifts, you may have more freedom than a staffer, and enjoy working on several publications each week.

Feature writers, who may have a contract to write a column each week, or a certain number of features in a year, are often freelance.

Take advantage of every opportunity to study. Try to get to know at least one subject in depth which could be used if you ever turn freelance. Being too much of a generalist when freelance is a disadvantage. STEVE TURNER, FREELANCE ROCK JOURNALIST AND AUTHOR

Freelancing is also common in broadcasting. The advent of a forest of independent production companies has meant that the old, established career structure has fragmented. Many broadcasters have set up their own production companies or now offer their services to these independents.

Another way of thriving as a freelance is to become an expert in some key area that is regularly in the news but which is too specialised for most publications to hire a staffer to cover. You might know everything about budget airlines, for example, and write about them for a range of newspapers, magazines and websites. You might find you can get a book commissioned on the subject, and then you will find that TV and radio programmes regularly ask you to appear.

If freelancing is thrust upon you, you need to fall back on your resources. This is where having NCTJ training can stand you in good stead. Perhaps for the first time in years, people want to see your CV, and to ensure that you know what you are doing.

While working on the newsdesk I freelanced for a London court agency and the Sunday Mirror in my holidays; then became full-time freelance working mainly for Mirror Group Newspapers. Late I changed course to work in Northern Ireland on a couple of local and regional papers with a short stint at Ulster TV. JACKIE MCKEOWN, NEWS EDITOR, BELFAST NEWS LETTER

At such times, journalists often have to take one or more steps down the ladder. News editors may find themselves doing reporting shifts or features editors doing **down-table** subbing.

Even those who reach the very top and become editors can find it necessary to go freelance. There are few editors who retire in the top job. Often they go on to sell their skills, acting as consultants to publishers who need really high-level know-how while they launch a publication, or put right an ailing one.

Working out what you would do if you ever had to become freelance is a very useful exercise for any journalist. After all, you see few 65-year-olds still in staff jobs.

CROSS-MEDIA
CAREER PATHS

Introduction

Many journalists move between media. Increasingly, as media converge, the old distinctions between media, and the prejudices among those who have chosen a particular medium, are disappearing. But older journalists are sometimes slow to adapt to the modern media world. Many are still far more aware of the differences between rival media than they are of the similarities. There can be a general suspicion among well-established journalists of those from another medium. Some newspaper people may suspect magazine-trained journalists of being lightweights, who don't understand hard news and can't hit a deadline unless it is at least three weeks away. Broadcasters can suspect that print journalists will be far too wordy – and probably worthy – and won't understand how to tell a story with pictures and sounds.

I moved from the Surrey Advertiser *to an evening newspaper, then BBC local radio, ITV regional television, GMTV, Sky News, BBC national TV and radio.* – MARY GAHAN, NEWS EDITOR, BBC WORLD SERVICE

Such prejudice can work both ways. Some young online journalists know that they have a handle on the future, and may resent people from old media for their plodding ways and insistence on demarcation between, for example, those who write text and those who edit video.

After four years on the Brighton and Hove Gazette I switched to local radio for about four years, then shifts on national papers and a reporter's job on The Mail on Sunday. JOHN WELLINGTON, MANAGING EDITOR, MAIL ON SUNDAY

In fact, journalists in any one branch of the media have key skills that they can transfer to any other medium, if they are open-minded enough to have a go, and if employers are enlightened enough to let them. There is nothing to say that a newspaper-trained writer, sub-editor or section head can't work very well in magazines, for example. Or that someone who speaks well on TV or radio can't write a newspaper column.

Career Path 11:
Cross-media Career Paths – Reporting

Reporting skills are the same, whichever medium they are practised in. What differs is the format in which you express your message. On a newspaper, your key method of expression is clearly through words. In an illustrated magazine, pictures may tell a large part of the story. On radio, you use spoken word and sound, and on TV spoken word and moving pictures. Online you can use any of the above, in whatever combination that suits your format, your story, and your audience.

I talked my way into the Thomson newspaper [graduate trainee] scheme – they owned The Times, Belfast Telegraph, The Scotsman, the Western Mail and other papers. I broke indentures, and was told I would 'never work in journalism again'. I got a job at the BBC, as a reporter on Spotlight. (Jeremy Paxman had previously worked on the programme.) After a couple of years at the BBC in Belfast I was offered a three-week stint as a Newsnight reporter. It turned into six weeks, then eventually they offered me a job. GAVIN ESLER, PRESENTER, BBC2 NEWSNIGHT

Here are some key cross-media moves reporters have made:

- Newspaper and press agency reporters move to TV and radio.
- Magazine reporters move to newspapers, TV and radio.

- Newspaper reporters move to online journalism.
- TV and radio reporters move to online journalism.
- Online reporters move to newspapers, magazines, TV and radio.

Career Paths 12:
Cross-media Career Paths – Production

Sub-editing and production are practised in every media. The skills involved are always the same, though their practice is adjusted depending on the format in which a story is being told.

I've subbed on local and national newspapers, consumer and business magazines and websites. I've used exactly the same skills in each, just adapting to the different audience and what they needed. RICHARD ABBOTT, FREELANCE WRITER

In every medium, it is necessary to ensure written text is checked and corrected. It is necessary in all media other than radio to ensure that words and pictures match up. In every medium it is important that a story is organised logically, that it fits the space or time allotted to it and that it does not contain serious errors.

Which attribute does a journalist most need? Accuracy, accuracy, accuracy. ROY SCOTT, EDITOR, JOHNSTON NEWSPAPERS, LOTHIAN

Here are some tried-and-tested cross-media career paths in sub-editing and production:

- From newspaper sub to magazine sub.
- From newspaper sub to online channel producer.
- From newspaper sub to TV and radio bulletin compiler.
- From TV producer to newspaper sub-editor.

- From magazine chief sub to newspaper chief sub.
- From radio producer to online bulletin editor.
- From newspaper production editor to magazine production editor.

Career Path 13:
Cross-media Career Paths – Editing

Good editing involves the selection of material which a particular audience finds interesting, and managing a team which can work together to create, gather and present that material to a consistently high standard. A good editor can work in any medium.

> *I started my own neighbourhood news sheet at the age of eight. [I finally] got the job I decided I wanted at that age: editor of my mother's favourite newspaper, the Sunday Express.* ROBIN ESSER, EXECUTIVE MANAGING EDITOR, DAILY MAIL

Here are some cross-media career paths that editors have followed:

- Newspaper editor to magazine editor.
- Magazine editor to newspaper editor.
- Newspaper or magazine editor to website editor.
- Website editor to TV or radio editor.
- TV or radio editor to website editor.
- Newspaper editor to TV programme editor.

Career Path 14:
Wild-card Career Paths

So far in this section, we have mapped out many of the key points in your career at which crossing between media is practical, and indeed very common.

But don't feel you need to be restricted by them. If you have the talent and flexibility, you can take your journalistic skills anywhere you like. As we said right at the start of this section, there are almost as many career paths as there are journalists.

[I've been through] local papers, news agency, local papers as news editor, sports editor and sub, sub on evening paper, sub on national, work on nationals, into magazines as editor/launch editor and columnist on The Independent, *running a training company but still working as a journalist (I write at least 5,000 words a week)* . KEITH ELLIOTT, MANAGING DIRECTOR, PMA TRAINING

Here are some wild-card career moves that have worked:

- From newspaper editor to TV presenter.
- From TV programme maker to radio presenter.
- From newspaper editor to newsreader.
- From magazine editor to sports writer.
- From sports reporter to online channel producer.
- From TV producer to magazine editor.
- From website editor to magazine editor.
- From news editor to news agency editor-in-chief.

Section 3

NCTJ–ACCREDITED JOURNALISM COURSES

Introduction

At the time of writing, the NCTJ accredits over 60 courses at 40 centres around the UK. This section comprises a full list of them. In each case, the institution was invited to sell itself to you, their potential students: to say why *you* should choose *them*. Variations in how that has been done are down to the institutions. In one or two cases, it was not possible to get information from the institution, in which case their entry has been compiled by us from information we have on file, and is less detailed. Those entries are marked with an*.

Please note that while all courses listed were accredited at the time of writing, you should double-check that any course you are interested in is still accredited before applying.

The NCTJ accredits courses in a variety of formats, including at undergraduate and postgraduate level. Here is a checklist of the different types of course on offer:

Block release
A block release course is designed for those who are employed on a newspaper and need to gain their NCTJ qualification.

Day release
Again, this course is designed for those already working on a newspaper but means they spend one day a week on a course studying for their NCTJ qualification.

BA (Hons) degree
A course which offers the opportunity to gain the NCTJ qualification while studying for a degree at university.

Foundation degree
A two-year course of study during which time the student sits their NCTJ exams. The option of topping up the foundation degree with an additional year of study to gain a BA is sometimes available.

One-year postgraduate
Usually an MA or Postgraduate diploma, this type of course would suit a graduate who is looking to gain their NCTJ qualification.

Fast-track
Ideal for those who want to study intensively for 18–20 weeks to gain the NCTJ pre-entry qualification.

Pre-entry academic year
Offered through further education centres, a one-year course to study for the NCTJ pre-entry qualification.

Two-year HND
An opportunity to gain the NCTJ pre-entry qualification while studying for a Higher National Diploma.

Magazine journalism
Suitable for anyone who wants to become a magazine journalist.

Photojournalism and press photography
Available for those wishing to become a press photographer or photojournalist.

BA (Hons) Sports Journalism degree
Offers the opportunity to train to be a journalist, while studying for a sports degree.

Part-time study
An ideal method of learning for anyone who cannot commit to full-time study.

Bournemouth University

BA (Hons) Multi-Media Journalism

They say

Our courses are designed to provide students with the professional skills needed to win jobs in journalism together with an informed understanding of the many issues and dilemmas faced by journalists in contemporary society. Journalists starting a career today can expect to move between print, radio, television, broadband and the internet. Our BA Multi-media Journalism course delivers an introduction to the range of available opportunities in all these media.

We have high graduate employment rates – graduates from our courses go straight into national and local broadcast news, national and local newspapers, national magazines and online news outlets, and have a wider choice of career options, often enjoying an accelerated rate of promotion in their chosen profession. Graduates are now working for the BBC, CNN and other major news organisations worldwide. Recent work placement opportunities have included BBC *Newsnight*, *The Sunday Times*, the Press Association, *The Independent* and ITN.

We have strong industry links with local and national media organisations, including guest lectures by industry professionals. Visiting Fellows include investigative journalist Duncan Campbell, Mark Brayne (Director Europe, Dart Centre for Journalism and Trauma), Kevin Marsh (Editor-in-Chief, BBC College of Journalism) and Eve Pollard (the second-ever female editor of a British national newspaper).

Every effort is made to ensure graduates are exposed to a wide range of current practitioners and to the underlying issues that the next generation of journalists will need to understand. An example of this is our recent 'Could you cover a bomb attack in London?' mock exercise. Bournemouth Media School, in partnership with the Dart Centre in Europe, is also leading research to investigate how journalists are trained in the UK to cover traumatic events and stories that deal with difficult emotional issues.

Former students say

'I felt I was completely ready for the industry when I started out and due to the high emphasis on work experience and hands-on learning, I was well prepared for becoming a professional.'

'The reputation is good and also the links with the NCTJ. You have to have that sort of journalism training really. People you speak to, you say Bournemouth and there's that association with the media.'

'The course left me with a passion for journalism and my ability to contribute to it.'

The assessors say

Eve Pollard, a Visiting Fellow to Bournemouth Media School since 1995, said: 'I like coming down to Bournemouth and passing on my experiences to a whole generation of young people hoping to go into the media. The School has a good reputation and is very highly respected within the media industry. Students leaving Bournemouth University are real ambassadors and the name really does get around for all the right reasons.'

At the latest NCTJ re-accreditation, the inspection panel, including two newspaper editors, said that BA (Hons) Multi-Media Journalism goes 'from strength to strength'. The panel praised its multimedia ethos and its 'excellent combination of the professional and academic' in a 'well-balanced curriculum'. The programme exceeded NCTJ standards in some areas. NCTJ Chief Executive Joanne Butcher said: 'The programme has huge strengths in terms of teaching and technology and the use of visiting lecturers and is ahead of the game in terms of embracing multimedia skills.' She added that BA (Hons) Multi-Media Journalism could be summed-up in terms of 'motivation, enjoyment and enthusiasm on the part of both students and staff'.

Find out more

www.media.bournemouth.ac.uk

Course details for BA (Hons) Multi-Media Journalism: www.bournemouth.ac.uk/courses/bammj

Contact details

www.media.bournemouth.ac.uk
media@bournemouth.ac.uk

01202 965360
Dorset House,
Talbot Campus,
Fern Barrow,
Poole,
Dorset BH12 5BB

Brunel University

MA Journalism

They say

A brand new programme offering a unique combination of cutting-edge skills and contextual knowledge.

Devised in close consultation with senior journalists, the syllabus provides a rigorous foundation to a career in this dynamic, challenging and often controversial industry.

Students are trained in print/online journalism, with the option to specialise in broadcast journalism in the second term. Throughout the programme, students gain a reflexive understanding of the journalism industry, particularly the ethical, legal, political and other contextual factors that impact upon journalists' daily working lives.

Taught by highly-experienced practitioners and academics, the programme also benefits from input from prestigious guest speakers. Students have the flexibility of completing the course in one year full-time or two years part-time.

Find out more

http://www.brunel.ac.uk/courses

Contact details

Donna White 01895 267214. donna.white.@brunel.ac.uk
School of Arts
Brunel University
Uxbridge, Middlesex
UB8 3PH

Cardiff University

Postgraduate Diploma in Journalism Studies – Broadcast, Magazine or Newspaper

They say

The Cardiff School of Journalism, Media and Cultural Studies is quite simply the premier centre for journalism scholarship, education and training in Europe. In 1970, Cardiff pioneered journalism education in British universities and has subsequently built a world-renowned centre for the study of all aspects of journalism, mass media and cultural studies.

In recent years, £140 million has been spent to ensure that these buildings contain the equipment and other facilities needed by today's students. Cardiff has first-class library and information technology resources, excellent lecture theatres and private study areas, a number of new residences and extensive sports facilities.

The measure of our success is that our students are in such heavy demand from employers, who are the most unforgiving judges. Our alumni can be found in top broadcasting, magazine and newspaper jobs across Britain. They include Ben Brown, the BBC's star television news correspondent; Donald Macintyre of *The Independent*; Dawn Bebe, managing director of Emap Elan; Oliver Holt, chief sports writer of the *Daily Mirror*; and John Witherow, editor of the *Sunday Times*, along with many others.

Former students say

'Cardiff was always my first choice for studying journalism, given its reputation and its alumni. The course prepared me for my career, it's a cliché but the diploma really is a passport into that first job. The standard of teaching and facilities is first class and news editors' eyes still light up when they hear work placement students are "at Cardiff".'

'Most people came to Cardiff knowing they wanted to be a reporter but not sure where or how to get a start in the profession. Those who arrived with pretensions of becoming a leader writer for *The Guardian* within 12 months quickly learned that they were more likely to be starting on the *Cambridge Evening News*. The lecturers could be tough but only because they wanted to be producing journalists rather than student essay writers.'

The assessors say

The course is praised by the NCTJ for the resources available, including equipment and the library.

Find out more

www.cardiff.ac.uk/jomec/
www.cardiff.ac.uk
www.cardiffstudents.com/

Contact details

David English: 02920 874786   englishdm@Cardiff.ac.uk

Cardiff School of Journalism, Media & Cultural Studies,
Cardiff University,
Bute Building,
King Edward VII Avenue,
Cardiff CF10 3NB

Cardonald College, Glasgow

HND in Journalism Studies
Day release – Newspaper journalism

They say

The journalism course at Cardonald College is based in Scotland's media capital, Glasgow, and is one of the country's longest-running and most widely respected journalism training courses, with long-standing NCTJ accreditation. It is a practical course designed by experienced journalists and newspaper editors to offer the real skills demanded by the industry. Course co-ordinators work closely with the NCTJ, the National Union of Journalists and the Scottish Journalism Training Forum to maintain an excellent record of helping students get their big break in journalism.

Modern facilities and equipment, experienced journalists, low class numbers, excellent industry links and a proven track-record of success ensure that studying journalism at Cardonald is a valuable experience which will set you on the right track to success.

Add to that the fact that you will be studying in one of Europe's most vibrant cities, with unparalleled student life and media links and you know that you are on to a winner on a course which has also produced *The Herald*'s college publication of the year for the last two years.

The HND course, which includes all NCTJ preliminary examinations, is open to graduates, school leavers and anyone interested in changing career path, while the day-release course is open to working journalists aiming to complete the NCTJ prelim exams.

Former students say

'The course is excellent and really set me on my way in journalism. I've met a lot of people who studied at universities where things like shorthand are optional. That's quite amazing considering how important it is. The staff are great – they clearly care about the students and won't fill your head with nonsense. The focus is on the realities of the job.'
–Stefan Lach, reporter with the *Paisley Daily Express* and Write Stuff Scottish Journalist of the Year 2004 and 2005

'I always wanted to break into magazines and film writing and Cardonald helped me do just that. I'd recommend this course as a really strong, relevant grounding in journalism which will give you a realistic chance of employment.'
–Sam Ashurst, Future Publishing, Bath

'The course is excellent because it prepared me for anything. There are a lot of courses out there that place emphasis on writing but don't spend enough time on all the other things you need. The course at Cardonald covers it all, and I started my job confident that I could tackle everything that could be thrown at me.'
–Gillian Stewart, reporter with *The Lennox*, Dumbarton

The assessors say

Having first won NCTJ accreditation in 1999 the course was re-accredited once again in 2003, when the re-accreditation chairman said: 'I was very impressed with the course and the quality of all of the work undertaken by the students.'

The Media and Communications section of Cardonald College, which houses journalism, was also praised by Her Majesty's Inspectorate. Inspectors praised both the standard of tuition and students' work.

In addition, the *Cardonald Courier* was named *The Herald*'s college publication of the year in 2005 and 2006, and numerous Cardonald students have been winners of the Write Stuff Scottish Student Journalism Awards.

Find out more

www.cardonald.ac.uk

Contact details

Contact course co-ordinator and senior lecturer: Martin Boyle: mboyle@cardonald.ac.uk
Course administrator: Rena McAdam: 0141 272 3242

Cardonald College,
690 Moss Park Drive,
Glasgow, G52 3AY

City College, Brighton and Hove

Fast-track PgDip in Newspaper Journalism (18 weeks)
Fast-track PgDip in Magazine Journalism (18 weeks)
One-year part-time in Newspaper Journalism
One-year part-time in Magazine Journalism

They say

A new media suite was set up in 2005. Lecturing staff include respected working journalists, some with as many as 20 years experience in the field, plus one of the best shorthand teachers in the country. We focus on the practical aspects of the discipline with the emphasis on equipping students for both staff and freelance jobs after the course. We encourage students with a wide range of guest speakers, from local MPs to editors of national music magazines. There are visits to parliament and Crown Courts and we use trained actors for mock interview exercises.

Former students say

'I enjoyed the course – it was well organised and the course leaders really were dedicated.'

'Freelance advice was sound and the stuff on contacts.'

'Teaching was good, they knew what they were talking about.'

The assessors say

We achieved a 2 in the last OfSTED inspection for the department as a whole.

Find out more

www.ccb.ac.uk
www.ccb.ac.uk/public/support/students_union.html

Contact details

Alan Gill: 01273 667788 ext 431   AG3@ccb.ac.uk
01273 667788 for admissions and guidance

City College,
Journalism Department,
Wilson Avenue,
Brighton,
East Sussex BN2 5PB

City of Wolverhampton College

Full-time Academic Year Course in Newspaper Journalism
Part-time Day-release Course in Newspaper Journalism for trainee journalists already in the newspaper industry
Refresher courses to prepare candidates for the NCE

They say

NCTJ full-time students at the City of Wolverhampton College are treated like journalists from their first week of study. The two principal lecturers have more than 60 years' experience as journalists on weekly, daily, Sunday and national daily titles and they combine informality with sound, modern teaching practice. There is a strong emphasis on practical work, informed by lectures, discussions and input from visiting speakers.

Visits are arranged to other newspapers, police headquarters, courts and council meetings. And interwoven with their journalism, law, public affairs and shorthand tuition is the requirement to produce their own full-colour college magazine.

The course also has strong links with many editors of newspapers throughout the Midlands who are all keen to offer work placement opportunities to our students for up to two days a week for 12 consecutive weeks. Many are recruited to these publications before the end of the course. Learning takes place in a room dedicated to our NCTJ students so work placement cuttings can be displayed along with vacancies and a map showing the dozens of newspapers that have employed our young people. Full-time students accepting employment during the course can transfer to the day-release course which the college also offers for reporters already in the industry. This runs alongside the full-time course.

Former students say

'The course provided a strong and stimulating foundation for a career in reporting, with teaching from experienced journalists who passed on both their knowledge and enthusiasm. The emphasis on work experience was particularly useful for establishing contacts which eventually led to a job on a successful local paper.'
–Martyn Smith, *Stourbridge News*

'Experienced college tutors combined their knowledge of the core principles of law, politics and writing with advice based on their own experiences. We received a thorough grounding in journalism skills and were fully supported in our new jobs. The department also created a friendly environment where students helped each other to succeed.'
–Alicia Kelly, *Redditch Standard*

'One of the best aspects of the course was that the tutors were very supportive and encouraging. I had a mock job interview with them which was very

helpful. I felt less nervous and more relaxed when it came to the real thing because of the advice I had received.'
–Heather Large, *Kidderminster Shuttle*

Find out more

www.wolverhamptoncollege.ac.uk

Contact details

Course Leader: Sue Green: 01902 317564   greens@wolvcoll.ac.uk

City of Wolverhampton College,
Wulfrun Campus,
Paget Road,
Wolverhampton WV6 0DU

Cornwall College

Foundation Degree (FdA) in Newspaper and Magazine Journalism (full-time over two years)
Postgraduate Journalism – fast-track (18 weeks)

They say

Journalism courses were established at Cornwall College more than a decade ago after close collaboration with the National Council for the Training of Journalists (NCTJ).

Our purpose-built newsroom is equipped with a bank of 16 computers, all with internet access and offering a variety of programmes including Quark and Photoshop, an A3 scanner, digital satellite TV and video equipment. It is the base for journalism teaching and the place where most of the story writing is done.

Successful students can expect to find work as a reporter in newspapers, magazines and news agencies. There are also many opportunities to develop your skills in radio and television. Over the past five years more than 80 per cent of our students have gone straight into jobs as reporters.

Cornwall College has trained more than 450 newspaper reporters and now has former students working with the BBC, national newspapers, news agencies and a range of provincial newspapers around Britain, as well as in public relations and marketing. Former students from the course are working for organisations as diverse as the *News of the World* and Oxfam. The course provides excellent links with the local media, with most journalists in Cornwall trained at Cornwall College.

Former students say

'I studied journalism at Cornwall College six years ago and still use the skills I learned there every day. The course dealt with the numerous disciplines needed to cover a news story, whether it be major incidents such as a gun siege or train crash or lighter news such as the Beast of Bodmin or outrage at the WI.'
–Luke Mendham, *News of the World*

'The skills I learned at Cornwall College have always been a resource on which I have been able to rely, and I have very happy memories of my time there.'
–Becky Morris, *Daily Mail*

'I would recommend the foundation degree at Cornwall College to anyone who is serious about a career in journalism because it prepares you for the real world.'
–Danielle Tatton

The assessors say

During a recent re-accreditation NCTJ inspectors found the course to be well taught by enthusiastic staff. All journalism is taught by current and ex-journalists.

Find out more

www.cornwall.ac.uk

Contact details

Mark Benattar, Head of Journalism/Course Manager Postgraduate Journalism – fast-track (18 weeks): 01209 616650   mark.benattar@cornwall.ac.uk
Peter Ryder, Course Manager, FdA Newspaper and Magazine Journalism: 01209 616651   peter.ryder@cornwall.ac.uk
Course enquiries: (01209) 611611

Cornwall College Camborne,
Opie Building,
Trevenson Road,
Pool,
Redruth,
Cornwall TR15 3RD

Cumbria Institute of the Arts

BA (Hons) Journalism

They say

Students studying at Cumbria Institute of the Arts will find themselves within a vibrant and creative student community. Our cohorts are small, which means students are able to benefit from focused workshops and, often, one-to-one tuition. The teaching staff are all former journalists from print or broadcast backgrounds, and our emphasis is very much on preparing our graduates for a demanding and challenging profession. All students are expected to contribute to the student newspaper, which is produced to professional standards and printed by the region's newspaper group. Carlisle provides a wealth of opportunity for work experience. Based in the city are the headquarters of the regional newspaper group, two local radio stations (BBC and Independent Local Radio), plus the region's ITV station. Our students have regularly worked for all four organisations.

Former students say

'I really enjoyed the course – it was practical, challenging and extremely interesting. It helped me to get the skills I needed to work in the real world.'
–Mike Boorman

'My degree at Cumbria Institute of the Arts set me up perfectly for a career in journalism, and gave me all the skills needed to succeed. The broad skills range was exactly what the Press Association wanted from new staff, and meant I have been able to rise up the company quickly and gave me a huge advantage over other people without my training.'
–Luke Thornhill, the Press Association

'The thing I most value about the course was the professional way in which it was delivered. Because the tutors were fresh from the industry, they dealt with us in a realistic way. As a result I had a practical and professional approach to my career and work. The opportunity to get involved in print, broadcast and online projects meant I gained multi-platform experience. In turn this meant I had vital skills and more importantly a realistic attitude when applying for jobs and entering the world of work. That said, the tutors value more traditional aspects of journalism, such as shorthand, a skill which is delivered in a digestible fashion – you can work at your own speed! After graduating I joined the BBC.'

'When I joined the BBC I was told I would never get a contract until I got a degree from Preston – or somewhere similar. Now they realise I did practically the same course with a bit more experience thrown in.'
–Helen Skelton

The assessors say

NCTJ report: 'Students were very enthusiastic about the course and appreciated the commitment and professionalism of their lecturers. The panel members were impressed by the dynamism and dedication of the students they met. Journalism students work extremely hard and are admired for this by other students at the institute. The course is viewed as excellent value for money given its intensity, practicality and professionalism.'

Find out more

www.cumbria.ac.uk

Contact details

Ms Helen Hutchinson: 01228 400300   helen.hutchinson@cumbria.ac.uk
0845 6076563
info@cumbria.ac.uk

Cumbria Institute of the Arts,
Brampton Road,
Carlisle,
Cumbria CA3 9AY

Darlington College

NCTJ Pre-entry Newspaper Journalism (20-week fast-track)
NCTJ Block Release Newspaper Journalism (20-week fast-track)

They say

Darlington College has been delivering high-quality NCTJ journalism training for more than 30 years and has helped launch the careers of hundreds of journalists. Former Darlington students are to be found in newsrooms and editor's chairs around the world.

In the summer of 2006 the college relocated to a striking new purpose-built campus. The school of journalism forms part of the media design centre and has been awarded Centre of Vocational Excellence status.

The pre-entry journalism courses on offer at Darlington will equip you with the skills and experience you will need to apply for jobs as a trainee reporter. The block release courses will develop trainees who are already working on newspapers.

You will receive expert tuition in practical journalism, media law and public affairs from experienced journalists and shorthand tuition from experts using resources devised specifically for journalists. These courses are practical, highly vocational and intensive. We offer start dates in September and February.

Former students say

'This course gave me the skills I needed to get a job.'

'I had a great time, even though I worked like a dog!'

'The most positive thing about this course is that it prepares you completely for being a journalist and for what it is like to work on a newspaper.'

Find out more

www.darlington.ac.uk

Contact details

NCTJ pre-entry programme leader Sue Kelly: 01325 503050   skelly@darlington.ac.uk

NCTJ block release programme leader Jon Smith: 01325 503050   jsmith1@
darlington.ac.uk

Darlington College,
Central Park,
Haughton Road,
Darlington,
Co. Durham DL1 1DR

De Montford University

Postgraduate Diploma, Newspaper Journalism

They say

Launched a decade ago with a mission to provide high-quality journalism education and training geared to each individual student's strengths and weak-
nesses, the PGDip at De Montford University has proved hugely successful with
students and the newspaper industry alike.

Almost 100 per cent of our graduates get jobs in newspapers or related
industries, if not before they even finish the course (as many do), then within
a few months of graduating. And they return to tell us what they learned here
helped secure their next job and the ones after that too – a real 'education for life'.

The course is run and taught by people who have decades of successful
experience in local, regional and national newspapers and magazines, most of
whom are NCTJ-qualified.

Our students not only learn the basics and material needed to pass exams, but
gain extensive experience in putting that knowledge into practice in 'real world'
journalism – making the mistakes we all make when we start out, developing their
own individual aptitudes and strengths, and learning to be true professionals.

The course features an excellent staff/student ratio, unrivalled individual
and class contact time, and all the benefits you'd expect from a thriving and
cosmopolitan city-centre university.

Former students say

'[The course] has totally lived up to my expectations, and more. The work has
been challenging (but fun), necessary, interesting and most importantly

career-orientated. I would also say that the amount of variety was superlative. It was impossible to get bored. I can speak for everyone on the course when I say that we have all thoroughly enjoyed it. And we all respect the superb head-start that you have given our (hopefully!) glittering careers.'
–Alex Blackwell, news editor, *Harborough Mail*

'I can honestly say that I loved this course to pieces, I made some fantastic friends, had a brilliant time and learnt so much. Without it I wouldn't be in my dream job that I'm currently enjoying! The co-ordinators of the course were fab and really supportive and passionate about it and I would highly recommend it to anyone wanting to get into journalism.'
–Robyn Greenacre, reporter, *Eastern Daily Press*

Find out more

www.dmu.ac.uk/humanities
DMU Student Union website: www.mydsu.com

Contact details

Ms Ali Haynes: 0116 250 6163   ahaynes@dmu.ac.uk
De Montfort University,
The Gateway,
Leicester LE1 9BH

Edge Hill University

BA (Hons) Journalism with NCTJ Preliminary Certificate (3 years, full-time)
From 2007 we will also offering a one-year graduate course in journalism

They say

To survive, the journalist of the future will need to know how and where to find stories and how to produce and present them for a range of different media, including newspapers, magazines, radio, television and the internet. This degree course offers tuition in all areas of journalism: print, broadcast and online, and there is a good mixture between the practical and theoretical elements.

The teaching team have a wide range of professional experience in all fields of the news industry as well as research interests in contemporary developments in journalism and the media. The practical elements of print, radio, TV and online journalism are taught by former or current industry practitioners, and facilities for journalists are excellent, with newsrooms and radio and TV studios equipped with industry-standard hardware and software. Practical news-based exercises replicate industry working conditions and there are work placements in both the second and third year. Study becomes more self-directed and independent as the course progresses, leading to a final year major practical project and 10,000-word dissertation of the student's choice.

Assessment for the degree is a mixture of coursework, essays, practical projects and exams, with the NCTJ prelim exams taken alongside the degree assessment.

Former students say

'Thanks – the course was great, tutors very supportive and knowledgeable, facilities excellent.'

'I certainly will not look at a news story in the same "innocent" light ever again!'
'I have just got my dream job as a reporter . . . thanks to you and the team at Edge Hill.'

The assessors say

The Media Department, which includes journalism, gained 20 out of a maximum of 24 points on the six aspects assessed during the last Higher Education Funding Council for England inspection.

Find out more

www.edgehill.ac.uk

Contact details

Angela Birchall: 01695 584172   birchalla@edgehill.ac.uk
Enquiries unit: 0800 195 5063 (freephone)
enquiries@edgehill.ac.uk

Edge Hill University,
St Helens Road,
Ormskirk,
Lancashire L39 4QP
01695 575171

Glasgow Caledonian University

BA (Hons) Journalism

They say

This is the only NCTJ-accredited BA Journalism in Scotland which includes compulsory teaching in broadcast journalism (radio, TV, online), in all-digital TV and radio studios/edit suites (Avid/Audition). Print production and subbing are also included. Shorthand, law and government are all compulsory parts of the single-honours course and marks in each count towards the degree. Work experience of four weeks has to be completed during the course, and marks are awarded for detailed reports on achievements and learning during work experience, at the end of each academic year. The two main full-time practical lecturers are former newspaper and magazine editors. There is a core practical journalism and a core academic journalism module in every semester. The course is based in the Caledonian Business School and one third of the curriculum is made up of a selection of useful business subjects, including economics, marketing, IT and statistics, accounting.

Of the first graduates in July 2006, 50 per cent were in journalism jobs by the end of August 2006. The main emerging first destination job market is local weekly Scottish papers, Scottish commercial radio newsrooms, sports departments and sports broadcasting.

Former students say

'I have the usual job of a reporter: interviewing, writing stories, arranging pictures, and I accompany a reporter usually once a week to court. Shorthand, news writing and feature writing were also important, and I found the doorstop interview exercise very helpful in hopefully preparing myself for a real one in the future.'
–Laura Cummings, trainee reporter, *The Dunfermline Press*

'The BA Journalism degree programme at Caledonian gave me the best possible grounding for a career in this field. The fact it allows you to tackle both print and broadcast journalism with excellent professional input, means that you leave with more than one string to your bow which, to a working journalist in the 21st century, is very important.'
–Liam McLeod, broadcast/online journalist, BBC *Sport Scotland*

'The main strength of the degree is how much of the journalism industry it covers – all talents are catered for. I've found work in both print and broadcasting and can always call on the valuable lessons I learned here. It is a great course for those who want to develop their all-round game or who want to find which area of journalism suits them best.'
–Stuart Wilson, news reporter, *Ayrshire Post*

The assessors say

The University was rated 'Highly Satisfactory' in 95–96 Teaching Quality Assessment in Media/Communication. Assessors were particularly impressed by the teaching they observed, and the student work produced. In every year since 2000, Glasgow Caledonian University has been rated in the UK Top 20 universities – and top two in Scotland – for the teaching of media, by *The Times Good University Guide*. In 2005, the newspaper rated GCU best for media in Scotland. GCU's media team is also the only one in Scotland to improve its ranking in each Research Assessment Exercise (3a).

Find out more

www.caledonian.ac.uk/cbs/study/bajo/index.html

Contact details

Ken Garner, programme organiser: 0141 331 3258   k.garner@gcal.ac.uk
Julian Calvert, admissions tutor: 0141 331 3844   julian.calvert@gcal.ac.uk

Caledonian Business School,
City Campus,
Cowcaddens Road,
Glasgow G4 0BA

Harlow college

One-year Journalism: Newspapers
Postgraduate Journalism: Newspapers
Postgraduate Journalism: Magazines

They say

From national, regional and local newspapers to household names, our centre is well known in the media industry. Former students include Piers Morgan, Alan Rusbridger, Steve Lamacq, Mark Knopfler, Kelvin McKenzie, Tim Lott and Richard Madeley.

In April 2004 the new Journalism Centre accommodation was officially launched by Martin Bell and Mike Wooldridge (another former student).

National, local and regional newspapers as well as well-known magazine titles and publishers both recruit from us and send their staff to us.

Many of our lecturers are also highly successful freelancers, writing for *The Guardian*, the *Daily Telegraph*, *Press Gazette*, *The Sunday Times Magazine*, *Vogue*, *Essex Magazine* and *Yes!* Past experience includes investigative journalism in the United States and Canada, foreign correspondent for *The European*, editor of the *Nursing Times*, editor of the *Braintree and Witham Times* and a former magazine proprietor. Many of our lecturers are also examiners and sit on industry panels, including NCTJ Examination Board members.

Former students

Tom Jackson was only 17 when the *Cambridge Times* sponsored him on his studies with a guaranteed job at the end of his studies.

Jessica Huie. With all the responsibilities of being a single mother, Jessica found work experience with Max Clifford in her third year of studies. Max was very generous, presenting Jessica with a large cheque at the end of her work experience which allowed her to finish her studies. Jessica now works for Max and also freelances for *The Mirror* and *3 am magazine*.

Paul Carter. Despite Paul's severe physical disabilities, he graduated from the course with high grades and was immediately appointed as a web writer for *ZOO* magazine.

The assessors say

In 2004 the official OfSTED and Adult Learning Inspectorate (ALI) Inspection Report awarded the Journalism Centre a Grade 1, viewing the teaching and learning as 'Outstanding'. The report praised the teaching staff and accommodation, citing: 'There are good specialist accommodation and resources for journalism ... this has a professional newsroom ethos which is highly valued by the students. Students are highly motivated and produce high-quality practical work which matches the requirements of the industry. There is very good teaching in journalism which draws upon the wealth of industrial experience and links that staff bring'.

Find out more

www.harlow-college.ac.uk

Contact details

The Learning Link: 01279 868100
learninglink@harlow-college.ac.uk

Harlow College,
Velizy Avenue,
The Hides,
Harlow CM20 3LH

Highbury College, Portsmouth

NCTJ Pre-entry Certificate in Newspaper Journalism (Fast-track, 20-week)
NCTJ part-time Pre-entry Certificate in Newspaper Journalism (one year)

They say

*journalism@***highbury** is renowned as a centre of excellence for journalism training on the south coast. Every year dozens of Highbury graduates gain a job in journalism – many of them snapped up by newspapers, magazines and radio and television stations before their course has finished.

Employers know our students are highly-trained, highly-motivated and well-prepared for the pressures of the newsroom. That's why Highbury graduates are in demand, and why thousands of our former students now hold senior posts in the industry – top professionals such as ITN's Mark Austin, the BBC's Jon Pienaar and CNN's Chris Cramer.

And a wide range of employers put their faith in our training programmes every year, either by sending staff for training at Highbury or by asking us to deliver tailor-made in-house training. They include the *Sunday Times*, the BBC, Northcliffe, Archant, Newsquest, Johnston Press, Guardian Media Group and many, many more.

What can *journalism@**highbury*** give you?

- Real journalism – we concentrate on hands-on training
- Real equipment – industry-standard digital studios and newsrooms
- Real journalists – all our trainers are highly-experienced journalists

Visiting editors, reporters and specialists also work on our practical training programmes. Many editors come to *journalism@**highbury*** for our students, and many of them recruit exclusively from our ranks.

Industry-standard newsrooms
Four Mac newsrooms
Two digital radio studios with digital newsroom
Three-camera, full colour digital television studio
Digital TV editing suite

Former students say

'The course at Highbury was time well spent in every sense of the word. It is excellent preparation for the industry and worth three times as much as on-the-job experience.'
–Jon Pienaar, BBC

'What Highbury College gives aspiring journalists is a solid foundation for a reporting career, the basics of the job whether they end up in newspapers, radio or television.'
–Mark Austin, ITN

'The advice and support that I received at Highbury was second to none and helped me secure a job very quickly on a newspaper. I fully believe there is no better place to study journalism.'
–Gemma Wheatley, *Croydon Guardian*

The assessors say

This is what the NCTJ accreditation panel said about us: 'The panel believes the NCTJ journalism courses at Highbury are of a very high standard and has no hesitation in recommending full accreditation. There is a strong emphasis on contact-making and patch-reporting. Competition between students for stories is actively encouraged. The course goes well beyond the minimum NCTJ requirements for accreditation. Equipment and facilities offered are first class.'

Find out more

www.highbury.ac.uk

Contact details

Joy Young: 02392 313287   journalism@highbury.ac.uk

Highbury College,
Department of Media, Creative & Visual Arts,
Dovercourt Road,
Cosham,
Portsmouth,
Hampshire PO6 2SA

The Journalist Works*

Fast track Diploma in Production Journalism. (12 weeks)

They say

The Diploma in Production Journalism is a brand new qualification. The Journalist Works is the first centre in the country to run the course and successful graduates stand a high chance of gaining employment as production journalists on newspapers, magazines and websites, as there is a national and international shortage of suitably qualified sub-editors.

We work in partnership with *The Argus*, Brighton's regional daily newspaper, and train our students in their HQ

The diploma consists of four modules: sub-editing; media law; practical journalism and public affairs. The latter three modules form the basis of the well-established NCTJ Pre-Entry Diplomas in both Newspaper and Magazine Journalism which are available at other training centres nationally. So that means that our graduates are also able to apply for jobs as reporters. Just add shorthand at 100wpm and you are doubly qualified. (And we can get you a discount rate at Brighton's top shorthand provider.) If you would like to study for the diploma on a part-time basis you can take modules individually – contact us for more details.

Find out more

www.thejournalistworks.co.uk

Contact details

Paula O'Shea 01273 324351 info@thejournalistworks.co.uk

The Journalist Works
The Argus
Crowhurst Road
Hollingbury
Brighton
BN1 8AR

Lambeth College

Foundation degree in journalism – (two years) the course, run in partnership with London Metropolitan University, offers a third-year option to top up to a BA Honours Degree in Journalism Studies at London Metropolitan University.

Postgraduate pre-entry newspaper journalism (18 weeks) starting in February and September each year

They say

Lambeth College is recognised throughout the industry as providing students with the knowledge necessary for a career in journalism. Each year 72 post-graduate students study for the NCTJ pre-entry certificate. There are also, each year, a further 18 students enrolled on the foundation degree in journalism.

The success of the courses is measured by good results and the high number of students gaining employment as trainee reporters, trainee sub-editors or trainee multimedia journalists across local and national titles, the BBC, the Press Association and Reuters.

To date 100 per cent of students passing the foundation degree have opted to top it up to a full BA Honours Degree in Journalism Studies by studying for a third year at London Metropolitan University.

All students benefit from a staff of qualified teachers who between them have a wealth of journalistic experience at both local and national level. The college is equipped with up-to-date newspaper industry computer programmes for writing, design and research. Students have open access to the internet. The college has strong links with industry and many publications offer work experience to our students.

Former students say

'I thought I could write before, but the NCTJ course at Lambeth really taught me how to write good, clean copy. It also sharpened my news senses.'
–**Ali Martin,** *Sun online*

'The thing that sets one NCTJ course apart from another is the teaching. The great thing about Lambeth is if you listen to the sound advice and stay focused, you will get through with relatively little pain'
–**Aline Nassif,** *Barking and Dagenham Post*

The assessors say

The NCTJ says: 'Lambeth College is a long-standing centre for journalism training with a sound structure for learning and a good reputation within the industry.'

The Quality Assurance Agency (QAA) reported that Lambeth College provided a strong focus upon the technical and professional skills required in journalistic practices and that the professional expertise of staff provided students with a key learning resource. QAA also reported that students considered staff supportive, helpful and readily available.

The London Metropolitan University external examiner reported that student achievement formed a good basis for entering the industry.

Find out more

www.lambethcollege.ac.uk

Contact details

Wendy McClemont, course manager: 020 7501 5489 wmcclemont@lambethcollege.ac.uk

Lambeth College,
Vauxhall Centre,
Belmore Street,
Wandsworth Road,
London SW8 2JY

Leeds Trinity and All Saints

MA/Postgraduate Diploma in Print Journalism

They say

We give our trainees the essential skills and knowledge underpinning all journalism practice, starting with the basics: what news is, where it comes from, how to conduct interviews, how to write news, how to behave in an ethical way and so on.

Our trainees study law, public affairs, ethics and shorthand, but they also have lots of practical experience with the emphasis on learning by doing in a modern, fully equipped newsroom.

The senior print tutor is an award-winning former journalist and her deputy is a working freelance. Between them they are able to offer individual tuition and provide constant feedback.

In the newsroom, we work on 'real news in real time' and produce the weekly *West Riding Post,* not a student magazine, but a paper that is distributed to newsdesks, authorities, organisations and other contacts throughout the region.

Our contacts in the regional newspaper industry are second to none; we have editors calling us when vacancies arise. Our employment record is impressive with 95 per cent of our graduates employed in the industry within six months of finishing the course. But, importantly, our trainees leave the college ready, keen and able to walk into any newsroom and get on with the job.

Former students say

'Without the TAS course, there's absolutely no way I'd be where I am today working at the *Yorkshire Evening Post*. I got the job here following a placement arranged by my tutors and it gave me the chance to show what I had learned and what I was capable of doing.'
–Suzanne

'I think the course has prepared me very well for my future career. By covering law, shorthand and public affairs we have the technical knowledge. By producing a paper we are able to effectively experience the ressures/demands of a newsroom.'
–Sunita

The assessors say

'The panel was unanimous in declaring that the pre-visit documentation was more than adequate and that it was a pleasure to visit the college. Both staff and trainees exuded confidence about the course and panel members were hard put to find any criticisms.'
–NCTJ accreditation visit, May 2001

'The panel visited the dedicated and well-equipped newsroom where production of the *West Riding Post* for that week was underway. Each of the twelve trainees took it in turn to be editor and during the one-to-one confidential session the panel held with most of the class it became clear all interviewed found the course enjoyable, hard work and value for money. Many of the students hoped to start their careers on the regional/provincial press.'
–NCTJ accreditation visit, June 2004

The next visit is due in 2007.

Find out more

www.leedstrinity.ac.uk/cfj

Former students say

'The degree at John Moores offers students a chance to gain a real feel for journalism. With specific assessment suited to each student's choices it presents the opportunity to develop essential skills while building up a portfolio of work. In the final year a four-week work placement gives the chance to gain on-the-job experience and impress prospective employers.'
–John Hynes, Trinity Mirror Sports Media

'The course gave me an insight into the world of journalism from politics to magazine, it gave me the opportunity to see what area of journalism I wanted to get into.'
–Ngunan Adamu, Radio Merseyside

The assessors say

The course was awarded an 'Excellent' grade (22 points out of a possible 24) by the Teaching Quality Assessment undertaken by the Quality Assurance Agency for Higher Education. The QAA said: 'The School can genuinely claim ... to be at the leading edge of development, geared to the needs of students and other clients.'

Find out more

www.ljmu.ac.uk and follow links or type in: http://www.livjm.ac.uk/ StudyLJMU/Courses/58643.htm

Contact details

Julie Quine, Admissions and Information Officer: 0151 231 5119   Fax: 0151 231 5049   j.quine@ljmu.ac.uk
Lynne Gilbertson, Admissions Assistant: 0151 231 5127   Fax: 0151 231 5049 l.gilbertson@ljmu.ac.uk

Glyn Mon Hughes, Admissions Tutor: 0151 231 5044   Fax: 0151 231 5049
r.g.Hughes@ljmu.ac.uk

Liverpool John Moores University,
School of Media, Critical and Creative Arts,
Dean Walters Building,
St James Road,
Liverpool L1 7BR

Midland News Association*

Midland News Association training scheme

They say

The traineeship scheme is designed to recruit the reporters needed for the
Midland News Association's newspapers, which include the *Express &
Star, Shropshire Star* and 20 weeklies. Trainees sign a three-year contract,
which includes five months at the Rock House training centre in
Wolverhampton.

There are usually two intakes of trainees a year, in March and September.
Competition for places is fierce because those selected become paid members
of staff and have a job to go to at the end, providing they have successfully
completed the Rock House course.

At the end of the course they join one of the weekly papers where they
work towards full senior status. Most trainees will have reached senior status
within about two years of joining the course and will be pushing to move on
to the evening paper.

Find out more

www.expressandstar.com/aboutus/training/index.php
www.shropshirestar.com/aboutus/careerinjournalism

Contact details

Crispin Clark: 01902 742126   c.clark@expressandstar.co.uk

Midland News Association Training Scheme,
Rock House,
Old Hill,
Tettenhall,
Wolverhampton,
West Midlands WV6 8QB

Nosweat Journalism Training*

Part-time 41-week course in Newspaper Journalism
Fast-track 21-week course in Newspaper Journalism

They say

At noSWeat we believe that journalism is caught, not taught. We try to encourage an informal and friendly atmosphere with tutors available for help and advice at all times. We also have a programme of guest speakers from the top of their profession to build and channel the already boundless enthusiasm of our selected students.

Students themselves are encouraged to mix and contact each other both within and outside the centre. With this combined approach we have achieved considerable success. Above-average exam results have led to some students finding jobs before the end of their course. Others, already in the industry, come to us for training needed for career advancement.

Most graduates go on to well-established local papers such as the *Camden New Journal,* the *Hampstead and Highgate Express* and the *Romford Recorder.* Some go directly to evening provincials and others to the nationals.

We are situated in a quiet close in the heart of London with all of the city's facilities on our doorstep. Facilities include up-to-the-minute computer suites all on broadband and networked. There is also a comfortable common room.

All students study journalism in its various forms. There are no other subjects studied at noSWeat.

Former students say

'My mother had a little cry when I told her I'd got the reporter's job. What can I say – it's what I always wanted.'
–Former student on a west London weekly, previously in advertising sales

'I started as an editorial assistant. Now I am a junior reporter.'
–Former student on a national Sunday

'I am working as a photo journalist now after the course. It is the first rung on the ladder and I intend to work my way up.'
–Former student now working as a photojournalist on a Kent weekly, formerly in advertising sales

The assessors say

The NCTJ assessors said: 'The college has moved to excellent facilities in Clerkenwell Close. Great emphasis is placed on getting students through exams. Feedback was extremely positive about all aspects of the course.'

Find out more

www.nosweatjt.co.uk

Contact details

info@nosweatjt.co.uk
020 7490 2006

noSWeat Journalism Training,
16/17 Clerkenwell Close,
London EC1R 0AN

Nottingham Trent University*

MA/Postgraduate Diploma in Newspaper Journalism

They say

The Centre for Broadcasting and Journalism leads the way in providing professional training and education for the journalists and broadcasters of the future. Supported by a consortium of leading media organisations, the centre is based in a purpose-built newsroom and studios with cutting-edge technology.

Each member of the centre's teaching staff is a current or former media professional. Together they offer substantial experience of broadcasting or journalism in television, radio, newspaper and online.

Our professionally-oriented courses provide practical experience through work placements, which are essential for gaining the expertise necessary to launch a rewarding and successful career.

Graduates of both our undergraduate and postgraduate courses have gone on to successful careers around the world, many winning prestigious awards for their work, both during and after their studies.

Former students say

'The teaching on the MA was brilliant, completely changed the way I wrote and showed me how to look for the real story when a person is talking. My studies easily saw me through my NCTJ exams and I wouldn't have got my job without those.'
–Katharine Barney, senior reporter, *London Evening Standard*

'I think it would have been hard to get into the industry and reach this point in my career without an accredited journalism course behind me.'
–Lisa Dowd, Midlands correspondent, *Sky News*

'The broadcasting facilities are really impressive, and the course has strong links with industry. It's good training, particularly if you also get some experience of working in a professional environment.'
–Sarah Dolman, awarded the BBC East Midlands Traineeship in 2004 and went on to win the 96 Trent FM award for Best Student Radio News Reporter in her final year

Find out more

www.ntu.ac.uk/cbj

Contact details

Ms Sarah Murphy: 0115 848 5803   sarah.murphy@ntu.ac.uk
If you would like to visit the university, call the course administrator for
details of open events on 0115 848 5806

Nottingham Trent University,
Centre for Broadcasting and Journalism,
Room 106, York House,
Mansfield Road,
Nottingham NG1 3JA

Press Association Training Centre*

Editorial Foundation Course in Newspaper Journalism

They say

As the national news agency of the UK and Ireland, the Press Association is
able to offer one of the best and most comprehensive training opportunities
in the media industry. Through a mix of formal classroom training, the environment of a modern multimedia newsroom, professional tutors and working
with talented and experienced people, we are able to offer a choice of training
across the gamut of the industry.

You can rest assured that if you are fortunate enough to gain a place on one
of the Press Association Training's foundation courses, you will be getting the
best training there is in the UK.

Our training centre in Newcastle is the only one in the country to be based
in a working newspaper office. The course runs for 16 weeks at our fully
equipped facility in the headquarters of the *Newcastle Evening Chronicle*,
Journal and *Sunday Sun* newspapers. It is unique in allowing reporters the
chance to get stories published in some of the biggest regional titles as you

train. That means as well as leaving the course with the right qualifications, you can also expect a healthy cuttings' file with which to impress editors.

At the end of the course, delegates sit preliminary exams in shorthand, government and law. They will have the chance to apply for jobs in the media during the course. Over the past 10 years no one who has successfully completed the course has failed to be offered a job in newspapers.

Former students say

'There is a plethora of so-called journalism training centres but Newcastle is the real thing. Unlike many courses it is based in a newspaper office NOT on a university campus. The staff there will arm you with the skills to tackle tough stories and tough news desks.'
–Michael Greenwood, assistant news editor, *Daily Mirror*

'After leaving Newcastle, I was given a permanent job with Birmingham's Sunday tabloid, *The Sunday Mercury,* where I had a great two years. I've no doubt that Newcastle gave me the tools to succeed in Birmingham, where I landed some solid splashes and gained a great deal of useful experience. I moved away from Birmingham in November 2005 to take up a job with Ferrari Press Agency. It's one of the most respected agencies in the business, and I work with and for the nationals on a daily basis. But even now – three years after Newcastle – I still find myself falling back on tips I'd picked up during the course. It was the best type of journalism training – practical, very professional, and great fun too.'
–Tom Wells, Ferrari Press Agency

Find out more

www.editorial-centre.co.uk

Contact details

Tony Johnston: 0191 201 6043   tony.johnston@pa-training.co.uk

Press Association Training Centre,
Thomson House,
Groat Market,
Newcastle Upon Tyne NE1 1ED

Scottish Centre for Journalism Studies*

Postgraduate Diploma/MLitt in Journalism Studies

They say

The Scottish Centre for Journalism Studies is a collaboration between the University of Strathclyde and Glasgow Caledonian University. Its courses are accredited by the National Council for the Training of Journalists and it has the support of the Scottish Newspaper Publishers' Association. Students have the choice of studying the Postgraduate Diploma in Journalism Studies or progressing to the MLitt.

The Postgraduate Diploma prepares students for careers as journalists in the newspaper, magazine and broadcasting industries and is aimed at graduates in any discipline and media professionals with relevant experience who seek a formal qualification. Diploma students study for nine months and pursue a broad range of relevant practical and theoretical journalism studies – news reporting, feature writing, news gathering, and research and Scots law, government and public administration, journalism and society, and Teeline shorthand. Students also have the opportunity to specialise in print journalism or broadcasting, as well as arts, sports or magazines.

On successful completion of the Diploma at a specific standard, students may progress to the MLitt, in which they prepare a dissertation on an approved journalistic topic.

Former students say

'I chose the journalism course at Strathclyde because of its excellent reputation. It also offers a good mix of theory and practice. The centre has great facilities and the staff are very friendly and helpful. We got the chance to produce our own weekly newspaper and that was fantastic preparation for going out into the industry.'
–Jacqueline McGhie, winner of Young Journalist of the Year Award at the Scottish Press Awards 2005

'I decided on Strathclyde because I knew the course had a good reputation and was NCTJ-accredited. I found the course both challenging and fulfilling.

The thought of living and working in Glasgow was also appealing. It's a vibrant city and I enjoyed every minute of my time there.'
–Beth Neil, winner of the Press Gazette Young Journalist of the Year 2004, Best Newcomer at the Norwich Union Medical Journalism Awards and the Rosemary Goodchild Prize for excellence in sexual health journalism

Find out more

www.strath.ac.uk/Departments/scjs/

Contact details

Gordon Smith: 0141 950 3281   gordon.j.smith@strath.ac.uk

Scottish Centre for Journalism Studies,
University of Strathclyde/Glasgow Caledonian,
Crawfurd Building,
Jordanhill Campus,
76 Southbrae Avenue,
Glasgow G13 1PP

Sheffield College, Norton

Academic year course in Newspaper Journalism
Academic year course in Press Photography or Photojournalism
Postgraduate fast-track in Newspaper Journalism
12-week block release in Newspaper Journalism
12-week block release in Press Photography

They say

Would you get a buzz from chasing stories, interviewing people about the serious issues of life — or life's oddities? And would you enjoy writing to deadlines? If you have an aptitude for news gathering — an interest in people and what's happening around you — our journalism courses could equip you for an exciting career.

We're the biggest and oldest in the journalism training business. We achieve exceptional exam results. and we are very proud of our success in the jobs market. Of 27 students on a recent fast-track course, for example, 22 went straight from college into careers as journalists. Many of them had the job in the bag weeks before the end of the course.

If you're keen to become a reporter, show us. We'll be pleased to hear you have some news-gathering work experience, and have a basic grasp of news-writing style. And we'll be getting quite excited if you tell us you've started to learn Teeline shorthand. In short, impress us with your commitment and determination, and reinforce that impression with good people skills at the selection interview. After all, interviewing is going to be a major part of your working life.

Digital Press Photography/Photo Journalism

It's described as the country's toughest course, geared to the twenty-first century needs of the newspaper industry. Its students consistently win national and regional awards, and places on the country's only NCTJ-accredited press photography/photojournalism course are available for those who demonstrate skill, commitment, drive and personality.

The selection panel will expect candidates to have a good knowledge of photography and bring along some striking images. They're impressed with candidates who have a capacity to look at the obvious and see something different — or better — by way of a news line and picture.

Paul Sanders, picture editor of *The Times*, said: 'Three of the last four winners of the Times Tabasco scholarship have been from Norton College in Sheffield. This year's entries – nearly 200 – were of an even higher standard than in previous years, and the winner was yet again from Norton College. That speaks volumes.'

Former students say

'I won a job as a reporter straight away – thanks to the dedicated and detailed training I received at Norton College, and because of its strong links with the newspaper industry.'
–Matt Westby, *Barnsley Chronicle*

'Norton College changed my approach to photography, greatly improving quality and consistency – and gave me a keen journalistic sense for the better image and story.'
–Chris Pledger, winner of the Times Tabasco award

'Going to Norton was a great learning experience.'
–Julian Thorpe, *Barnsley Chronicle*

Find out more

http://my.sheffcol.ac.uk

Contact details

Academic Year Newspaper Journalism
Terry Wootton: 0114 260 2359   terry.wootton@sheffcol.ac.uk
Photo Journalism/Press Photography
Paul Delmar:
0114 260 2600   Paul.Delmar@sheffcol.ac.uk

Sheffield College,
Norton Centre,
Dyche Lane,
Sheffield S8 8BR

Southampton Solent University

BS (Hons) Journalism (provisional accreditation)

They say

Southampton Solent is one of only a handful of university colleges to run a BA (Hons) Journalism degree course incorporating NCTJ training. This means a student can acquire a meaningful degree and essential pre-entry qualifications at the same time.

This distinction enables students to concentrate on all academic aspects of journalism while learning and using all practical skills that the industry demands.

The Institute is situated in the centre of this lively south coast city, which has a large and cosmopolitan student population. It is convenient for access to the media with BBC and Meridian TV, a variety of radio stations, two competing south coast evening newspapers and several lifestyle magazines within a 20-mile radius.

Graduates go on to a variety of media-related jobs with local radio stations, regional newspapers, and PR companies.

Former students

Alumni include:
Sarah Lagan who secured a job with the *Press Gazette*.
Lee Honeyball is assistant editor with *Observer Sports Monthly*
Zoe Richards is editor of *Hair and Beauty* magazine.

Find out more

www.solent.ac.uk/

Contact details

Glyn Mottershead: 02380 319000   glyn.mottershead@solent.ac.uk

Southampton Solent University
East Park Terrace
Southampton SO14 OYN

Sportsbeat

Pre-entry Certificate in Newspaper Journalism (Fast-track, 19 weeks). Intakes in March and September. (Provisional accreditation)

They say

The ability to train as a journalist with a leading reporting agency offers students an opportunity that is unparalleled at other places of learning.

Our team of lecturers will tell you how it should be done against the background of a busy newsroom in which most of them actively play a part. As part of the NCTJ family, we are helping the industry's training body shape its curriculum to the changing needs of news organisations such as ourselves. We also pride ourselves on the individual attention we can offer to those studying to take their place in this, the most satisfying of professions.

Former students say

'Ever since I can remember I have wanted to be a journalist. I have always had a passion for writing and I'm nosey by nature, so it made sense really. The course has only given me a thirst for more. I get such a buzz from opening a newspaper and seeing an article that I've written, especially when I've put all my time and energy into it.'
–Lauren Margrave

'One of the things that attracted me to the Sportsbeat course was the idea that a real working journalist would be there to give me advice when I needed it. I've already helped put together their coverage from the Commonwealth Games and attended my share of football matches. Building your portfolio is the best way to get a job.'
–Pippa Davis

'The only way to survive this course is to live it and breathe it. Shorthand is a tough nut to crack but if you put in the work then you will reap the rewards. You just have to work like a dog and never give up. I hit the 100 words per minute but I was transcribing everything in sight from billboards to TV programmes. It's already an invaluable skill for me.'
–Nadia Mendoza

Find out more

www.newsassociates.co.uk

Contact details

Richard Parsons on training@sportsbeat.co.uk

Staffordshire University

BA (Hons) Journalism

They say

Excellence in journalism is at the heart of the most diverse range of media courses offered by any UK university. Core awards in journalism and broadcast journalism are accredited by the country's leading journalism training organisations. They have praised our state-of-the-art facilities, and the university is committed to maintaining a lead in this field.

The journalism team's wealth of continuing professional experience and grasp of the enormous changes in the industry have fuelled the development of specialist awards. Sports journalism, music journalism and broadcasting, ethical world journalism and an array of joint honours courses have been tailored to students' professional ambitions and real jobs in the twenty-first century.

All modules, theoretical and practical, focus totally on producing content to trade standards for all platforms. Students have to submit work for broadcast, print or online use as part of their assessments. Fully-assessed work placements bolster the stress on professional practice. The result is graduates going directly into an impressive and exciting variety of jobs (from Sky News to *Your Cat* magazine) and postgraduate study.

Staff include an award-winning BBC producer, a former Sky, BBC and ITV correspondent, an ITV sports producer, a BBC political pundit, senior newspaper editorial staff, and widely published and respected academics. We are passionate about what we do.

Former students say

'The best thing was that I learnt an array of skills which I am now improving on in my working career. The encouragement from the tutors/lecturers was invaluable and certainly made a difference to me personally. The facilities at the university were also impressive and all the factors prepared us for the "working world".'
–Mark Bowering, sports reporter, Press Association

'My course taught me the "real" world of journalism. It's not all fame and fortune, and the wages can be a bit of a joke. But if you work hard and are determined, you will succeed. All the tutors were extremely helpful, friendly and approachable, which made my experience one I will treasure forever.'
–Antonia Merola, chief reporter, *North Wales Pioneer*

The assessors say

'One of the best equipped training newsroom facilities in the country.'
–National Council for the Training of Journalists

Our teaching standards are some of the very best in the university sector – over the last three years we have achieved 12 consecutive excellences in all subject reviews carried out by the Quality Assurance Agency (QAA).

Find out more

www.staffs.ac.uk
Union website: www.staffsunion.com

Contact details

Sarah Rowlands: 01782 294415
s.rowlands@staffs.ac.uk
Journalism

Faculty of Arts, Media and Design,
Staffordshire University,
College Road,
Stoke-on-Trent ST4 2DE

Sutton Coldfield College*

Pre-entry course in Newspaper Journalism

They say

Sutton Coldfield College launched the pre-entry course in 1996 and its journalism graduates are now working for national, regional daily and weekly newspapers all over the country. They are also working with news agencies and magazines. Others have moved into broadcasting and public relations.

The college has excellent relationships with the local media and students have often been recruited following successful work-experience placements.

Students are taught in a dedicated base room equipped with Apple MACs and PCs incorporating all the latest software. Members of staff teaching on the course have appropriate industry and academic backgrounds.

As well as offering the core subjects (journalism, law, public affairs and shorthand) students also have an opportunity to develop their page design skills using Quark Xpress and contribute to their own college online newspaper www.newshub.org.

Find out more

www.sutcol.ac.uk

Contact details

Argentina Menendez:
0121 355 5671 ext 5618   amenendez@sutcol.ac.uk

Sutton Coldfield College
Lichfield Road,
Sutton Coldfield,
West Midlands B74 2NW

University of Brighton*

BA (Hons) Sports Journalism (provisional accreditation)

They say

The BA Sport Journalism degree at the University of Brighton was the first sport journalism degree in the country to be accredited by the NCTJ. The course offers the opportunity to train to be a journalist, while studying the sociology of sport. The university's excellent sports facilities are right on the doorstep.

In the first year of the course a student was a finalist in the Daily Telegraph Young Sportswriter of the Year competition.

With opportunities for work experience at both *Observer Sport Monthly* and BBC Sport, the course is attracting huge numbers of applicants.

Find out more

www.bton.ac.uk

Contact details

Ms Jackie Errigo: 01273 643703   j.j.errigo@brighton.ac.uk

University of Brighton (Eastbourne Campus),
Gaudick Road,
Eastbourne,
East Surrey BN20 7SP

University of Central Lancashire

BA (Hons) Journalism
Postgraduate Diploma/MA in Magazine Journalism
MA in Magazine Journalism

They say

UCLan is recognised as one of the leading institutions for journalism training in the country. Journalism has been taught at Preston for well over 40 years and many well-known journalists began their careers at Preston, such as Simon Kelner, Angelique Chrisafis, Victoria Derbyshire, Ian Payne and Catherine Marston.

Journalism courses are very practical. The single honours undergraduate and postgraduate journalism courses are accredited by the National Council for the Training of Journalists and the Broadcast Journalism Training Council.

BA students are given a thorough grounding in print, broadcasting and online journalism in the first two years. They can specialise in print, online, radio or television the final year. Work placements are in the final year. Students also take their NCTJ exams in final year.

The Masters degree builds on the strengths of the postgraduate diploma course. In the third semester students choose to produce either a radio or television documentary programme, or a 15,000-word dissertation.

There are more than 20 lecturers in the Department of Journalism and all have a professional background in media industries.

Students work in a busy newsroom atmosphere, undertaking realistic tasks, involving live issues in the city and surrounding area.

The department boasts some of the best facilities in the UK with fully digital radio, television and production facilities. It has six radio studios, a TV studio, two video edit suites, three print rooms, live news feeds from the Press Association and Independent Radio News. Students have the use of mini-disc recorders, digital stills cameras and digital video cameras. More than £400,000 has been invested in new equipment in the last four years.

Former students say

'When I began the postgraduate course, I had no idea the doors it was about to open for me. I remember feeling a little out of my depth, as everyone else seemed to have so much experience, but we were all pretty well level by Christmas. Once the practical aspects such as editing had been mastered, the serious business of "news days" form the mainstay of the course. You learn so much from these simulated days; how to do the job quickly, how to work under pressure and how to get on with your colleagues despite that pressure!'
– Sally Naden, BBC Radio Lancashire

The assessors say

The Journalism department received a glowing report from the 2004 institutional audit by the Quality Assurance Agency for Higher Education (www.qaa.ac.uk). It is also consistently singled out as one of the leading UK journalism centres in higher education surveys conducted by top British newspapers.

Find out more

www.ukjournalism.org
www.uclan.ac.uk
www.uclan.ac.uk/induction
www.yourunion.co.uk

Contact details

Mike Green: 01772 894730   mtgreen@uclan.ac.uk
or dlbenton@uclan.ac.uk
Enquiry management at: 01772 892400
cenquiries@uclan.ac.uk

The Department of Journalism,
University of Central Lancashire,
Preston PRI 2HE

University of Portsmouth*

BA (Hons) Journalism and Media Studies/English Literature or English Language
(provisional accreditation)

They say

The course is designed to provide accredited pre-entry training to enable you
to pursue a professional career in newspapers, magazines or online journalism.
You will also be expected to develop your creative skills, learning how to lay
out newspapers, magazines and websites and eventually to design your own.

The English literature half of the course concentrates on the study of literary
texts and the cultural, historical and theoretical interpretation of literature.
You will analyse, interpret and criticise literature in different ways through
studying topics such as textual analysis, period-based investigation, literary
genres and literary history. After the core studies of your first year, you will

have ample scope to choose different periods and literary context, from Shakespeare to contemporary literature.

This course offers you the chance to browse the whole realm of written English along with the opportunity to develop your own writing and research skills as a journalist. You also have the opportunity to show your creative skills as a journalist in the areas of newspaper, magazine and web design.

Find out more

www.port.ac.uk

Contact details

Barry O'Shea: 02392 842287   barry.oshea@port.ac.u

University of Portsmouth,
LB 3.04 Milldam,
Burnaby Road,
Portsmouth PO1 3AS

University of Salford*

BA Journalism (combined honours)

They say

All degrees are joint honours (e.g. Journalism and English, Journalism and Politics, Journalism and Sociology, Journalism and Broadcast, Journalism and Design). The aim is to offer as wide and as solid an educational experience as possible along with an introduction to the core skills and knowledge base that underpins modern journalism.

The undergraduate programme is presently accredited by the NCTJ and all students are encouraged to take all seven preliminary papers before graduating.

All the full-time and part-time staff teaching these courses are experienced professional journalists. The four full-time staff members, Tom Gill, Mike Henfield, Pete Leydon and Steve Panter, have together just under 100 years experience as working journalists in newspapers, TV and radio.

Find out more

www.salford.ac.uk

Contact details

Ms Cynthia Martin: 0161 295 4142   course-enquiries@salford.ac.uk

University of Salford,
School of Media, Music & Performance,
Adelphi House,
The Crescent,
Salford M3 6EN

University of Sheffield

BA (Hons) Journalism Studies and BA (Hons) Journalism and a modern language MA/Postgraduate Diploma in Print Journalism

They say

Courses are taught by former industry professionals from the national and regional press – e.g. *The Guardian, The Independent, The Observer, The Sunday Times*, the PA – and from regional and national radio and television – e.g. BBC and Yorkshire TV. Well-equipped newsrooms, with radio and TV studios, simulate the workplace environment. There are work placements for all students. We have strong industry links, with visits to media employers, guest lectures and workshops from leading industry professionals. We encourage active research into the practice of journalism from lecturers who have published widely in books and journals as well as continuing to publish in newspapers and to broadcast.

Former students say

'I enjoy working among the buzz of the national news. It is pressurised, but satisfying and rarely boring.'
–Fran Booth, *Daily Telegraph*

'I've been the *Guardian*'s night reporter, covering everything from artistic chimpanzees to Prince Harry's ill-advised decision to attend a fancy dress party in Nazi uniform.'
–Sam Jones, *The Guardian*

'Working in local television news is just as fast-paced and exciting as working for a big national network. I've covered events such as the 60th anniversary of D-Day and the Athens Olympics. I was nominated as best TV newcomer by the Yorkshire Royal Television Society.'
–Marco Van Belle, BBC TV

The assessors say

'The University of Sheffield has built up a first-class reputation for journalism training and has excellent links with the industry.'
–National Council for the Training of Journalists

'The standing of the Department of Journalism Studies in industry as well as academia is endorsed most strongly by graduates and employers. The Department attracts very strong students, produces highly qualified and satisfied graduates and engages positively with issues relating to quality and standards.'
–Quality Assurance Agency

Find out more

www.sheffield.ac.uk/journalism

Contact details

Course leaders Jonathan Foster (undergraduate), David Holmes (print post-graduate): 0114 222 2500

University of Sheffield,
Department of Journalism Studies,

Minalloy House,
Regent Street,
Sheffield S1 3NG

University of Strathclyde*

BA (Hons) Journalism and Creative Writing (provisional accreditation)
MA/Postgraduate Diploma

They say

The Scottish Centre for Journalism Studies (SCJS) is a collaborative venture of
the Universities of Strathclyde and Glasgow Caledonian. Since its creation in
1990, the centre has built an unrivalled reputation for training journalists to
the highest standards.

In addition to the excellent employment record of graduates, our courses
have enjoyed continuous accreditation by the NCTJ. If you want to pursue a
career in journalism, SCJS can help give you the ideal start.

Find out more

www.strath.ac.uk

Contact details

Brian McNair: 0141 548 3054   brian.mcnair@strath.ac.uk

University of Strathclyde,
522 Livingstone Tower,
Richmond Street,
Glasgow G1 1XQ

University of Sunderland*

BA (Hons) Journalism (provisional accreditation)
MA/Postgraduate Diploma in Newspaper Journalism

They say

BA (Hons) Journalism offers a wide range of flexibility in the field of journalism to give you essential multiple skills for employment. It is structured around core modules in journalism and media studies, allowing you to study and practise journalism alongside theoretical subjects.

In the first year, you will learn general journalism skills such as interviewing, research and writing. From your second year, you can choose to specialise in either newspaper journalism or magazine journalism. Alternatively, you can opt for a more general, theory-based route.

The newspaper and magazine pathways are provisionally accredited by the National Council for the Training of Journalists. This allows and prepares you to take the NCTJ preliminary examinations which form the industry's accepted pre-entry qualification. It would then allow you to take the final professional examination, the NCTJ's National Certificate, once you're in employment and ready to become a senior reporter.

Practical elements of the course include print journalism, magazine writing, design and production, media law and reporting public affairs. In addition, shorthand is taught to professional standards – this is an essential requirement if you want to report for newspapers. You can also opt to take radio journalism, or modules in TV, new media or video production.

The MA/Postgraduate Diploma combines practical and theoretical approaches to journalism. It includes a route provisionally accredited by the National Council for the Training of Journalists. This allows and prepares students to take all the NCTJ preliminary examinations which, together, form the newspaper industry's accepted pre-entry qualification.

The programme is designed to prepare students for their first job in print journalism and will be closely allied to accepted industry standards. It is not expected that students will have previous experience of journalism studies. The programme will provide them with an intensive grounding in the provision of vocational skills together with a critical awareness of the responsibilities and roles of the modern journalist.

Students will work in a realistic newsroom environment in the new £9.4 million purpose-built Media Centre at the Sir Tom Cowie Campus at St Peter's. They will learn the basics of print journalism, including writing, interviewing, news gathering, news values and ethics. They will also be given the opportunity to work on placements at local newspapers. Students will also study media law and public administration as it operates in England and Wales. Shorthand is also taught and students are expected to attain a speed of at least 100 words per minute. Masters students will go on to complete a major dissertation or project.

All staff members teaching on the programme are experienced journalists who have worked at a senior level in the regional and/or national media.

The assessors say

The University of Sunderland forms part of the media and cultural studies provision, and was rated 'excellent' in 1998 by the Quality Assurance Agency.

Find out more

http://welcome.sunderland.ac.uk/

Contact details

Chris Rushton: 0191 515 2188   chris.rushton@sunderland.ac.uk

University of Sunderland
The Media Centre,
St Peter's Campus,
Sunderland SR6 0DD

University of Ulster

MA/Postgraduate Diploma in Newspaper Journalism, (including NCTJ preliminary exams)

They say

The course provides comprehensive training in news reporting and production for print and broadcast using the latest digital newsroom facilities. Previous students have won the top student journalism awards in both Ireland and the UK, and have one of the highest employment and completion records of any course. Students undertake a placement with a news organisation and are given assistance in obtaining the all-important first job in journalism. As well as law, the course also explores issues such as ethics, conflict reporting and how the media industry works.

Former students say

'The course is highly respected within the industry and gave me a great start. It is intensive but with small classes there was a great rapport between students and lecturers.'

Find out more

www.ulster.ac.uk

Contact details

MA Journalism: c.murphy@ulster.ac.uk
BA Journalism: g.mclaughlin@ulster.ac.uk

University of Ulster,
Coleraine,
Co. Londonderry BT52 1SA

Up to Speed Journalism*

Fast Track Multi-Media Journalism (22 weeks)

They say

Up To Speed Journalism is the only UK Multi-Media Journalism training centre owned and run by a top TV journalist.

Up To Speed runs the only NCTJ-accredited Fast-Track course in the country starting in July. That means you can take NCTJ exams before Christmas and qualify in the same year that you graduate, or leave school. And our location on the south coast makes Up To Speed the ideal place to study in the summer months.

You spend 18 weeks studying on our Newspaper Journalism course, taking exams in News Writing, Law, Public Affairs and Shorthand. Then, equipped with those skills, you devote four weeks to training as an Online Journalist, learning web and video skills and taking the NCTJ's new exams in those subjects. These skills are vital as newspapers increasingly need qualified journalists capable of working for both their print and online editions.

Former students say

'I now have a much better understanding of how the news really works. The teaching is excellent and I have enjoyed every aspect of the course – even if it is really hard work!'
–Sophia Hough, Up To Speed Fast-Track student.

The assessors say

Stephen Chambers, the NCTJ's Head of Accreditation, said: 'In terms of its focus on practical skills and knowledge, the quality of the teaching staff and their familiarity with the NCTJ syllabus and the facilities available to students, this course is doing exactly what it says on the tin by delivering the NCTJ syllabus in full and to a standard that should produce well-qualified and highly employable trainee journalists.'

Find out more

www.uptospeedjournalism.com

Contact details

info@uptospeedjournalism.com

Up To Speed Journalism Training Limited,
Thornton House,
16, Parkstone Road,
Poole,
Dorset BH15 2PG

Warwickshire College*

Academic year course in Newspaper Journalism

They say

A regular feature of the NCTJ full-time pre-entry course at Warwickshire College is that each year two local weekly newspapers, the *Courier* and *Observer* groups, seem to be almost entirely staffed by our previous year's student intake.

Within two weeks of completing his final exam for the NCTJ Certificate in June this year, Josh Layton had a by-lined front page lead in the *Leamington Courier*. News editor on his weekly rival, the *Observer*, is past student Greg Aris.

Our 2002–03 Journalism Student of the Year, Jeanette Scott, moved quickly from local weeklies on to the *Coventry Evening Telegraph* where she is now one of the principal news reporters. She was also nominated in three categories for West Midlands Journalist of the Year awards.

www.warkscol.ac.uk/

Contact details

Peter McGarry: 01926 832655   pmcgarry@warkscol.ac.uk

Warwickshire College,
Warwick New Road,
Leamington Spa,
Warwickshire CV32 5JE

West Kent College

Pre-entry (academic year) course in Newspaper Journalism

They say

Worried about being just one more face in the crowd with tutors who don't know your name? West Kent College is the affordable alternative. We are a small course taking 12–16 students a year, allowing tutors to work closely with individual students. Our tutors are all practising journalists and work as freelances when not involved in the course – so they have up-to-date industry knowledge and contacts.

As well as law, public affairs, journalism and shorthand, we teach Indesign and Photoshop. Several former students have gone on to subbing jobs as a result of this.

We work with students to arrange relevant work experience either in the Kent area or further afield. We have good relationships with local papers whose staff come in as guest speakers and sit on our selection panels. We don't believe our job finishes with the exams: we will offer you practical advice and assistance in finding a job at the end of the course. We offer sessions on job search, CV preparation, covering letters and interview practice, and can offer advice and insight into different career paths. We have a well-equipped newsroom with modern computers equipped with Adobe Creative Suite and Word.

We will consider postgraduates and mature applicants who want to change careers. We may also be able to consider post-A level candidates.

Former students say

'The course set me on a path for a career in journalism, a profession which seemed impossible to penetrate until I passed the NCTJ. It also opened my eyes to the importance of local newspapers as the voice of the community.'

'We studied local newspapers from our area, and outside the area when possible, and it helped develop my sense of a good story. We then produced two pages of news a week with a small group, gathering stories, writing them up before deadline and subbing the pages. It was great fun, and prepared me for work on a local newspaper. And, vitally, I passed the exams, an invaluable ticket into a horribly underpaid career which I still believe is the best job in the world.'
–Megan Reynolds, Newsquest

The assessors say

West Kent College was inspected by OfTED in 2006 and was judged to be 'good.' OfSTED praised:

- its excellent support for learners;
- its partnership with employers and the community;
- the enterprising and highly responsive curriculum;
- the high level of student performance.

Find out more

www.wkc.ac.uk

Contact details

Alison Moore, course leader: 01732 358101   alisonmoore@wkc.ac.uk

West Kent College,
Brook Street,
Tonbridge,
Kent TW9 2PW

Section 4

DATABASE OF EMPLOYERS

How to use these listings

The listings here are organised under the following headings:

- Newspapers and newspaper-related websites
- Magazines and magazine-related websites
- Television and radio broadcasters and related websites
- News, sport and picture agencies
- Online publishers

These listings provide an extensive database of opportunities for work experience, training and jobs. But this is really just a starting point. There is no use firing off a standard letter or e-mail to dozens of organisations on the lists, asking for work experience, training or a job.

As has been made clear in Section 1 of this book, the best way to go about it is to make individual, tailored approaches to newspapers, magazines, programmes or websites where you can demonstrate a genuine knowledge and interest.

So, when thinking of local papers, contact editors of papers you read, or perhaps your parents read, and of which you can show some knowledge. They need to cover areas of the country that you know well – ideally, where you were brought up. Editors will be interested if you say you only read them online – perhaps you can tell them how to get the website right?

With magazines, you need to be able to demonstrate that you are a reader, and know the magazine well enough to be able to talk intelligently about what it does.

With a broadcast news service or programme you need to demonstrate that you know that news service or programme. Likewise with a website.

Editors get dozens of approaches from those who have not done their homework and can demonstrate no knowledge of, or interest in, their newspaper, magazine, website or programme. These approaches are – justifiably – rejected out of hand.

Your approach needs to stand out from the dross. You want the editor to think: 'Ah, here's a useful person. They live in the town or read/watch/listen to us regularly.'

Of course, everyone has to start somewhere, and when you are applying for work experience at the age of 18 it is understandable that you don't have any previous experience. But if you are any older than this, the person you contact is going to want to see that you have relevant experience. And once you are in your early twenties they will expect someone who is serious about journalism to have undertaken several work placements and have something to show for it – cuttings from a newspaper, glowing references from an editor, that sort of thing.

Finally, these lists are extensive, but they are not always entirely comprehensive. If the contact information you want is not here, go to your reference library or use the internet to find it. Knowing how to research is a vital part of becoming a journalist.

NEWSPAPERS AND NEWSPAPER-RELATED WEBSITES

National newspapers

Daily Express
The Northern & Shell
Building,
10 Lower Thames Street,
London, EC3R 6EN
08714 341010
www.express.co.uk

Daily Mail
Northcliffe House,
2 Derry Street,
London W8 5TT
020 7938 6000
www.dailymail.co.uk

Daily Mirror
1 Canada Square,
Canary Wharf,
London E14 5AP
020 7293 3000
www.mirror.co.uk

Daily Star
The Northern & Shell
Building,
10 Lower Thames Street,
London EC3R 6EN

08714 341010
www.dailystar.co.uk

Daily Star Sunday
The Northern & Shell
Building,
10 Lower Thames Street,
London EC3R 6EN
08714 341010
www.megastar.co.uk

Daily Telegraph
1 Canada Square,
Canary Wharf,
London E14 5DT
020 7538 5000
www.telegraph.co.uk

Financial Times
1 Southwark Bridge,
London SE1 9HL
020 7873 3000
www.ft.com

The Guardian
119 Farringdon Road,
London EC1R 3ER

020 7278 2332
www.guardian.co.uk

The Independent
Independent House,
191 Marsh Wall,
London E14 9RS
020 7005 2000
www.independent.co.uk

**The Independent on
Sunday**
Independent House,
191 Marsh Wall,
London E14 9RS
020 7005 2000
www.independent.co.uk

The Mail on Sunday
Northcliffe House,
2 Derry Street,
London W8 5TT
020 7938 6000
www.mailonsunday.co.uk

Metro
(see regional and local

listing for Metro regional editions)
Northcliffe House,
2 Derry Street,
London W8 5TT
020 7651 5242
www.metro.co.uk

The News of the World
1 Virginia Street,
London E98 1NW
020 7782 4000
www.thenewsoftheworld.
co.uk

The Observer
119 Farringdon Road,
London EC1R 3ER
020 7278 2332
www.observerguardian.co.uk

The People
1 Canada Square,
Canary Wharf,

London E14 5AP
020 7293 3000
www.people.co.uk

The Sun
1 Virginia Street,
London E98 1SN
020 7782 4000
www.thesun.co.uk

The Sunday Express
The Northern & Shell Building,
10 Lower Thames Street,
London EC3R 6EN
08714 341010
www.express.co.uk

Sunday Mirror
1 Canada Square,
Canary Wharf,
London E14 5AP
020 7293 3000
www.sundaymirror.co.uk

Sunday Sport
19 Great Ancoats Street,
Manchester M60 4BT
0161 236 4466
www.sundaysport.com

The Sunday Telegraph
1 Canada Square,
Canary Wharf,
London E14 5DT
020 7538 5000
www.telegraph.co.uk

The Sunday Times
1 Pennington Street,
London E98 1ST
020 7782 5000
www.sunday-times.co.uk

The Times
1 Pennington Street,
London E98 1TT
020 7782 5000
www.timesonline.co.uk

Main regional newspaper publishing groups

Archant
Prospect House,
Rouen Road,
Norwich NR1 1RE
01603 628311
www.archant.co.uk

Daily Mail & General Trust
Northcliffe House,
2 Derry Street,
London W8 5TT
020 7938 6000
www.dmgt.co.uk

DC Thompson
185 Fleet Street,
London EC4A 2HS
020 7400 1030
www.dcthompson.co.uk

Guardian Media Group
164 Deansgate,

Manchester M3 3RN
0161 832 7200
www.gmgplc.co.uk

Independent News and Media
2023 Bianconi Avenue,
Citywest Business Campus,
Nass Road,
Dublin 24, Ireland
00 353 1 466 3200
www.independentnews
media.com

Johnston Press
53 Manor Place,
Edinburgh EH3 7EG
0131 255 3361
www.jptalk.co.uk

Midland News Association
51–53 Queen Street,

Wolverhampton WV1 1ES
01902 313131
www.expressandstar.com

Newsquest Media
58 Church Street,
Weybridge,
Surrey KT13 8DP
01932 821212
www.newsquest.co.uk

Northcliffe Newspapers Group
31–32 John Street,
London WC1N 2QB
020 7400 1100
www.thisisnorthcliffe.
co.uk

Scotsman Publications
Barclay House,

BROOKLANDS COLLEGE LIBRARY
WEYBRIDGE, SURREY KT13 8TT

108 Holyrood Road,
Edinburgh EH8 8AS
0131 620 8620
www.scotsman.com

Trinity Mirror
UK Head Office,
Chronicle House,
Commonhall Street,

Chester CH1 2AA
01244 687000
www.trinitymirror.
com

Main regional newspapers

Aberdeen Press and Journal
Aberdeen Journals,
Lang Stracht, Mastrick,
Aberdeen AB15 6DF
01224 690222
www.pressandjournal.co.uk

Belfast News
028 9068 0000
www.icnorthernireland.
co.uk

Belfast Telegraph
124–144 Royal Avenue,
Belfast BT1 1EB
028 9026 4000
www.belfasttelagraph.co.uk

Birmingham Evening Mail
Weaman Street,
Birmingham,
West Midlands B4 6AT
0121 236 3366
www.icbirmingham.co.uk

Bristol Evening Post
Temple Way,
Bristol BS99 7HD
0117 934 3000
www.thisisbristol.co.uk

Connacht Tribune
00 353 91 536222
www.connacht-tribune.ie

Cork Evening Echo
00 353 21 480 2142
www.eveningecho.ie

Courier and Advertiser
DC Thomson & Co,
2 Albert Square,

Dundee DD1 9QJ
01382 223131
www.thecourier.co.uk

**Coventry Evening
Telegraph**
Corporation Street,
Coventry CV1 1FP
024 7663 3633
www.iccoventry.co.uk

**The Daily Mirror (Northern
Ireland)**
028 9056 8000

Daily Record
One Central Quay,
Glasgow G3 8DA
0141 309 3000
www.dailyrecord.co.uk

Derby Evening Telegraph
Northcliffe House,
Meadow Road,
Derby,
Derbyshire DE1 2DW
01332 291111
www.thisisderbyshire.co.uk

Eastern Daily Press
Prospect House,
Rouen Road,
Norwich NR1 1RE
01603 628311
www.edp24.co.uk

Edinburgh Evening News
Barclay House,
108 Holyrood Road,
Edinburgh EH8 8AS
0131 620 8620
www.edinburghnews.com

Evening Chronicle
Groat Market,
Newcastle Upon Tyne NE1
1ED
0191 232 7500
www.icnewcastle.co.uk

**Evening Herald
(Dublin)**
00 353 1 705 5333

Evening Standard
Northcliffe House,
2 Derry Street,
London W8 5TT
020 7938 6000
www.thisislondon.co.uk

Express & Star
51–53 Queen Street,
Wolverhampton,
West Midlands WV1 1ES
01902 313131
www.expressandstar.com

Glasgow Evening Times
200 Renfield Street,
Glasgow G2 3QB
0141 302 7000
www.eveningtimes.co.uk

Glasgow Herald
200 Renfield Street,
Glasgow G2 3QB
0141 302 7000
www.theherald.co.uk

Ireland on Sunday
00 353 1 637 5800

Irish Daily Star
00353 1 490 1228

Irish Examiner
00 353 21 427 2722
www.examlner.ie

Irish Independent
00 353 1 705 5333
www.independent.ie

Irish News
028 9032 2226
www.irishnews.com

Irish Times
00 353 1 675 8000
www.ireland.com

Kerryman
00 353 66 71 45500
www.kerryman.ie

Leicester Mercury
St George Street,
Leicester LE1 9FQ
0116 251
www.leistermercury.co.uk

Leinster Leader
00 353 45 897302
www.leinsterleader.ie

Limerick Leader
00 353 61 214503/6
www.limerick-leader.ie

Limerick Post
00 353 61 413322
www.limerickpost.ie

Liverpool Post & Echo
Old Hall Street,
Liverpool L3 9JQ
0151 227 2000
www.icliverpool.co.uk

Manchester Evening News
164 Deansgate,
Manchester M3 3RN
0161 832 7200
www.manchesteronline.
co.uk

The News (Portsmouth)
Portsmouth Publishing &
Printing,
The News Centre,
Military Road,
Hilsea, Portsmouth,
Hampshire PO2 9SX
023 9266 4488
www.thenews.co.uk

News Letter (Belfast)
028 9068 0000
www.newsletter.co.uk/www.
newsletter.co.uk/
www.icnorthernireland.co.uk

**Northern Echo (North
East England)**
Priestgate,
Darlington,
Co. Durham DL1 1NF
01325 381313
www.thisisthenortheast.co.uk

**The People (Northern
Ireland edition)**
028 9056 8000

Scotland on Sunday
Barclay House,
108 Holyrood Road,
Edinburgh EH8 8AS
0131 620 8620
www.scotlandonsunday.com

The Scotsman
Barclay House,
108 Holyrood Road,
Edinburgh EH8 8AS
0131 620 8620
www.scotsman.com

**The Sentinel (Stoke-on-
Trent)**
Staffordshire Sentinel
Newspapers,
Sentinel House, Etruria,
Stoke-on-Trent, ST1 5SS
01782 602525
www.thesentinel.co.uk

Shropshire Star
Shropshire Newspapers,
Ketley,
Telford,
Shropshire TF1 5HU
01952 242424
www.shropshirestar.com

Southern Daily Echo
Newsquest (Southern),
Newspaper House,
Test Lane,
Redbridge,
Southampton SO16 9JX
023 8042 4777
www.dailyecho.co.uk

**South Wales Echo
(Cardiff)**
Thomson House,
Havelock Street,
Cardiff CF10 1XR
029 2058 3583
www.icwales.co.uk

**South Wales Evening Post
(Swansea)**
PO Box 14,
Adelaide Street,
Swansea SA1 1QT
01792 510000
www.swep.co.uk

The Star (Sheffield)
York Street,
Sheffield
South Yorkshire S1 1PU
0114 276 7676
www.sheffieldtoday.net

**Sunday Business Post
(Ireland)**
00 353 1 602 6000
www.sbpost.ie

Sunday Herald (Scotland)
200 Renfield Street,
Glasgow G2 3QB
0141 302 7800
www.sundayherald.com

Sunday Independent
(Ireland)
00 353 1 705 5333
www.independent.ie

Sunday Life (Northern
Ireland)
124–144 Royal Avenue,
Belfast BT1 1EB
028 9026 4000
www.sundaylife.co.uk

Sunday Mail (Scotland)
One Central Quay,
Glasgow G3 8DA
0141 309 3230
www.sundaymail.co.uk

Sunday Mercury
(Birmingham)
Weaman Street,
Birmingham,
West Midlands B4 6AT

0121 236 3366
www.icbirmingham.co.uk

Sunday Mirror (Northern
Ireland)
028 9056 8000

Sunday Post
DC Thomson & Co,
2 Albert Square,
Dundee DD1 9QJ
www.thesundaypost.co.uk

Sunday Sun (Newcastle)
Groat Market,
Newcastle Upon Tyne NE1
1ED
0191 232 7500
www.icnewcastle.co.uk

Sunday Tribune (Ireland)
00 353 1 631 4300
www.tribune.ie

Sunday World (Ireland)
00 353 1 490 2177
www.sundayworld.com

Sunday World (Northern
Ireland edition)
00 353 1 406 3500
www.sundayworld.com

Yorkshire Evening Post
PO Box 168,
Wellington Street,
Leeds LS1 1RF
0113 243 2701
www.leedstoday.net

Yorkshire Post
PO Box 168,
Wellington Street,
Leeds LS1 1RF
0113 243 2701
www.yorkshireposttoday.
co.uk

Other regional and local newspapers

Aberdeen & District
Independent
01224 618300
www.aberdeen-indy.co.uk

Aberdeen Evening Express
01224 690222

Abergavenny Chronicle
01873 852187
www.abergavenny.co.uk

Abingdon Herald
01865 425262
www.thisisoxfordshire.co.uk

Accrington Observer
01254 871444
www.accringtonobserver.co.uk

The Advertiser (Newbury)
01635 524111
www.newburynews.co.uk

Airdrie & Coatbridge
Advertiser
01236 748648
www.icscotland.co.uk

Aldershot News
01483 508700
www.aldershot.co.uk

Alloa & Hillfoots Advertiser
01259 214416

Andersonstown News
028 9061 9000
www.irelandclick.com

Andover Advertiser
01264 323456
www.andoveradvertiser.co.uk

Antrim Guardian
028 9446 2624
www.ulster-ni.co.uk

Antrim Times
028 3839 3939
www.mortonnewspapers.
com

Arbroath Herald
01241 872274
www.arbroathtoday.co.uk

Argyllshire Advertiser
01631 563058
www.argyllshireadvertiser.
co.uk

Armagh Observer
028 8772 2557

Armagh-Down Observer
028 8772 2557

Ashby & Coalville Mail
0116 251 2512
www.thisisleicestershire.co.uk

Ashby Times
01530 813101

Ashton-under-Lyne Reporter
0161 303 1910

Ayrshire Post
01292 261111
www.icscotland.co.uk

Ayrshire Weekly Press
01294 464321

Baldock Crow
01763 245241
www.royston-crow.co.uk

Ballyclare Advertiser
028 9336 3651
www.ulster-ni.co.uk

Ballymena Chronicle
028 8772 2557

Ballymena Guardian
028 2564 1221

Ballymena Times
028 2565 3300
www.mortonnewspapers.
com

Banbridge Chronicle
028 4066 2322
www.banbridgechronicle.com

Banbury Guardian
01295 227777
www.banburyguardian.
co.uk

Banff Gazette
01224 618300
www.aberdeen-indy.co.uk

Bangor Chronicle
01248 387 400
www.northwaleschronicle.
co.uk

Barnes, Mortlake & Sheen Times
020 8940 6030
www.richmondandtwicken-
hamtimes.co.uk

Barnet & Potters Bar Times
020 8359 5959
www.barnettimes.co.uk

Barnett & Whetstone Press
020 8367 2345
www.trinitymirrorsouthern.
co.uk

Barking & Dagenham Post
020 8491 2000
www.bdpost.co.uk

Barking & Dagenham Recorder
020 8478 4444
www.recorderonline.co.uk

Barnsley Chronicle
01226 734734
www.barnsley-chronicle.co.uk

Barrow Advertiser
01229 840150
www.cumbria-online.co.uk

Basildon and Wickford Recorder
01268 522792
www.thisisessex.co.uk

Basingstoke Observer
01256 694121
http://members.lycos.co.uk/
Tarantulauk/basobframe2.
html

Bath Chronicle
01225 322322
www.thisisbath.co.uk

Bath Times
01225 322322
www.thisisbath.co.uk

Beaconsfield Advertiser
01753 888333
www.buckinghamtoday.
co.uk

Berwick Advertiser
01289 306677
www.berwicktoday.co.uk

Berwick Gazette
01289 306677
www.berwicktoday.co.uk

Berwickshire News
01289 306677
www.berwickshiretoday.
co.uk

Bexhill-on-Sea Observer
01424 730555
www.bexhilltoday.co.uk

Bicester Advertiser
01865 425262
www.thisisoxfordshire.
co.uk

Biggleswade Chronicle
01767 222333
www.biggleswadetoday.co.uk

Birmingham Evening Mail
0121 236 3366
www.icbirmingham.co.uk

Birmingham News
0121 234 5073
www.icbirmingham.co.uk

Birmingham Post
0121 236 3366
www.icbirmingham.co.uk

Blackburn Citizen
01254 678678
www.thisislancashire.co.uk

Blackpool Gazette & Herald
01253 400888
www.blackpoolonline.co.uk

Blackpool Reporter
01253 400800
www.blackpoolonline.co.uk

Bognor Regis Observer
01243 828777
www.bognortoday.co.uk/

Bolton Evening News
01204 522345
www.thisisbolton.co.uk

Bolton Journal
01204 522345
www.thisisbolton.co.uk

Border Telegraph (Scottish Borders)
01896 758395
www.bordertelegraph.com

Bordon Post
01730 264811
www.petersfieldtoday.co.uk

Borehamwood & Elstree Times
020 8359 5959
www.borehamwoodtimes.co.uk

Boston Citizen
01205 311433
www.bostontoday.co.uk

Bracknell & Ascot Times
0118 936 6180
www.getbracknell.co.uk

Bracknell & Wokingham Standard
0118 936 6180
www.getbracknell.co.uk

Bradford Telegraph and Argus
01274 729511
www.thisisbradford.co.uk

Braintree Chronicle
01245 600700
www.thisisessex.co.uk

Brecon & Radnor Express
01874 610111
www.brecon-radnor.co.uk

Brent and Wembley Leader
020 8427 4404
www.trinitymirrorsouthern.co.uk

Brentford, Chiswich & Isleworth Times
020 8940 6030
www.richmondandtwicken-hamtimes.co.uk

Bridgnorth Journal
01746 761411
www.bridgnorthjournal.co.uk

Bridlington Free Pass
01262 606606
www.bridlingtontoday.co.uk

Brighouse Echo
01422 260200
www.brighousetoday.co.uk

Brighton Evening Argus
01273 544544
www.thisisbrightonandhove.co.uk

Bristol Evening Post
0117 934 3000
www.thisisbristol.co.uk

Bromley and Beckenham Times
020 8269 7000

Bromley and Orpington Express
020 8269 7000

Bromley News
01959 564766
www.bromley-today.co.uk

Buckinghamshire Advertiser
01753 888333
www.buckinghamtoday.co.uk

Bucks Free Post
01494 755000
www.bucksfreepress.co.uk

Burnley Citizen
01254 678678
www.thisislancashire.co.uk

Burnley Express
01282 426161
www.burnleytoday.co.uk

Burnley Journal
0161 764 9421
www.thisisbury.co.uk

Burton Mail
01283 512345
www.burtonmail.co.uk

Bury Times
0161 764 9421
www.thisisbury.co.uk

Caithness Courier
01955 602424
www.caithness-courier.co.uk

Camberley News & Mail
01252 339760
www.camberley.co.uk

Cambridge Evening News
01223 434434
www.cambridge-news.co.uk

Cambridge Weekly News
01223 434434
www.cambridge-news.co.uk

Camden Chronicle
020 8340 6868

Camden New Journal
020 7419 9000
www.camdennewjournal.co.uk

Camden Times
020 8962 6800
www.camdentimes.co.uk

Carlisle News & Star
01228 612600
www.news-and-star.co.uk

Carmarthen Journal
01267 227222
www.carmarthenjournal.co.uk

Carrick Times
028 3839 3939
www.mortonnewspapers.com

Caterham & District
Advertiser
020 8763 6666
www.icsurrey.co.uk

Central Fife Times &
Advertiser
01383 728201

Chelmsford Chronicle
01245 600700
www.thisisessex.co.uk

Cheltenham Independent
01453 762412
www.thisisstroud.com

Chepstow Free Press
01291 621882
www.thisismonmouthshire.
co.uk

Cheshunt & Waltham
Mercury
01992 414141
www.herts-essex-news.co.uk

Chester Chronicle
01244 340151
www.cheshirenews.co.uk

Chester Mail
01244 340151
www.cheshirenews.co.uk

Chichester Observer
01243 539389
www.chiobserver.co.uk

Chingford Guardian
020 8962 6800
www.chingfordguardian.co.uk

Chislehurst Times
020 8269 7000

Chronicle and Echo
(Northampton)
01604 467000
www.northantsnews.com

Chronicle Weekend
(Oldham)
0161 633 2121
www.oldham-chronicle. co.uk

City News (Northern
Ireland)
028 7127 2200

City of London & Dockland
Times
07957 961520

Clacton & Frinton Gazette
01255 221221
www.thisisessex.co.uk

Clitheroe Express
01200 422324

Clyde Weekly News
01294 273421
www.icscotland.co.uk

Clydebank Post
0141 952 0565
www.clydebankpost.co.uk

Coalville Times
01530 813101

Colchester Evening Gazette
01206 506000
www.thisisessex.co.uk

Coleraine Times
028 7035 5260
www.mortonnewspapers.com

Colne Times
01282 612561
www.pendletoday.co.uk

Corby Citizen
01536 506100
www.northantsnews.com

Cornish & Devon Post
01566 772424

Cornish Guardian
01208 78133
www.cornishguardian.co.uk

The Cornishman
01736 362247
www.thisiscornwall.co.uk

County Down Spectator
028 9127 0270

County Echo (Newport)
01348 874445
www.newport-today.co.uk

County Times & Gazette
(Powys)
01938 553354
www.countytimes.co.uk

Coventry Evening Telegraph
024 7663 3633
www.iccoventry.co.uk

Crawley News
01737 732000
www.icsurrey.co.uk

Crawley Observer
01293 562929
www.crawleyobserver.co.uk

Crewe & Nantwich Guardian
01925 434000
www.thisischeshire.co.uk

Croydon Advertiser
020 8763 6666
www.iccroydon.co.uk

Cumberland and Westmorland Herald
01768 862313
www.cwherald.com

Cumberland News
01228 612600
www.cumberland-news.co.uk

Cumbernauld News & Kilsyth Chronicle
01236 725578
www.falkirktoday.co.uk

Cynon Valley Leader
01685 873136
http://icwales.icnetwork.co.uk

Daily Echo (Bournemouth)
01202 554601
www.thisisbournemouth.co.uk

Daily Post
01492 574455
www.icnorthwales.co.uk

Dartford Express
020 8269 7000

Dartford Times
020 8269 7000
www.dartfordtimes.com

Dartmouth Chronicle
01548 853101
www.dartmouth-today.co.uk

Dawlish Gazette
01626 353555
www.dawlish-today.co.uk

Dawlish Post
01626 353555
www.dawlish-today.co.uk

Deeside Piper
01330 824955
www.deesidepiper.com

Denbighshire Free Press
01745 813535
www.denbighshirefreepress.co.uk

Derby Evening Telegraph
01332 291111
www.thisisDerbyshire.co.uk

Derbyshire Times
01246 504500
www.derbyshiretimes.co.uk

Derry Journal
028 7127 2200
www.derryjournal.com

Derry Journal (Sunday)
028 7127 2200
www.derryjournal.com

Derry News
028 7129 6600

Devizes, Melksham and Vale of Pewsey News
01793 528144
www.thisiswindon.co.uk

Didcot Herald
01865 425262
www.thisisoxfordshire.co.uk

Diss Express
01379 642264
www.disstoday.co.uk/

Diss Mercury
01603 628311
www.edp24.co.uk

Doncaster Star
01302 819111
www.doncastertoday.co.uk

Dorset Echo
01305 830930
www.thisisdorset.net

Dover Express
01227 767321
www.trinitymirrorsouthern.co.uk

Dover Mercury
01304 240380

Down Democrat
028 4461 4400
www.downdemocrat.com

Down Recorder
028 4461 3711
www.thedownrecorder.com

Droitwich Standard
01527 574111
http://droitwich.standardto-day.co.uk

Dromore Leader
028 3839 3939
www.mortonnewspapers.com

Dumfries & Galloway Standard
01387 240342
www.icscotland.co.uk

Dungannon Observer
028 8772 2557

Ealing and Acton Gazette
020 8579 3131

East Anglian Daily Times
01284 702588
www.eadt.co.uk

Eastbourne Gazette
01323 722091
www.eastbournetoday.co.uk

Eastern Daily Press
01603 628311
www.edp24.co.uk

East Grinstead Observer
01737 732000
www.icsurrey.co.uk

East Kent Gazette
01227 767321
www.trinitymirrorsouthern.
co.uk

East Lothian Courier
01620 822451
www.eastlothiancourier.
com

East Lothian Herald
01289 306677
www.berwickshire-news.
co.uk

East London Advertiser
020 7790 8822
www.eastlondonadvertiser.
co.uk

**Eltham and Greenwich
Times**
020 8269 7000

Enfield Gazette
020 8367 2345
www.trinitymirrorsouthern.
co.uk

Epping Guardian
01992 572285
www.eppingguardian.
co.uk

Essex Chronicle
01245 600700
www.thisisessex.co.uk

Essex County Standard
01206 506000
www.thisisessex.co.uk

Eton Observer
01753 523355

**Evening Advertiser
(Swindon)**
01793 528144
www.thisisswindon.co.uk

**Evening Chronicle
(Newcastle)**
0191 232 7500
www.icnewcastle.co.uk

Evening Echo (Basildon)
01268 522792
www.thisisessex.co.uk

Evening Gazette (Teeside)
01642 245401
www.icteeside.co.uk

Evening Leader (Chester)
01352 707707
www.chestereveningleader.
co.uk

Evening News (Norwich)
01603 628311
www.eveningnews24.co.uk

**Evening Telegraph
(Dundee)**
01382 223131
www.eveningtelegraph.
co.uk

**The Evening Telegraph
(Northampton)**
01536 506100
www.northantsnews.com

Exeter Express & Echo
01392 442211
www.thisisexeter.co.uk

**Express and Star (West
Midlands)**
01902 313131
www.expressandstar.co.uk

Falkirk Herald
01324 624959
www.falkirktoday.co.uk

Falmouth Packet
01326 21333
www.thisisthewestcountry.co.uk

Fareham & Gosport News
023 9266 4488
www.thisisportsmouth.co.uk

Faversham News
01227 475901
www.faversham.org/GENERAL

Faversham Times
01227 767321

Fermanagh Herald
028 8224 3444
www.fermanaghherald.com

Fermanagh News
028 8772 2557

Flintshire Chronicle
01244 821911
www.icnorthwales.co.uk

Folkestone Express
01233 623232

Folkestone Herald
01227 767321
www.trinitymirrorsouthern.
co.uk

Formby Times
01704 872237
http://icseftonandwestlancs

Fulham Chronicle
020 8572 1816
www.trinitymirrorsouthern.co.uk

Fulham Gazette
020 8579 3131
www.trinitymirrorsouthern.
co.uk

Galloway Gazette
01671 402503
www.gallowaygazette.com

Gateshead Herald and Post
0191 201 6405

Glamorgan Gazette
01656 304924
http://icwales.icnetwork.
co.uk

Gloucester Citizen
01452 424442
www.thisisgloucestershire.
co.uk

Gloucestershire County Gazette
01453 544000
www.thisisthesouth-
cotswolds.co.uk

Gloucestershire Echo
01242 271821
www.thisisgloucestershire.
co.uk

Grantham Journal
01476 562291
www.granthamjournal.co.uk

Great Yarmouth & Gorleston Advertiser
01493 601206
www.advertiser-online.co.uk

Grimsby Evening Telegraph
01472 360360
www.thisisgrimsby.co.uk

Gwent Gazette
01495 304589
www.buckinghamtoday.co.uk

Gwynedd Chronicle
01248 387400
www.chroniclenow.co.uk

Hackney Gazette
020 7790 8822
www.hackneygazette.co.uk

Halifax Evening Courier
01422 260200
www.halifaxtoday.co.uk

Hampshire Chronicle
01962 841772
www.thisishampshire.net/
hampshire/winchester

Hampstead and Highgate Express
020 7433 0000
www.hamhigh.co.uk/

Hants & Dorset Avon Advertiser
01722 426500
www.salisburyjournal.co.uk

Harefield Gazette
01895 451000
www.trinitymirrorsouthern.co.uk

Haringey Advertiser
020 8367 2345
www.trinitymirrorsouthern.
co.uk

Harlow Herald
01279 624331
www.thisisessex.co.uk

Harpenden Observer
01727 834411
www.stalbansobserver.co.uk

Harrogate Advertiser
01423 564321
www.harrogatetoday.co.uk

Harrow Observer
020 8427 4404
http://icharrow.icnetwork.
co.uk

Hartlepool Mail
01429 239333
www.hartlepoolmail.co.uk

Hastings & St Leonards Observer
01424 854242
www.hastingstoday.co.uk

Havant & Waterlooville News
023 9266 4488
www.thisisportsmouth.co.uk

Haverhill Echo
01440 703456
www.buryfreepress.co.uk

Hayes and Harlington Gazette
01895 451000
http://icuxbridge.icnetwork.
co.uk/

Heartland Evening News
024 7635 3534
www.hen-news.com

Heart of Wales Chronicle
01874 610111

Helensburgh Advertiser
01436 673434
www.helensburghadvertiser.
co.uk

Hemel Hempstead Gazette
01442 262311
www.hemelonline.co.uk

Hemel Hempstead Herald & Express
01442 262311
www.hemelonline.co.uk

Henley Standard
01491 419444
www.henleystandard.co.uk

Hertfordshire Mercury
01992 526625
www.herts-essex-news.
co.uk

Hexham Courant
01434 602351
www.hexam-courant.co.uk

Highbury & Islington Express
020 7433 0000
www.islingtonexpress.co.uk

Highland News
01463 732222
www.highland-news.co.uk

Hillingdon Times
01494 755000
www.hillingdontimes.co.uk

Hitchin Comet
01462 420120
www.thecomet.net

Hornsea Gazette
01964 612777

Hornsey & Crouch End Journal
020 8340 6868
www.hornseyjournal.co.uk

Hounslow Chronicle
020 8572 1816

Huddersfield Daily Examiner
01484 437747
www.ichuddersfield.co.uk

Hull Daily Mail
01482 327111
www.hulldailymail.co.uk

Hunts Post
01480 411481
www.huntspost.co.uk

Illford Recorder
020 8478 4444
www.recorderonline.co.uk

Impartial Reporter (Fermanagh)
028 6632 4422
www.impartialreporter.com

Ipswich Advertiser
01473 324700
www.advertiser-online.co.uk

Isle of Man Courier
01624 695695
www.iomonline.co.im

Isle of Man Examiner
01624 695695
www.iomonline.co.im

Isle of Thanet Gazette
01227 767321
www.trinitymirrorsouthern.co.uk

Isle of Wight CountyPress
01983 521333
www.iwcp.co.uk

Ivybridge, South Brent and South Hams Gazette
01548 853101
www.ivybridge-today.co.uk

John O'Groat Journal
01955 602424
www.johnogroat-journal.co.uk

The Journal (Newcastle-upon-Tyne)
0191 201 6230
www.icnewcastle.co.uk

Keighley News
01274 729511
www.keighleynews.co.uk

Kensington Times
020 8962 6800

Kent & Sussex Courier
01892 681000
www.thisiskentandeastsussex.co.uk

Kent Messenger
01622 695666
www.kentonline.co.uk

Kentish Times
020 8269 7000
www.archant.co.uk

Keswick Reminder
01768 772140
www.keswickreminder.co.uk

Kettering Evening Telegraph
01536 506100
www.northantsnews.com

Kilburn Times
020 8962 6800
www.kilburntimes.co.uk

Kingsbridge and Salcombe Gazette
01548 853101

Kingston & Surbiton Times
020 8940 6030

Kingston Guardian
020 8940 6030
www.kingstonguardian.co.uk

Knaresborough Post
01423 564321
www.knaresboroughtoday.co.uk

Lakeland Echo (Cumbria)
01524 833111
www.lakelandtoday.co.uk

Lanark Gazette
01555 663937
www.lanarktoday.co.uk

Lanarkshire World
01698 283200
www.icscotland.co.uk

Lancashire Evening Post
01772 838103
www.lep.co.uk

Lancashire Evening Telegraph
01254 298220
www.thisislancashire.co.uk

Lancaster Guardian
01524 32525
www.lancastertoday.co.uk

Larne Gazette
028 9336 3651
www.ulster-ni.co.uk

Launceston Journal Gazette
01566 772424

Leamington Spa Courier
01926 457777
www.leamingtononline.co.uk

Leatherhead Advertiser
01737 732000
www.icsurrey.co.uk

Leeds and Yorkshire Times
01926 431 1601

Leicester Mercury
0116 251 2512
www.leicestermercury.co.uk

Leyton & Leytonstone
Guardian
020 8498 3400
www.leytonguardian.co.uk

Lincolnshire Echo
01522 820000
www.thisislincolnshire.co.uk

Liverpool Post & Echo
0151 227 2000
www.icliverpool.co.uk

Llanelli Star
01554 745300
www.thisissouthwales.
co.uk

Londonderry Sentinel
028 7134 8889
www.mortonnewspapers.com

Loughborough Echo
01509 232632

http://icloughborough.
icnetwork.co.uk

Lurgan & Portadown
Examiner
028 8772 2557

Luton Herald & Post
01582 700600
www.lutontoday.co.uk

Luton News
01582 526000
www.lutontoday.co.uk

Macclesfield Express
01625 42445
www.macclesfield-
express.co.uk

Macclesfield Times
01625 424445
www.manchesteronline.
co.uk

Maidenhead Advertiser
01628 680680
www.maidenhead-
advertiser.co.uk

Manchester Evening News
0161 832 72090
www.manchesteronline.co.uk

The Manx Independent
01624 695695
www.iomonline.co.im

Market Harborough Herald
& Post
01604 614600
www.trinitymirror.com

Marlow Free Press
01494 755081
www.bucksfreepress.co.uk

Matlock Mercury
01629 582432
www.matlockmercury.co.uk

Medway Standard
01227 767321
www.trinitymirrorsouthern.co.uk

Merthyr Express
01685 856500
http://icwales.icnetwork.co.uk

Metro North East
0191 477 8200
www.metronortheast.co.uk

Metro North West
0161 832 7200
www.metronorthwest.co.uk

Metro Scotland
020 7651 5200
www.metroscot.co.uk

Metro Yorkshire
020 7651 5200

Middlesbrough Herald & Post
01642 245401
www.icteeside.co.uk

Mid Somerset Times
01749 672430
www.thisissomerset.co.uk

Mid-Ulster Mail
028 8676 2288
www.mortonnewspapers.com

Mid Wales Journal
01597 828060
www.midwalesjournal.co.uk

Milford & West Wales
Mercury
01646 698971
www.milfordmercury.co.uk

Milton Keynes Journal
0116 233 3635

Monmouth Free Press
01600 713631
www.thisismonmouthshire.co.uk

Monmouthshire Beacon
01600 712142
www.monmouth-today.co.uk

Montrose Review
01674 672605
www.montrosereview.net

Neath & Port Talbot Guardian
01639 778885
http://icwales.icnetwork.co.uk

Newark Advertiser
01636 681234
www.newarkadvertiser.co.uk

Newbury Weekly News
01635 524111
www.newburynews.co.uk

Newcastle Herald & Post
0191 201 6405
www.icnewcastle.co.uk

Newcastle Times
01332 205900

Newham Recorder
020 8472 1421
www.recorderonline.co.uk

Newmarket Journal
01638 564104
www.newmarketjournal.co.uk

Newry Democrat
028 3025 1250
www.newrydemocrat.com

The News (Portsmouth)
023 9266 4488
www.thenews.co.uk

Norfolk Citizen
01553 761188

Northampton Herald & Post
01604 614600

Northern Echo (north east England)
01325 381313
www.thisisthenortheast.co.uk

Northern Scot
01343 548777
www.northern-scot.co.uk

Northern Times (Scotland)
01408 633993
www.northern-times.co.uk

North London Herald
020 8340 6868

Northumberland Gazette
01665 602234
www.northumberlandtoday.co.uk

North Wales Chronicle
01248 3874400
www.chroniclenow.co.uk

North Wales Pioneer
01492 531188
www.northwalespioneer.co.uk

North Wales Weekly News
01492 584321
www.icnorthwales.co.uk

Northwest Evening Mail (Barrow)
01229 821835
www.nwemail.co.uk

North Yorkshire Herald & Post
01642 245401
www.ncjmediainfo.co.uk

Nottingham Evening Post
0115 948 2000
www.thisisnottingham.co.uk

Oldham Evening Chronicle
0161 633 2121
www.oldham-chronicle.co.uk

The Orcadian (Orkney)
01856 879000
www.orcadian.co.uk

Orpington & Petts Wood Times
020 8269 7000
www.trinitymirrorsouthern.co.uk

Oxford Journal
01235 553444
www.courier-newspapers-oxford.co.uk/journal.htm

Oxford Mail
01865 425262
www.thisisoxfordshire.co.uk

Paisley & Renfrewshire Extra
0141 427 7878
www.icscotland.co.uk

Paisley Daily Express
0141 887 7911
www.icscotland.co.uk

Peebleshire News
01896 758395
www.peebleshirenews.com

Petersfield Post
01730 264811
www.petersfield.co.uk

Penarth Times
029 2070 7234
www.thisispenarth.co.uk

Perthshire Advertiser
01738 626211
www.northshropshirechronicle.com

Peterborough Herald & Post
01733 318600
www.peterborough.net/heraldandpost

Pinner Observer
020 8427 4404
www.trinitymirrorsouthern.co.uk

Plymouth Evening Telegraph
01752 765529
www.thisisplymouth.co.uk

Pontypridd Observer
01443 665161
www.icwales.com

Portadown Times
028 3833 6111
www.mortonnewspapers.com

Preston & Leyland Citizen
01772 824631
www.thisislancashire.co.uk

**Preston & Leyland
Reporter**
01772 838103

Reading Chronicle
0118 950 3030
www.icberkshire.co.uk

Reading Evening Post
0118 918 3000
www.gettreading.co.uk

Reigate Post
020 8770 7171

Rhondda Leader
01443 665151
http://icwales.icnetwork.
co.uk

**Richmond and Twickenham
Times**
020 8940 6030
www.richmondandtwicken-
hamtimes.co.uk

**Ripon Gazette &
Boroughbridge Herald**
01423 564321
www.ripontoday.co.uk

Rochdale Observer
01706 354321
www.rochdaleobserver.co.uk

Romford Recorder
01708 771500
www.recorderonline.co.uk

Romney Marsh Herald
01227 767321
www.trinitymirrorsouthern.
co.uk

Romsey Advertiser
023 8042 4777
www.thisishampshire.net/
hampshire/romsey

Royston Crow
01763 245241
www.royston-crow.co.uk

Rugby Advertiser
01788 535363
www.rugbyadvertiser.co.uk

Runcorn Weekly News
0151 424 5921
www.cheshireonline.
icnetwork.co.uk

Saffron Walden Observer
01279 866355
www.herts-essex-news.co.uk

St Albans Observer
01727 834411
www.stalbansobserver.co.uk

St Helens Star
01925 434000
www.thisisst-helens.co.uk

St Ives Times & Echo
01736 795813
www.thisiscornwall.co.uk

Salford Advertiser
0161 789 5015
www.manchesteronline.co.uk

Scarborough Evening News
01723 363636
www.scarbor-
oughveningnews.co.uk

Scunthorpe Telegraph
01724 273273
www.thisisscunthorpe.co.uk

Sevenoaks Chronicle
01732 228000
www.thisiskentandsussex.
co.uk

Sheerness Times Guardian
01795 580300

Sheppey Gazette
01227 767321
www.trinitymirrorsouthern.
co.uk

Shepton Mallet Journal
01749 832300
www.thisissomerset.co.uk

Shetland News
01806 577332
www.shetlandtoday.co.uk

Shetland Times
01595 693622
www.shetlandtoday.co.uk

Shoreham Herald
01903 230051
www.shorehamtoday.co.uk

Shrewsbury Chronicle
01743 248248
www.shrewsburychronicle.
co.uk

Shropshire Star
01952 242424
www.shropshirestar.com

Sidmouth Herald
01392 888444
www.archantdevon.co.uk

Slough Express
01753 825111
www.lcberkshire.co.uk

Slough Observer
01753 523355
www.thisisslough.com

Somerset County Gazette
01823 365151
www.thisisthewestcountry.
co.uk

Somerset Guardian
01225 322322
www.thisissomerset.co.uk

Southall Gazette
020 8579 3131
www.trinitymirrorsouthern.
co.uk

Southampton Advertiser
023 8042 4777
www.southamptonadver-
tiser.co.uk

Southend Standard
01268 522792
www.thisisessex.co.uk

Southern Daily Echo
013 8042 4777
www.dailyecho.co.uk

South London Press
020 8769 4444
www.icsouthlondon.co.uk

South Shields Gazette
0191 455 4661
www.southynesidetoday.co.uk

South Wales Argus
01633 810000
www.thisisgwent.co.uk

South Wales Echo
029 2058 3583
www.icwales.co.uk

South Wales Evening Post
01792 510000
www.swep.co.uk

**South West News & Star
(Scotland)**
01228 612300
www.news-and-star.co.uk

Staines & Ashford News
01932 561111
www.trinitymirrorsouthern.
co.uk

Staines & Egham News
01932 561111
www.trinitymirrorsouthern.
co.uk

Stanmore Observer
020 8427 4404
www.trinitymirrorsouthern.co.uk

The Star (Sheffield)
0114 276 7676
www.sheffieldtoday.net

Stevenage Comet
01462 420120
www.thecomet.net

Stockport Express
0161 480 4491
www.stockportexpress.co.uk

**Stornoway Gazette & West
Coast Advertiser**
01851 702687
www.stornowaygazette.co.uk

Strabane Chronicle
028 8224 3444
www.strabanechronicle.com

Stratford-upon-Avon Herald
01789 266261
www.stratford-herald.co.uk

Stratford-upon-Avon Journal
01442 386555

www.stratford-upon-
avon.co.uk

Suffolk Advertiser
01473 324700
www.advertiser-online.co.uk

Suffolk Free Press
01787 375271
www.sudburytoday.co.uk

**Sunday Independent (south
west England)**
01752 206600
www.thisisthewestcountry.
co.uk

**Sunday Mercury
(Birmingham)**
0121 236 3366
www.icbirmingham.co.uk

Sunday Sun (Newcastle)
0191 232 7500
www.icnewcastle.co.uk

Sunderland Echo
0191 501 7208
www.sunderland-today.co.uk

Surrey Advertiser
01483 508700
www.surreyad.co.uk

Surrey Mirror
020 8770 7171
www.icsurrey.co.uk

Sussex Express
01273 480601
www.sussexexpress.co.uk

Sutton Coldfield News
0121 355 7070
http://icsuttoncoldfield.icnet
work.co.uk

Sutton Coldfield Observer
01827 848535
Sutton Guardian

020 8646 6336
www.suttonguardian.
co.uk

Swansea Herald
01792 514630
www.thisisnorthcliffe.co.uk

Tamworth Herald
01827 848535
www.tamworthherald.co.uk

Taunton Star
01823 365151
www.tauntonstar.co.uk

Tenterden Express
01233 623232

Tonbridge Courier
01892 681000
www.thisiskentandeastsus-
sex.co.uk

Torquay Herald Express
01803 676000
www.thisissouthdevon.
co.uk

Totnes News
01548 853 101

Towcester Post
01604 614600
www.trinitymirror.com

Truro Packet
01326 213333
www.thisisthewestcountry.
co.uk

Tunbridge Wells Courier
01892 681000
www.thisiskentandeastsus-
sex.co.uk

Tyrone Times
028 8775 2801
www.mortonnewspapers.
com

**Ulster Gazette & Armagh
Standard**
028 3752 2639
www.ulsternet-ni.co.uk

Ulster Herald
028 8224 3444
www.ulsterherald.com

Ulster Star
028 9267 9111
www.mortonnewspapers.
com

Wallingford Herald
01865 425262
www.thisisoxfordshire.
co.uk

Waltham Forest Guardian
020 8498 4300
www.walthamforest-
guardian.co.uk

Walthamstow Guardian
020 8498 3400
www.walthamstowguardian.
co.uk

Wandsworth Guardian
020 8646 6336
www.wandsworthguardian.
co.uk

Wantage Herald
01865 425262
www.thisisoxfordshire.co.uk

Warrington Guardian
01925 434000
www.thisischeshire.co.uk

Watford Times
01788 543077

**Wellingborough & East
Northants Evening
Telegraph**
01536 506100
www.northantsnews.com

Wembley Observer
020 8427 4404
www.trinitymirrorsouthern.
co.uk

The West Briton
01872 271451
www.thisiscornwall.co.uk

**West Cumberland Times
and Star**
01900 607600
www.times-and-star.co.uk

**Western Daily Press
(Bristol)**
0117 924 3223
www.westpress.co.uk

Western Gazette
01935 700500
www.westgaz.co.uk

Western Morning News
01752 765500
www.thisisplymouth.co.uk

**Western Telegraph (South
Wales)**
01437 763133
www.thisispembrokeshire.
net

West Lothian Courier
01506 633544
www.icscotland.co.uk

Westmorland Gazette
01539 720555
www.thisisthelakedistrict.
co.uk

West Somerset Free Press
01984 632731
www.west-somerset-
today.co.uk

West Sussex County Times
01403 751200
www.horshamonline.co.uk

West Sussex Gazette
01243 534155
www.chichester.co.uk

Wharfedale & Airedale Observer
01943 465555
www.wharfdaleobserver.co.uk

Whitby Gazette
01947 602836
www.whitbytoday.
co.uk

Whitstable Gazette
01227 768181

Whitstable Times
01227 771515

Wigan Evening Post
01772 838103
www.wigantoday.net

Wigan Observer
01772 838103
www.wigantoday.net

Willesden Observer
020 8427 4404
http://icharrow.icnetwork.
co.uk

Wilts & Gloucestershire Standard
01285 642642
www.thisiscirencester.com

Wiltshire Gazette and Herald
01793 528144
www.thisisswindon.
co.uk

Wiltshire Times
01225 777292
www.thisiswiltshire.co.uk

Wokingham News
01344 456611

Wokingham Times
0118 366180
www.getwokingham.
co.uk

Woking News & Mail
01483 755755
www.woking.co.uk

Worcester Evening News
01905 748200
www.thisisworcestershire.co.uk

Worksop Guardian
01909 500500
www.worksoptoday.co.uk

Worthing Guardian
01903 282398
www.worthingtoday.co.uk

Worthing Herald
01903 230051
www.worthingtoday.co.uk

Wrexham Evening Leader
01978 355151
www.eveningleader.co.uk

Yeovil Express
01823 365151
www.thisisthewestcountry co.uk

MAGAZINES AND MAGAZINE-RELATED WEBSITES

How to use this listing

This listing is divided into two parts. First comes a list of the major magazine publishers, then an alphabetical list of individual magazines. Remember that many of these magazines will have a related website, and many of those will have journalists of their own. If online journalism interests you, there are plenty of leads here.

Main magazine publishers

BBC Worldwide
Woodlands,
80 Wood Lane,
London W12 0TT
020 8433 2000
www.bbcworldwide.com

Brooklands Group
Medway House,
Lower Road,
Forest Row,
East Sussex RH18 5HE
01342 828700
www.brooklandsgroup.com

Cedar
Pegasus House,
37–43 Sackville Street,
London W15 3EH
020 7534 2400
info@cedarcom.co.uk
www.cedarcom.co.uk

Cenatur
50 Poland Street,
London W1F 7AX
020 7970 4000
www.cenatur.co.uk

CMP Information
Ludgate House,
245 Blackfriars Road,
London SE1 9UY
020 7921 5000
nmain@cmpinformation.com
www.cmpinformation.com

Condé Nast
Vogue House,
Hanover Square,
London W1S 1JU
020 7499 9080
www.condenast.co.uk

DC Thomson
185 Fleet Street,
London EC4A 2HS
020 7400 1030
www.dcthomson.co.uk

Dennis Publishing
30 Cleveland Street,
London W1T 4JD
020 7907 6000
www.dennis.co.uk

Emap
40 Bernard Street,
London WC1N 1LW
020 7278 1452
www.emap.com

Emap communications
Scriptor Court,
155 Farringdon Road,
London EC1R 3AD
020 7841 6600

Emap Consumer Media
Endeavour House,
189 Shaftesbury Avenue,
London WC2H 8JG
020 7437 9011

Emap Performance
Mappin House,
4 Winsley Street,
London W1W 9HF
020 7436 1515

Future
Beauford Court,
30 Monmouth Street,
Bath BA1 2BW
01225 442244
www.futurenet.com

London Office
99 Baker Street,
London W1M 1FB
020 7317 2600

H Bauer
Academic House,
24–28 Oval Road,
London NW1 7DJ
020 7241 8000
www.bauer.co.uk

Hachette Filipacchi
64 North Row, London
W1K 7LL
020 7150 7000
www.hachettefilipacchiuk.
co.uk

Haymarket
174 Hammersmith Road,
London W6 7JP
020 8267 5000
hpg@haymarketgroup.com
www.haymarketgroup.co.uk

**Haymarket Consumer
Publishing**
38–42 Hampton Road,
Teddington,
Middlesex TW11 OJE
haycustpub@haynet.com
www.haycustpub.com

Highbury Entertainment
53–79 Highgate Road,
London NW5 1TW
020 7331 1000

**Highbury House
Communications**
1–3 Highbury Station Road,
London NW1 1SE
020 7226 2222
www.hhc.co.uk

Highbury Leisure
8–10 Knoll Rise,
Orpington,
Kent BR6 OPS
01689 887200

IPC Media
King's Reach Tower,

Stamford Street,
London SE1 9LS
0870 444 5000
www.ipc.co.uk

John Brown Citrus
The New Boathouse,
136–142 Bramley Road,
London W10 6SR
020 7565 3000
www.jbcp.co.uk

Mediamark
11 Kingsway,
London WC2B 6PH
020 7212 9000
info@mediamark.co.uk
www.mediamark.co.uk

**National Magazine
Company**
National Magazine House,
72 Broadwick Street,
London W1F 9EP
020 7439 5000
www.natmags.co.uk

New Crane Publishing
20 Upper Ground,
London SE1 9PD
020 7633 0266
enquiries@newcrane.
co.uk
www.newcrane.com

Publicis Blueprint
Whitfield House,
83–89 Whitfield Street,
London W1A 4XA
020 7462 7777
www.publicis-blueprint.
com

Magazines A–Z

Absolute Horse
01473 461515
www.ahmagazine.com

Accountancy
020 8247 1387
www.accountancymagazine.com

Accountancy Age
020 8606 7505
www.accountancyage.com

Accounting & Business
020 7396 5966
www.accaglobal.com

Activity Wales
01437 766888
www.activitywales.co.uk

Adventure Travel
01789 450000
www.atmagazine.co.uk

AFF Families Journal
01908 615517
www.aff.org.uk

Amateur Gardening
01202 440840
www.amateurgardening.co.uk

Amateur Photographer
020 7261 5100
www.amateurphotographer.
com

Angler's Mail
020 7261 5829
www.anglersmail.co.uk

Angling Times
01733 465520
www.greatmagazines.co.uk

Another Magazine
020 7336 0766
www.anothermag.com

Antique Collecting
01394 389950
www.antique-acc.com

Architecture Today
020 7837 0143
www.architecturetoday.
co.uk

The Arsenal Magazine
020 7704 4010
www.arsenal.com

Asda Magazine
020 7462 7777
www.publicis-blueprint.co.uk

Astronomy Now
01903 266165
www.astronomynow.com

Athletics Weekly
01733 898440
www.athletics-weekly.com

Autocar
020 8267 5000
www.autocarmagazine.co.uk

Auto Express
020 7907 6000
www.autoexpress.co.uk

Autosport
020 8267 5000
www.autosport.com

Auto Trader
020 8544 7000
www.autotrader.co.uk

Auto Weekly
01392 442211
www.autoweekly.co.uk

Baby & You
020 7226 2222
www.baby-marketing.co.uk

BBC Gardeners' World
020 8433 3593
www.gardenersworld.com

BBC Good Food
020 8433 3781
www.bbcmagazines.com/goo
dfood

BBC Good Homes
020 8433 3483
www.bbcmagazines.com/goo
dhomes

BBC History Magazine
020 8433 3289
www.bbchistorymagazine.
com

BBC Homes & Antiques
020 8433 3483
www.bbcmagazines.com/
homesandantiques

BBC Music Magazine
020 8433 3283
www.bbcmagazines.com/
music

BBC Top Gear
020 8433 3710
www.topgear.com

BBC Wildlife Magazine
0117 973 8402
www.bbcwildlifemagazine.
com

Beautiful Brides
0117 934 3742
www.thisisbristol.co.uk/
beautifulbrides

Bella
020 7241 8000
www.bauer.co.uk

Best
020 7439 5000
www.natmags.co.uk

Big Issue
020 7562 3200
www.bigissue.com

Big Issue in Scotland
0141 418 7000
www.bigissuescotland.
com

Big Issue in the North
0161 834 6300
www.bigissueinthenorth.com

Bike
01733 468000
www.emap.com

Bizarre
020 7907 6000
www.bizarremag.com

Bloomberg Money
020 7484 9771
www.bloomberg.com

Boxing Monthly
020 8986 4141
www.boxing-monthly.co.uk

Boxing News
020 7618 3456
www.boxingnewsonline.net

The Brighton Source
01273 561617
www.brightonsource.
co.uk

Broadcast
Emap Media
33–39 Bowling Green
Lane,
London ECIR 0DA
020 7505 8000
www.broadcastnow.co.uk

Builder & Engineer
0161 236 2782
www.excelpublishing.co.uk

Building
020 7560 4000
www.building.co.uk

Business Week
020 7176 6060
www.businessweek.com

Camping & Caravanning
024 7669 4995
www.campingandcaravan-
ningclub.co.uk

Camping Magazine
01778 391000
www.campingmagazine.co.uk

Canal & Riverboat
01603 708930
www.canalandriverboat.com

**Canal Boat & Inland
Waterways**
0118 977 1677
www.canalboatmag.co.uk

Caravan Club Magazine
01342 336804
www.caravanclub.co.uk

Caravan Life
01778 391000
www.caravanlife.co.uk

Caravan Magazine
020 8774 0737
www.caravanmagazine.co.uk

The Cat
01403 221936
www.cats.org.uk

Cat World
01403 711511
www.catworld.co.uk

Caterer and Hotelkeeper
020 8652 3500
www.caterer-online.com

Chat
020 7261 6559
www.ipcmedia.com/
magazines/chat

Child Education
01926 887799
www.scholastic.co.uk

Classic and Sports Car
020 8267 5000
www.classicandsportscar.com

Classic Bike
01733 468 000
www.emap.com

Classic FM The Magazine
020 8267 5000
www.haymarketpublishing.
co.uk

Classic Music
020 7333 1742
www.rhinegold.co.uk

Classic Rock
020 7317 2654
www.classicrockmagazine.com

Climber
01778 391000
www.climber.co.uk

Closer
020 7859 8463
www.closermag.co.uk

**CN Traveller (Condé Nast
Traveller)**
020 7499 9080
www.cntraveller.com

Coarse Fisherman
07971 241484
www.coarsefisherman.co.uk

Community Care
020 8652 3500
www.communitycare.co.uk

Company
020 7439 5000
www.company.co.uk

Computeractive
01858 438881
www.computeractive.co.uk

Computer Buyer
020 7907 6000
www.computerbuyer.co.uk

Computer Shopper
020 7907 6000
www.computershopper.co.uk

Computer Weekly
020 8652 8979
www.reedbusinessinforma-
tion.co.uk

Computing
020 8606 7505
www.computing.co.uk

Computing Which?
0845 301 8000
www.computingwhich.co.uk

**Connect Magazine
(Greenpeace)**
020 7865 8100
www.greenpeace.org.uk

Cosmopolitan
020 7439 5000
www.cosmopolitan.co.uk

Country Life
020 7261 6969
www.countrylife.co.uk/

Country Living
020 7439 5000
www.countryliving.co.uk

Country Music People
020 8854 7217
www.countrymusicpeople.com

Cricket World Magazine
01476 561944
www.cricketworld.com

Cycle
0870 873 0060
www.ctc.org.uk

Cycle Sport
020 8774 0703
www.cyclesport.co.uk

Cycling Plus
01225 442244
www.cyclingplus.co.uk

Cycling Weekly
020 8774 0703
www.cyclingweekly.co.uk

**Daily Mail Ski & Snowboard
Magazine**
020 8515 2000
www.skiingmail.com

Dazed & Confused
020 7336 0766
www.confused.co.uk

Decanter
020 7261 3929
www.decanter.com

Design Week
020 7970 4000
www.designweek.co.uk

Details
020 7240 0420
www.details.com

Director
020 7766 8950
www.iod.com

DIVE Magazine
020 8940 3333
www.divemagazine.co.uk

Diver
020 8943 4288
www.divermet.com

Doctor
020 86522500
www.doctorupdate.net

Dogs Today
01276 858880
http://dogstodaymagazine.
co.uk/

Dog World
01233 621877
www.dogworld.co.uk

Drapers
020 7391 3300
www.drapersonline.com

DVD Monthly
01392 434477
www.predatorpublishing.co.uk

DVD Review
01202 299900
www.dvdreview.net

**Earth Matters (Friends of
the Earth)**
020 7490 1555
www.foe.co.uk

Easyjet Magazine
020 7269 7480
www.easyjetinflight.com

Ecologist
020 7351 3578
www.theecologist.org

The Economist
020 7830 7000
www.economist.com

Education Today
020 7947 9536
www.educationtoday.
com.au/

Education Travel Magazine
020 7440 4025
www.hothousemedia.com

Electronics Weekly
020 8652 3650
www.electronicsweekly.com

Elle
020 7150 7000
www.hf-uk.com

Elle Decoration
020 7150 7000
www.hf-uk.com

Empire
020 7182 8000
www.empireonline.co.uk

The Engineer
020 7970 4000
www.e4engineering.com

England Rugby
01707 273999
www.tmg.co.uk

Enjoy Dorset & Hampshire
Magazine
01202 737678
www.enjoydorset.co.uk

Esquire
020 7439 5000
www.esquire.co.uk

Essentials
020 7261 6970
www.essentialsmagazine.
com

Essex Life & Countryside
01206 571348
www.archant.co.uk

Euromoney
020 7779 8888
www.euromoneyplc.com

European Business
020 7269 7416
www.cnbceb.com

Family Circle
020 7261 6195
www.familycircle.co.uk

Farmers Guardian
01772 799411
www.farmersguardian.com

Farmers Weekly
020 8652 4911
www.fwi.co.uk

FHM
020 7436 1515
www.fhm.com

The Field
020 7261 5198
www.thefield.co.uk

Film Review
020 8875 1520
www.visimag.com

Financial Advisor
020 7382 8000
www.ftadvisor.com

Financial Management
020 8849 2313
www.cimaglobal.com

Financial News
020 7426 3333
www.efinancialnews.com

Financial World
01227 818609
www.financialworld.co.uk

Fitness First
01932 841450
www.fitnessfirst.com

Flybe, Uncovered
020 8649 7233
www.bmipublications.
com

Foodchain Magazine
020 8332 9090
www.foodchain-
magazine.com

Fortean Times
020 7907 6000
www.forteantimes.com

FourFourTwo
020 8267 5000
www.fourfourtwo
premiumtv.co.uk

Gap Year
0870 241 6704
www.gapyear.com

The Garden
01733 775775
www.rhs.org.uk

Garden Answers
01733 282683
www.gardeningmags.co.uk

Garden News
01733 282680
www.gardeningmags.co.uk

Gardening Which?
0845 903 7000
www.which.co.uk/gardening-
which

Gardens Illustrated
020 8433 1354
www.bbcmagazines.com/
gardensillustrated

Gardens Monthly
01689 887 200

Glamour
020 7499 9080
www.glamour.com

Glasgow Magazine
0141 287 0901
www.glasgow.gov.uk

Golf International
020 7828 3003
www.golfinternationalmag.co.uk

Golf Monthly
020 7261 7237
www.golf-monthly.co.uk

Golf News
01273 777994
www.golfnews.co.uk

Golf Weekly
01733 288035
www.golfweek.com

Golf World
01733 288011
www.golfworld.com

Good Housekeeping
020 7439 5000
www.goodhousekeeping.
co.uk

Good Ski Guide
020 7332 2000
www.goodskiguide.com

GP
020 8267 5000
www.gponline.com

GQ
020 7499 9080
www.gq.com

Granta
020 7704 9776
www.granta.com

Green Futures
020 7324 3660
www.greenfutures.org.uk

The Grocer
01293 610259
www.grocertoday.co.uk

The Gymnast
0116 247 8766
www.british-gymnastics.
org

Harpers Bazaar
020 7226 2222
www.harpersbazaar.co.uk

Harvey Nichols Magazine
020 7747 0700
www.redwoodgroup.net

Heat
020 7437 9011
www.emap.com

Hello!
020 7667 8901
www.hellomagazine.com

Hi-Fi Choice
020 7317 2495
www.hifichoice.co.uk

Hi-Fi News
020 8774 0850
www.hifinews.com

Hi-Fi World
01275 371386
www.hi-fiworld.co.uk

Higher Education Review
020 8341 1366
www.highereducationreview.
com

High Life
020 7534 2400
www.cedarcom.co.uk

History Today
020 7534 8000
www.historytoday.com

Holiday Which?
0845 309 4000
www.which.co.uk

Homes & Gardens
020 7261 5678
www.homesandgardens.com

Horse
020 7261 7969
www.horsemagazine.co.uk

Horse & Hound
020 7261 6453
www.horseandhound.co.uk

Horse & Rider
01428 601020
www.horseandrider-
magazine.co.uk

House & Garden
020 7499 9080
www.houseandgarden.co.uk

The House Magazine
020 7878 1520
www.epolitix.com

Illustrated London News
020 7805 5555
www.iln.org.uk

Information Age
020 7612 9300
www.information-age.com

Inside Soap
020 7150 7000
www.insidesoap.co.uk

In-Store
020 7970 4000
www.centaur.co.uk

In Style
020 7261 4747
www.ipcmedia.com

Insurance Age
020 7484 9700
www.insuranceage.com

Investors Chronicle
020 7382 8000
www.investorschronicle.
co.uk

IT Week
020 8606 7505
www.itweek.co.uk

Kerrang!
020 7436 1515
www.kerrang.com

The Lady
020 7261 5177
www.lady.co.uk

The Lancet
020 7611 4100
www.lancet.com

Liberty
020 7403 3888
www.liberty-human-
rights.org.uk

Loaded
020 7261 5562
www.uploaded.com

London Cyclist
020 7928 7220
www.lcc.org.uk

**London Review of
Books**
020 7209 1101
www.lrb.co.uk

London Student
020 7664 2054

MacFormat
01225 442244
www.macformat.co.uk

MacUser
01225 442244
www.macuser.co.uk

Macworld
020 7831 9252
www.macworld.co.uk

Management Today
020 8267 5000
www.mtmagazine.co.uk

**Manchester United
Magazine**
020 7317 2614
www.manutd.com

M&S Magazine
020 7747 0871
www.redwoodgroup.net

Marie Claire
020 7261 5177
www.marieclaire.co.uk

Marketing Week
020 7970 4000
www.marketingweek.co.uk

Maxim
020 7907 6000
www.maxim-magazine.
co.uk

Max Power
01733 468000
www.maxpower.co.uk

Men's Fitness
0207 907 6000
www.mensfitnessmagazine.
co.uk

Men's Health
020 7439 5000
www.menshealth.
co.uk

Mixmag
020 7182 8000
www.mixmag.net

Mojo
020 7312 8716
www.mojo4music.com

Money Observer
020 7713 4188
www.moneyobserver.
com

Morning Advertiser
01293 610344
www.morningadvertiser.
co.uk

**Mortgage Advisor & Home
Buyer**
020 8334 1600
www.mortgageadvisormag.
co.uk

Mortgage Finance Gazette
020 7827 5454
www.mfgonline.co.uk

Mortgage Introducer
020 7827 5454
www.mortgageintroducer.com

Mother & Baby
020 7347 1869
www.motherandbaby-
magazine.com

Motorcycle Mechanics
01507 523456
www.classicmechanics.com

Motor Sport
020 8267 5000
www.motorsportmagazine.
co.uk

Motorsport News
020 8267 5385
www.haymarketgroup.com

Mountain Bike Rider
020 8774 0600
www.mountainbikerider.co.uk/

Mountain Biking UK
01225 442244
www.mbuk.com

National Geographic
01483 522068
www.nationalgeographic.com

National Trust Magazine
020 7222 9251
www.nationaltrust.co.uk

Nature
020 7833 4000
www.nature.com

.net
01225 442244
www.netmag.co.uk

New Humanist
020 7436 1151
www.newhumanist.org.uk

New Media Age
020 7970 4000
www.nma.co.uk/

New Scientist
020 7331 2735
www.newscientist.com

New Statesman
020 7730 3444
www.newstatesman.com

Newsweek
020 7851 9799
www.newsweek.com

New Woman
020 7437 9011
www.newwoman.co.uk

NHS Magazine
0113 306 0000
www.nhs.uk/nhsmagazine

NME
020 7261 5564
www.nme.com

Now
020 7261 6274
www.nowmagazine.
co.uk

Nursery Education
01926 887799
www.scholastic.co.uk

Nursery World
020 7782 3120
www.nurseryworld.co.uk

Nursing Standard
020 8423 1066
www.nursing-standard.
co.uk

Nursing Times
020 7874 0500
www.nursingtimes.net

Nuts
020 7261 5661
www.nutsmag.co.uk

OK!
020 7928 8000
www.ok-magazine.com

The Oldie
020 7436 8801
www.theoldie.co.uk

Opera
020 8563 8893
www.opera.co.uk

Opera Now
020 7333 1740
www.rhinegold.co.uk

PC Advisor
020 72915939
www.pcadvisor.co.uk

PC Answers
01225 442244
www.pcanswers.co.uk

Pensions Age
020 7426 0101
www.pensions-age.com

People
020 7322 1134
www.people.com

The People's Friend
01382 223131
www.dcthomson.co.uk

Personal Computer World
01858 438881
www.pcw.co.uk

Personnel Today
020 8652 3705
www.personneltoday.com

Practical Boat Owner
01202 680593
www.pbo.co.uk

Practical Caravan
020 8267 5000
www.practicalcaravan.com

Practical Photography
01733 282736
www.photographymags.co.uk

Press Gazette
020 7936 6402
www.pressgazette.co.uk

Prima
020 7439 5000
www.primamagazine.co.uk

Private Eye
020 7437 4017
www.private-eye.co.uk

Prospect
020 7255 1281
www.prospect-
magazine.co.uk

PSM2
01225 442244
www.futurenet.com/psm

Q
020 7312 8182
www.q4music.com

Radio Times
020 8433 2235
www.radiotimes.com

The Railway Magazine
020 7261 5821
www.railwaymagazine.co.uk

Readers Digest
020 7715 8000
www.readersdigest.co.uk

Recruiter Magazine
020 7296 4200
www.recruitermagazine.
co.uk

Red
020 7150 7000
www.redmagazine.co.uk

Red Pepper
020 7255 1281
www.redpepper.org.uk

Ride
01733 468000
www.emap.com

Rugby Times
01484 401895
www.rugbytimes.com

Rugby World
020 7261 6810
www.rugbyworld.com

Runners World
020 7439 5000
www.runnersworld.co.uk

Running Fitness
01733 347559
www.running-fitness.
co.uk

Saga Magazine
01303 77 1523
www.saga.co.uk

Sainsbury's magazine
020 7633 0266
www.sainsburysmagazine.co.uk

Science
01223 326500
www.sciencemag.org

Screen International
020 7505 8080
www.screendaily.com

Sea Angler
01733 465702
www.emap.com

Select
01484 437737
http://icsolihull.icnetwork.
co.uk/select/

She
020 7439 5000
www.she.co.uk

Sight & Sound
020 7255 1444
www.bfi.org.uk/sightand
sound

Slimming
020 7347 1854
www.emapesprit.com

Slimming World
01773 546360
www.slimming-world.com

Somerfield Magazine
0117 989 7800
www.somerfield.co.uk

Spectator
020 7405 1706
www.spectator.co.uk

The Stage
020 7403 1818
www.thestage.co.uk

Stuff
020 8267 5000
www.stuffmagazine.co.uk

Supermarket News
020 7240 0420
www.supermarketnews.com

The Tablet
020 8748 8484
www.thetablet.co.uk

Take a Break
020 7241 8000
www.bauer.co.uk

Tatler
020 7499 9080
www.tatler.co.uk

The Teacher
020 7380 4708
www.teachers.org.uk

That's Life!
020 7241 8000
www.bauer.co.uk

Time
020 7499 4080
www.time.com

Time Out
020 7813 3000
www.timeout.com

**Times Educational
Supplement**
020 7782 3000
www.tes.co.uk

**Times Higher Education
Supplement**
020 7782 3000
www.tes.co.uk

Times Literary
Supplement
020 7782 3000
www.the-tls.co.uk

Total Carp
01327 311999
www.total-fishing.com

Total Film
020 7317 2449
www.totalfilm.co.uk

Travel Trade Gazette
020 7921 8029
www.ttglive.com

Travel Weekly
020 8652 8230
www.travelweekly.co.uk

Tribune
020 7433 6410
www.tribuneweb.co.uk

TV & Satellite Week
020 7261 7534
www.tvandsatelliteweek.
com/

TV Choice
020 7241 8000
www.bauer.com

TV Quick
020 7261 7740
www.bauer.co.uk

TV Times
020 7261 7740
www.tvtimes.co.uk

Ulster Bride
028 9068 1371
www.ulstertatler.com

Ulster Tatler
028 9068 1371
www.ulstertatler.com

Vanity Fair
020 7499 9080
www.vanityfair.co.uk

The Vegetarian
0161 925 2000
www.vegsoc.org

Vnvnet.com
020 7316 9000
www.vnunet.com

Vogue
020 7499 9080
www.vogue.com

W
020 7240 0420
www.wmagazine.com

Waitrose Food Illustrated
020 7565 3000
www.jbcp.co.uk

Web User
020 7261 7294
www.webuser.co.uk/

The Week
020 7907 6000
www.theweek.co.uk

What Camcorder?
020 7331 1000
www.whatcamcorder.net

What Camera?
020 7261 5266
www.ipcmedia.com/
magazines/whatcamera

What Home Cinema?
020 7331 1000
www.whathomecinemamag.
com

What Mountain Bike?
01225 442244
www.whatmtb.co.uk

What Satellite and
Digital TV?
020 7331 1000
www.wotsat.com

What's on in London
020 7278 4393
www.whatsoninlondon.
co.uk

What's on TV
020 72617535
ww.ipcmedia.com/
magazines/whatsontv

When Saturday Comes
020 7729 1110
www.wsc.co.uk

Which?
0845 307 4000
www.which.co.uk

White Lines Snowboarding
Magazine
01235 536229
www.whitelines.com

Windsurf Magazines
01993 811181
www.windsurf.co.uk

Wine
020 7549 2567
www.wineint.com
Woman & Home
020 7261 5176
www.womanandhome.
co.uk

Woman's Own
020 7261 5500
www.ipcmedia.com/maga-
zines/womansown

Woman's Wear Daily
(WWD)
020 7240 0420
www.wwd.com

Woman's Weekly
020 7261 6131
www.lpcmedia.com/
magazines/womansweekly

World Soccer
020 7261 5714
www.worldsoccer.com

Yachting World
020 7261 6800
www.ybw.com

Yachts & Yachting
01702 582245
www.yachtsandyachting.
com

The Yorkshire Journal
01756 701033
www.dalesman.co.uk

Your Cat
01708 766199
www.yourcat.co.uk

Your Dog
01708 766199
www.yourdog.co.uk

Your Horse
01733 282750
www.yourhorse.co.uk

Zoo Weekly
020 7208 7397
www.zooweekly.co.uk

TELEVISION AND RADIO BROADCASTERS AND RELATED WEBSITES

How to use this listing

This listing is divided into three main areas. First is a list of major broadcasters – the BBC and major commercial TV and radio companies. Second is a comprehensive list of BBC local radio stations. Third is an extensive list of local commercial and community radio stations. Remember that many of these broadcasters will have websites allied to their TV and radio concerns, and many of those websites will have their own journalists. You can use the links provided to investigate the websites you are interested in.

Major broadcasters

BBC

Principal BBC addresses:
Television Centre
Wood Lane,
London W12 7RJ

BBC White City
201 Wood Lane,
London W12 7TS

Broadcasting House
Portland Place,
London W1A 1AA
020 8743 8000
www.bbc.co.uk

BBC Television

Television Centre
020 8743 8000

General Enquiries
info@bbc.co.uk
www.bbc.co.uk/television

BBC Channels

BBC One
Television Centre
020 8743 8000
www.bbc.co.uk/bbcone

BBC Two
Television Centre
020 8743 8000
www.bbc.co.uk/bbctwo/

BBC Three
Television Centre
020 8743 8000
www.bbc.co.uk/bbcthree

BBC Four
Television Centre
020 8576 3193
www.bbc.co.uk/bbcfour

BBC Food
PO Box 5054,
London W12 0ZY
020 8433 2221
bbcfood@bbc.co.uk
www.bbcfood.com

BBC News 24
Television Centre
020 8743 8000
bbcnews24@bbc.co.uk
www.bbc.co.uk/bbcnews24

BBC Parliament
4 Millbank,
London SW1P 3JA
020 7973 6216
parliament@bbc.co.uk
www.bbc.co.uk/
bbcparliament

BBC World
Television Centre
020 8576 2308
bbcworld@bbc.co.uk
www.bbcworld.com

*BBC national and regional
stations*

BBC Scotland
Broadcasting House,
Queen Margaret Drive,

Glasgow G12 8DG
0141 339 8844
www.bbc.co.uk/scotland

BBC Wales
Broadcasting House,
Llantrisant Road,
Llandaff,
Cardiff CF5 2YQ
029 2032 2000
www.bbc.co.uk/wales

BBC Northern Ireland
Broadcasting House,
Ormeau Avenue,
Belfast BT2 8HQ
028 9033 8000
www.bbc.co.uk/
northernireland

BBC East
The Forum,
Millennium Plain,
Norwich NR2 1BH
01603 619 331
look.east@bbc.co.uk
www.bbc.co.uk/england/look
east

BBC East Midlands
London Road,
Nottingham NG2 4UU
0115 955 0500
emt@bbc.co.uk
www.bbc.co.uk/england/east
midlandstoday

BBC London
35c Marylebone High Street,
London W1U 4QA
020 7224 2424
yourlondon@bbc.co.uk
www.bbc.co.uk/london

BBC North
Broadcasting Centre,
Woodhouse Lane,
Leeds LS2 9PX
0113 244 1188

look.north@bbc.co.uk
www.bbc.co.uk/england/look
northyorkslincs

**BBC North East and
Cumbria**
Broadcasting Centre,
Barrack Road,
Newcastle Upon Tyne
NE99 2NE
0191 232 1313
look.north.northeast.Cumbri
a@bbc.co.uk
www.bbc.co.uk/england/look
northnecumbria

BBC North West
New Broadcasting House,
Oxford Road,
Manchester M60 1SJ
0161 200 2020
nwt@bbc.co.uk
www.bbc.co.uk/manchester

BBC South
Broadcasting House,
Havelock Road,
Southampton S014 7PU
02380 226 201
south.today@bbc.co.uk
www.bbc.co.uk/england/sout
htoday

BBC South East
The Great Hall,
Mount Pleasant Road,
Tunbridge Wells TN1 1QQ
01892 670 000
southeasttoday@bbc.co.uk
www.bbc.co.uk/england/sout
heasttoday

BBC South West
Broadcasting House,
Seymour Road,
Mannamead,
Plymouth PL3 5BD
01752 229201
spotlight@bbc.co.uk

www.bbc.co.uk/england/
spotlight

BBC West
Broadcasting House,
Whiteladies Road,
Bristol BS8 2LR
0117 973 2211
pointswest@bbc.co.uk
www.bbc.co.uk/england/
pointswest

BBC West Midlands
The Mailbox,
Birmingham B1 1XL
0121 567 6767
midlands.today@bbc.
co.uk
www.bbc.co.uk/birmingham

BBC News

BBC News
Television Centre
020 8743 8000
http://news.bbc.co.uk

BBC Television News
Room 1502,
Television Centre
020 8624 9043

Political Programmes Unit
BBC Westminster,
4 Millbank,
London SW1P 3JA
020 7973 6000

BBC News Online
Television Centre
http://news.bbc.co.uk

*Major news and political
programmes*

Breakfast
Room 1605,
News Centre,
Television Centre

020 8624 9700
breakfasttv@bbc.co.uk

Newsnight
Television Centre
020 8624 9800

Panorama
Room 1118,
BBC White City
020 8752 7152
panorama@bbc.
co.uk

Politics Show
4 Millbank,
London SW1P 3JQ
020 7973 6199
politicsshow@bbc.co.uk

Question Time
Mentorn,
43 Whitfield Street,
London W1T 4HA
020 7258 6800

Six O'Clock News
Television Centre
020 8624 9996

Ten O'Clock News
Television Centre
020 8624 9999

ITV

ITV Network
200 Gray's Inn Road,
London WC1X 8HF
020 7843 8000
www.itv.com

The ITV Network controls
programme commissioning
and scheduling across the
entire ITV network, including
stations not owned by the
major independent television
company, ITV plc.

ITV regions

Owned by ITV plc

ITV Anglia
Anglia House,
Prince of Wales Road
Norwich NR1 3JG
01603 615 151
www.angliatv.com

News at Anglia
0870 240 6003
news@angliatv.com

Cambridge regional office
ITV Anglia,
26 Newmarket Road,
Cambridge CB5 8DT
01223 467 076

Chelmsford regional office
64–68 New London Road,
Chelmsford CM2 0YU
01245 357 676

Ipswich regional office
Hubbard House,
Ipswich IP1 2QA
01473 226 157

Luton regional office
16 Park Street,
Luton LU1 2DP
01582 729 666

Northampton regional office
77b Abington Street,
Northampton NN1 2BH
01604 624343

Peterborough regional office
6 Bretton Green,
Peterborough PE3 8DY
01733 269 440

ITV Border
The Television Centre,
Durranhill,

Carlisle CA1 3NT
01228 525 101
www.border-tv.com

ITV Central
Gas Street,
Birmingham B1 2JT
0121 643 9898
www.itv.com.central

ITV Granada
Quay Street,
Manchester M60 9EA
0161 832 7211
www.granadatv.com

Blackburn regional news centre
Daisyfield Business Centre,
Appleby Street,
Blackburn BB1 3BL
01254 690 099

Chester regional news centre
Bridgegate House,
5 Bridge Place,
Lower Bridge Street,
Chester CH1 1SA
01244 313 966

Lancaster regional news centre
White Cross,
Lancaster LA1 4XQ
01524 60688

ITV London
London Television Centre,
Upper Ground,
London SE1 9LT
020 7620 1620
www.itv.com/london

London News Network
200 Gray's Inn Road
London WC1X 8HF

020 7430 4000
www.itvlondon.co.uk

ITV Meridian
Television Centre,
Southampton SO14 0PZ
023 8022 2555
news@meridiantv.com
www.meridiantv.co.uk

Maidstone news office
ITV Meridian,
Westpoint,
New Hythe,
Kent ME20 6XX
01622 882 244

Newbury news office
ITV Meridian,
Strawberry Hill House,
Strawberry Hill,
Newbury,
Berkshire RG14 1NG
01635 552266

Tees Valley & North Yorkshire news office
Tyne Tees Television,
Belasis Hall Technology Park,
Billingham,
Teesside TS23 4EG
Newsroom: 01642 566 999
newstoday@tynetees.tv

Tyne Tees Television
City Road,
Newcastle Upon Tyne NE1 2AL
0191 261 0181
news@tynetees.tv
www.tynetees.tv

ITV Wales
The Television Centre,
Culverhouse Cross,
Cardiff CF5 6XJ
029 2059 0590
info@itvwales.com

news@itvwales.com
www.itvwales.com

Carmarthen news office
ITV Wales,
Top Floor, 19–20 Lammas Street,
Carmarthen SA31 3AL
01267 236 809

Colwyn Bay news office
ITV Wales,
Celtic Business Centre,
Plas Eirias, Heritage Gate,
Abergele Road,
Colwyn Bay LL29 8BW
01492 513 888

Newtown news office
ITV Wales,
St David's House,
Newtown SY16 1RB
01686 623 381

Wrexham news office
ITV Wales,
Crown Buildings,
31 Chester Street,
Wrexham, LL 138 XN
01978 261 462

ITV West
Television Centre
Bath Road,
Bristol BS4 3HG
0117 972 2722
reception@itv.com
www.itv1west.com

Newsdesk
0117 972 2151/2152
itvwestnews@itv.com

ITV Westcountry
Language Science Park,
Western Wood Way,
Plymouth PL7 5BQ
01752 333 333
www.westcountry.co.uk

Main news desk
01752 333 329
news@westcountry.co.uk

Barnstaple news office
ITV Westcountry
1 Summerland Terrace,
Barnstaple EX32 8JL
01271 324 244

Exeter news office
ITV Westcountry,
St Luke's Campus,
Magdalene Road,
Exeter EX4 4WT
01392 499 400

Penzance news office
ITV Westcountry,
Parade Chambers,
10 Parade Street,
Penzance TR18 4BU
01736 331 483

Taunton news office
ITV Westcountry,
Foundry Cottage,
Riverside Place, St James
Street,
Taunton TA1 1JH
01823 322 335

Truro news office
ITV Westcountry,
Courtleigh House,
Lemon Street,
Truro TR1 2PN
01872 262 244

Weymouth news office
ITV Westcountry,
8 King Street,
Weymouth DT4 7BP
01305 760 860

ITV Yorkshire
The Television Centre,
Kirkstall Road,
Leeds LS3 1JS

0113 243 8283
www.yorkshiretv.com

**Calendar (ITV Yorkshire
news programme)**
0845 121 1000
calendar@yorkshiretv.com

Grimsby Office
Image Studios,
Margaret Street,
Immingham,
Grimsby DN40 1LE
01469 510 661

Hull Office
23 Brook Street,
Hull HU2 8PM
01482 324 488

Lincoln Office
88 Bailgate,
Lincoln LN1 3AR
01522 530 738

Sheffield Office
23 Charter Square,
Sheffield S1 3EJ
0114 272 7772

York Office
York St John's College,
Lord Mayors Walk,
York YO31 7EX
01904 610 066

*Owned by Scottish Media
Group*

Grampian TV
Television Centre,
Craigshaw Business Park,
West Tullos,
Aberdeen AB12 3QH
01224 848 848
www.grampiantv.co.uk

Scottish TV
200 Renfield Street,

Glasgow G2 3PR
0141 300 3000
News desk: 0141 300 3360
www.scottishtv.co.uk

Owned independently

BskyB
British Sky Broadcasting,
Grant Way,
Isleworth TW7 5QD
0870 240 3000
www.sky.com

Channel 4 News
ITN,
200 Gray's Inn Road,
London WC1X 8XZ
020 7833 3000
www.channel4.com/news

Channel Television
Television Centre,
La Pouquelaye,
St Helier,
Jersey JE1 3ZD
01534 816 816
Newsroom: 01534 816 688
broadcast@channeltv.co.uk
www.channeltv.co.uk

CNN
Turner House,
16 Great Marlborough
Street,
London W1F 7HS
020 7693 1000
http://edition.cnn.com

Five
22 Long Acre,
London WC2E 9LY
020 7550 5555
News and current affairs:
020 7421 7122
www.five.tv

Five News
See BSkyB

Guernsey Office
Television House,
Bulwer Avenue,
St Sampson,
Guernsey GY2 4LA
01481 241 888
broadcast.gsy@channeltv.co.uk

ITN
200 Gray's Inn Road,
London WC1X 8XZ
020 7833 3000
www.itn.co.uk

London Office
Unit 16A, 3rd Floor,
Enterprise House,
59–65 Upper Ground,
London SE1 9PQ
020 7633 9902

Sky News
www.skynews.co.uk

Teletext
Building 10,
Chiswick Park,

566 Chiswick High
Road,
London W4 5TS
0870 731 3000
editor@teletext.
co.uk
www.teletext.co.uk

UTV
Ormeau Road,
Belfast BT7 1EB
028 9032 8122
www.utv.plc

BBC Radio

Broadcasting House,
Portland Place,
London W1A 1AA
020 7580 4468

BBC Radio 1/1xtra
Yalding House,
152–156 Great Portland
Street,
London W1N 6AJ
www.bbc.co.uk/radio1
www.bbc.co.uk/1xtra

BBC Radio 2
Western House,
99 Great Portland Street,
London W1A 1AA
www.bbc.co.uk/radio2

BBC Radio 3
Broadcasting House,
Portland Place,
London W1A 1AA
www.bbc.co.uk/radio3

BBC Radio 4
Broadcasting House,
Portland Place,
London W1A 1AA
www.bbc.co.uk/radio4

**BBC Radio Five Live & Five
Live Sports Extra**
Television Centre,
Wood Lane,
London W12 7RJ
www.bbc.co.uk/fivelive

BBC Asian Network
Epic House,
Charles Street,
Leicester LE1 3SH
0116 251 6688
www.bbc.co.uk/asian
network

BBC World Service
Bush House,
Strand,
London WC2B 4PH
020 7557 2941
www.bbc.co.uk/world
service

BBC national and regional stations

BBC Radio Scotland
Queen Margaret Drive,
Glasgow G12 8DG
0141 339 8844
scottishplanning@bbc.co.uk
www.bbc.co.uk/scotland

**BBC Radio Nan
Gaidheal**
52 Church Street,

Stornoway,
Isle of Lewis HS12LS
01851 705 000
feedback@bbc.co.uk
www.bbc.co.uk/
scotlandalba/radio

BBC Radio Wales/Cymru
Broadcasting House,
LLANT RISANT ROAD

Llandaff,
Cardiff CF5 2YQ
0870 010 0110
radiowales@bbc.co.uk
www.bbc.co.uk/
radiowales

BBC Radio Ulster
Broadcasting House,
Belfast BT2 8HQ

028 9033 8000
radioulster@bbc.co.uk
www.bbc.co.uk/radioulster

BBC Radio Foyle
Northland Road,
Londonderry BT48 7GD

028 7137 8600
radiofoyle@bbc.co.uk
www.bbc.co.uk/radiofoyle

BBC local radio

BBC Radio Berkshire
PO Box 1044,
Reading RG4 8FH
0118 946 4200
berkshireonline@bbc.co.uk
www.bbc.co.uk/berkshire

BBC Radio Bristol and Somerset Sound
PO Box 194,
Bristol BS99 7QT
01179 741 111
radio.Bristol@bbc.co.uk
www.bbc.co.uk/radiobristol
and www.bbc.co.uk/bristol

BBC Radio Cambridgeshire
PO Box 96,
104 Hills Road,
Cambridge CB2 1LD
01223 259 696
cambs@bbc.co.uk
www.bbc.co.uk/cambridgeshire

BBC Radio Cleveland
PO Box 95FM,
Newport Road,
Middlesbrough TS1 5DG
01642 225 211
bbcradiocleveland@bbc.co.uk
www.bbc.co.uk/tees

BBC Radio Cornwall
Phoenix Wharf,
Truro,
Cornwall TR1 1UA
01872 275 421
radio.cornwall@bbc.co.uk
www.bbc.co.uk/cornwall

BBC Radio Cumbria
Annetwell Street,
Carlisle CA3 8BB
01228 592 444
radio.cumbria@bbc.co.uk
www.bbc.co.uk/radiocumbria

BBC Radio Derby
PO Box 104.5,
Derby DE1 3HL
01332 361 111
radio.derby@bbc.co.uk
www.bbc.co.uk/radioderby

BBC Radio Devon
PO Box 1034,
Plymouth PL3 5BD
01752 260 323
radio.devon@bbc.co.uk
www.bbc.co.uk/devon

BBC Essex
198 New London Road,
Chelmsford,
Essex CM2 9XB
01245 616 000
essex@bbc.co.uk
www.bbc.co.uk/essex

BBC Radio Gloucestershire
London Road,
Gloucester GL1 1SW
01452 308 585
radio.gloucestershire@bbc.co.uk
www.bbc.co.uk/gloucestershire

BBC GMR
PO Box 951,
Oxford Road,
Manchester M60 1SD

0161 200 2000
gmr.newsdesk@bbc.co.uk
www.bbc.co.uk/england/gmr

BBC Radio Guernsey
Bulwer Avenue,
St Sampsons,
Guernsey GY2 4LA
01481 200 600
radio.guernsey@bbc.co.uk
www.bbc.co.uk/guernsey

BBC Hereford and Worcester
Hylton Road,
Worcester WR2 5WW
01905 748 485
bbchw@bbc.co.uk
www.bbc.co.uk/worcester or
www.bbc.co.uk/hereford

BBC Radio Humberside and BBCi Hull
Queens Court,
Queens Gardens,
Hull HU1 3RP
01482 323 232
radio.humberside@bbc.co.uk
www.bbc.co.uk/humber

BBC Radio Jersey
18 Parade Road,
St Helier,
Jersey JE2 3PL
01534 870 000
radio.jersey@bbc.co.uk
www.bbc.co.uk/jersey

BBC Radio Kent
The Great Hall,
Mount Pleasant Road,
Tunbridge Wells,

Kent TN1 1QQ
01892 670 000
radio.kent@bbc.co.uk
www.bbc.co.uk/kent

BBC Radio Lancashire
26 Darwen Street,
Blackburn,
Lancs BB2 2EA
01254 262 411
radio.lancashire@bbc.co.uk
www.bbc.co.uk/lancashire

BBC Radio Leeds
Broadcasting Centre,
2 St Peters Square,
Leeds LS9 8AH
0113 244 2131
radio.leeds@bbc.co.uk
www.bbc.co.uk/leeds

BBC Radio Leicester
Epic House,
Charles Street,
Leicester LE1 3SH
0116 251 6688
radio.leicester@bbc.co.uk
www.bc.co.uk/leicester

BBC Radio Lincolnshire
PO Box 219,
Newport,
Lincoln LN1 3XY
01522 511 411
radio.lincolnshire@bbc.
co.uk
www.bbc.co.uk/lincolnshire

BBC London 94.9
35 Marylebone High Street,
London W1U 4QA
020 7224 2424
yourlondon@bbc.co.uk
www.bbc.co.uk/london

BBC Radio Merseyside
55 Parades Street,
Liverpool L1 3BP
0151 708 5500

radio.merseyside@bbc.co.uk
www.bbc.co.uk/liverpool

BBC Radio Newcastle
Broadcasting Centre,
Barrack Road,
Newcastle Upon Tyne NE99
1RN
0191 232 4141
radio.newcastle@bbc.co.uk
www.bbc.co.uk/england/radi
onewcastle

BBC Radio Norfolk
The Forum,
Millennium Plain,
Norwich NR2 1BH
01603 617 411
radionorfolk@bbc.co.uk
www.bbc.co.uk/norfolk

BBC Radio Northampton
Broadcasting House,
Abington Street,
Northampton NN1 2BH
01604 239 100
northampton@bbc.co.uk
www.bbc.co.uk/northamp-
tonshire

BBC Radio Nottingham
London Road,
Nottingham NG2 4UU
0115 955 0500
radio.nottingham@bbc.co.uk
www.bbc.co.uk/nottingham

BBC Radio Oxford
PO Box 95.2,
Oxford OX2 7YL
01865 311 444
radio.oxford@bbc.co.uk
www.bbc.co.uk/radiooxford

BBC Radio Sheffield
54 Shoreham Street,
Sheffield S1 4RS
0114 273 1177
radio.sheffield@bbc.co.uk

www.bbc.co.uk/england/radi
osheffield

BBC Radio Shropshire
2–4 Boscobel Drive,
Shrewsbury SY1 3TT
01743 248 484
radio.shropshire@bbc.co.uk
www.bbc.co.uk/shropshire

BBC Radio Solent
Broadcasting House,
Havelock Road,
Southampton SO14 7PW
02380 631 311
solent@bbc.co.uk
www.bbc.co.uk/radiosolent

**BBC Southern Counties
Radio**
Broadcasting Centre,
Guildford GU2 7AP
01483 306 306
southern.counties.radio@bbc.
co.uk
www.bbc.co.uk/southern-
counties

BBC Radio Stoke
Cheapside,
Hanley,
Stoke-on-Trent ST1 1JJ
01782 208 080
radio.stoke@bbc.co.uk
www.bbc.co.uk/stoke

BBC Radio Suffolk
Broadcasting House,
St Matthew's Street,
Ipswich,
Suffolk IP1 3EP
01473 250 000
radiosuffolk@bbc.co.uk
www.bbc.co.uk/suffolk

BBC Radio Swindon
PO Box 1234,
Swindon SN1 3RW
01793 513 626

radio.swindon@bbc.co.uk
www.bbc.co.uk/wiltshire

BBC Three Counties Radio
PO Box 3CR,
Luton,
Bedfordshire LU1 5XL
01582 637 400
3cr@bbc.co.uk
www.bbc.co.uk/threecounties

BBC Radio Wiltshire
Broadcasting House,

Prospect Place,
Swindon,
Wiltshire SN1 3RW
01793 513 626
radio.wiltshire@bbc.co.uk
www.bbc.co.uk/wiltshire

BBC WM (Birmingham)
Pebble Mill Road,
Birmingham B5 7QQ
0121 432 9000
radio.wm@bbc.co.uk
www.bbc.co.uk/blackcountry

BBC WM (Coventry)
1 Holt Court,
Greyfriars Road,
Coventry CV1 2WR
02476 860 086

**BBC North Yorkshire,
Radio York**
20 Bootham Row,
York YO30 7BR
01904 641 351
northyorkshire.news@bbc.co.uk
www.bbc.co.uk/northyorkshire

Commercial radio

**Commercial Radio
Companies Association**
77 Shaftesbury Avenue,

London W1D
5DU
020 7306 2603

info@crca.co.uk
www.crca.co.uk

Main commercial radio groups

Chrysalis Radio Group
The Chrysalis Building,
13 Bramley Road,
London W10 6SP
020 7221 2213
info@chrysalis.com
www.chrysalis.com

Classic Gold Digital
Network Centre,
Chiltern Road,
Dunstable LU6 1HQ
01582 676 200
www.classicgolddigital.com

Emap Performance Network
Mappin House,
4 Winsley Street,
London W1W 8HF
020 7436 1515
www.emap.com

GCap Media
30 Leicester Square,

London WC2H 7LA
020 7054 8000
www.gcapmedia.com

**The Local Radio
Company plc**
11 Duke Street,
High Wycombe,
Buckinghamshire HP13 6EE
01494 688200
Fax: 01494 688201

Scottish Radio Holdings
Clydebank Business Park,
Clydebank,
Glasgow G81 2RX
0141 565 2200
www.srhplc.com

SMG
200 Renfield Street,
Glasgow G2 3PR
0141 300 3300
www.smg.plc.uk

Tindle Radio Holdings
Weaver's Yard,
6 West Street,
Farnham,
Surrey GU9 7DN
01252 735 667
www.tindleradio.com

UKRD Group
Cam Brea Studios,
Wilson Way,
Redruth,
Cornwall TR15 3XX
01209 310 435
enquiries@ukrd.co.uk
www.ukrd.com

The Wireless Group
18 Hatfields,
London SE1 8DJ
020 7959 7800
www.talksport.net

National commercial radio stations

Capital Disney
30 Leicester Square,
London WC2H 7LA
020 7766 6000
www.capitaldisney.co.uk

Classic FM
7 Swallow Place,
Oxford Circus,
London W1B 2AG
020 7343 9000
www.classicfm.com

Core
PO Box 2269,
London W1A 5UQ

GWR Group
020 7911 7300
fresh@corefreshhits.com
www.corefreshhits.com

The Hits
Castle Quay,
Castlefields,
Manchester M15 4PR
0161 288 5000
studio@thehitsradio.com
www.thehitsradio.com

Jazz FM
26–27 Castlereagh Street,
London W1H 5DL
020 7706 4100
jazzinfo@jazzfm.com
www.jazzfm.com

Kerrang!
Kerrang House,

20 Lionel Street,
Birmingham B3 1AQ
Emap Performance Network
0845 053 1052
www.emapdigitalradio.com

Kiss
Mappin House,
4 Winsley Street,
London W1W 8HF
Emap Performance Network
020 7975 8100
www.kiss100.com

Life
30 Leicester Square,
London WC2H 7LA
020 7766 6000
studio@listentolife.com

Magic
900 Herries Road,
Sheffield S6 1RH
0114 209 1034
www.emapdigitalradio.com

Oneword Radio
Landseer House,
19 Charing Cross Road,
London WC2H OES
020 7976 3030
info@oneword.co.uk
www.oneword.co.uk

Planet Rock
PO Box 2269,
London W1A 5UQ
GWR Group
020 7911 7300

joinus@planetrock.com
www.planetrock.com

Prime Time Radio
PO Box 5050,
London SW1E 6ZR
0870 050 5050
www.primetimeradio.org

Q Radio
Mappin House,
4 Winsley Street,
London W1W 8HF
Emap Performance Network
020 7436 1515
www.q4music.com

Smash! Hits
Mappin House,
4 Winsley Street
London W1W 8HF
Emap Performance Network
020 7436 1515
www.emapdigitalradio.com

TalkSport
18 Hatfields,
London SE1 8DJ
The Wireless Group
020 7959 7800
www.talksport.net

Virgin Radio
1 Golden Square,
London W1F 9DJ
020 7434 1215
reception@virginradio.
co.uk
www.virginradio.co.uk

Commercial radio news services

ITN Radio
200 Gray's Inn Road,
London WC1X 8XZ
020 7430 4090
Newsdesk: 020 7430
4814

radio@itn.co.uk
www.itn.co.uk

Independent Radio News (IRN)
6th Floor,
200 Gray's Inn Road,

London WC1X 8XZ
020 7430 4090
Newsdesk: 020 7430 4814
irn@itn.co.uk
news@irn.co.uk
www.irn.co.uk

Commercial local radio

Many local radio stations take the number that identifies the wavelength they broadcast on as their name. This listing begins with those that use a number, followed by a conventional A–Z listing.

1

100.7 Heart FM
1 The Square,
111 Broad Street,
Birmingham B15 1AS
0121 695 0000
news@heartfm.co.uk
www.heartfm.co.uk
West Midlands

102.4 Wish FM
Orrell Lodge,
Orrell Road,
Orrell,
Wigan WN5 8HJ
01942 761 024
studio@wish_fm.com
Wigan

102.7 Hereward FM
PO Box 225,
Queensgate Centre,
Peterborough PE1 1XJ
01733 460 460
www.musicradio.com

102.8 RAM FM
35–36 Irongate,
Derby DE1 3GA
01332 205 599
ramfm@musicradio.com
www.musicradio.com
Derby

103.2 Power FM
Radio House,
Whittle Avenue,
Segensworth,
West Fareham
PO15 5SH
01489 589 911

info@powerfm.co.uk
www.powerfm.com

103.4 The Beach
PO Box 103.4,
Lowestoft,
Suffolk NR32 2TL
0845 345 1035
www.thebeach.co.uk

104.7 Island FM
12 Westbrook,
St Sampsons,
Guernsey GY2 4QQ
01481 242 000
www.islandfm.guernsey.net

106 Century FM
City Link,
Nottingham NG2 4NG
0115 910 6100
info106@centuryfm.co.uk
www.106centuryfm.com
East Midlands

106.3 Bridge FM
PO Box 1063,
Bridgend CF31 1WF
01656 647 777
www.bridge.fm
Bridgend

106.9 Silk FM
Radio House,
Bridge Street,
Macclesfield,
Cheshire
SK11 6DJ
01625 268 000
mail@silkfm.com
www.silkfm.com
Macclesfield

107 Oak FM
7 Waldron Court,
Prince William Road,
Loughborough,
Leicestershire LE11 5GD
01509 211 711
studio@oak107.co.uk
www.oak107.co.uk
Charnwood/NW
Leicestershire

107.1 Rugby FM
Dunsmore Business Centre,
Spring Street,
Rugby CV21 3HH
01788 541 100
mail@rugbyfm.co.uk
www.rugbyfm.co.uk
Rugby

107.2 Wire FM
Warrington Business Park,
Long Lane,
Warrington WA2 8TX
01925 445 545
info@wirefm.com
www.wirefm.com
Warrington

107.3 Time FM
Abbey Road,
London SE2 0EW
020 8311 3112
www.timefm.com

107.4 The Quay
Flagship Studios,
PO Box 1074,
Portsmouth PO2 8YG
023 9236 4141

mail@quayradio.com
www.quayradio.com

107.4 Telford FM
PO Box 1074,
Telford TF1 5HU
01952 280 011
staff@telfordfm.co.uk
www.telfordfm.co.uk
Telford

107.5 3TR FM
Riverside Studios,
Boreham Mill,
Bishopstow,
Warminster BA12 9HQ
01985 211 111
admin@3trfm.com
www.3trfm.com

107.5 Sovereign Radio
14 St Mary's Walk,
Hailsham,
East Sussex BN27 1AF
01323 442 700
info@1075sovereignradio.
co.uk
www.1075sovereignradio.
co.uk

107.6 Kestrel FM
Paddington House,
Festival Place,
Basingstoke RG21 7LJ
01256 694 000
studio@kestrelfm.com
www.kestrelfm.com

107.7 The Wolf
10th Floor,
Mander House,
Wolverhampton WV1 3NB
01902 571 070
www.thewolf.co.uk
Wolverhampton

107.8 Arrow FM
Priory Meadow Centre,
Hastings,
East Sussex TN34 1PJ

01424 461 177
info@arrowfm.co.uk
www.arrowfm.co.uk

107.8 Radio Jackie
The Old Post Office,
110–112 Tolworth
Broadway,
Surbiton,
Surrey KT6 7JD
020 8288 1300
info@radiojackie.com
www.radiojackie.com

107.8 Southciy FM
City Studios,
Marsh Lane,
Southampton SO14 3ST
023 8022 0020
info@southcityfm.
co.uk
www.southcityfm.
co.uk

2

2BR
Imex Lomeshaye
Business Village,
Nelson,
Lancs BB9 7DR
01282 690 000
info@2br.co.uk
www.2br.co.uk
Burnley

2CR FM
5–7 Southcote Road,
Bournemouth,
Dorset BH1 3LR
01202 259 259
newsbournemouth@
creation.com
www.musicradio.com

2-Ten FM
PO Box 2020,
Calcot,
Reading,
Berkshire RG31 7FG

0118 945 4400
www.musicradio.com

9

95.8 Capital FM
30 Leicester Square,
London WC2H 7LA
020 7766 6000
info@capitalradio.com
www.capitalfm.com

96 Trent FM
29–31 Castle Gate,
Nottingham NG1 7AP
0115 952 7000
www.musicradio.com
Nottinghamshire

96.2 The Revolution
PO Box 962,
Oldham OL1 3JF
0161 621 6500
info@therevolution.uk.com
www.revolutiononline.co.uk
Oldham

96.3 QFM
65 Sussex Street,
Glasgow G41 1DX
0141 429 9430
sales@q-fm.com
www.q96.net
Paisley

96.3 Radio Aire
51 Burley Road,
Leeds LS3 1LR
0113 283 5500
www.radioaire.co.uk
Leeds

96.4 FM BRMB
Nine Brindley Place,
4 Ozells Square,
Birmingham B1 2DJ
0121 245 5000
info@brmb.co.uk
www.brmb.co.k
Birmingham

96.4 The Eagle
Dolphin House,
North Street,
Guildford GU1 4AA
01483 300 964
onair@964eagle.co.uk
www.964eagle.co.uk

96.4 FM The Wave
PO Box 1170,
Swansea SA4 3AB
01792 511 964
info@thewave.co.uk
www.thewave.co.uk
Swansea

96.9 Chiltern FM
55 Goldington Road,
Bedford,
Beds MK40 3LT
01234 272 400
www.musicradio.com

96.9 Viking FM
The Boat House,
Commercial Road,
Hull HU1 2SG
01482 325 141
reception@vikingfm.
co.uk
www.vikingfm.co.uk
Hull

**97 FM Plymouth
Sound**
Earl's Acre,
Plymouth PL3 4HX
01752 275 600
mail@plymouthsound.
musicradio.com
www.musicradio.com

97.2 Stray FM
The Hamlet,
Hornbeam Park Avenue,
Harrogate HG2 8RE
01423 522 972
mail@972strayfm.co.uk
www.strayfm.com
Harrogate

97.4 Rock FM
PO Box 974,
Preston PR1 1YE
01772 477 700
www.rockfm.co.uk
Preston and Blackpool

97.4 Vale FM
Longmead Studios,
Shaftesbury,
Dorset SP7 8PL
01747 855 711
studio@valefm.co.uk
www.valefm.co.uk

97.6 Chiltern FM
Chiltern Road,
Dunstable,
Beds LU6 1HQ
01582 676 200
www.musicradio.com

A

All FM
Manchester
0161 273 4072
info@allfm.org
www.allfm.org

Alpha 103.2
Radio House,
11 Woodland Road,
Darlington,
Co. Durham DL3 7BJ
01325 255 552
sales@alpha1032.com
www.alpha1032.com
Darlington

**Angel Community
Radio**
Havant
02392 481 988
angelradio@37.com
www.cssd.com

Argyll FM
27–29 Longrow,
Campbeltown,

Argyll PA28 6ER
01586 551 800
argyllradio@hotmail.com
Kintyre, Islay and Jura

Asian Sound Radio
Globe House,
Southall Street,
Manchester M3 1LG
0161 288 1000
info@asiansoundradio.
co.uk
www.asiansoundradio.com
East Lancashire

B

Bath FM
Station House,
Ashley Avenue,
Lower Weston
Bath BA1 3DS
01225 471 571
news@bath.fm
www.bath.fm

The Bay
PO Box 969,
St Georges Quay,
Lancaster LA1 3LD
01524 848 747
information@thebay.fm
www.thebay.fm
Morecambe Bay

BCB 96.7 FM
Bradford
01274 771 677
info@bcb.yorks.com
www.bcb.yorks.com

BCRfm
Royal Clarence House,
York Buildings,
High Street
Bridgwater TA6 3AT
01278 727 701
studio@bcrfm.co.uk
www.bcrfm.co.uk
Bridgewater

Beacon FM
267 Tettenhall Road,
Wolverhampton WV6 ODE
01902 461 300
www.musicradio.com
Wolverhampton

Beat 106
Four Winds Pavillion,
Pacific Quay,
Glasgow G51 1EB
0141 566 6106
info@beat106.com
www.beat106.com
Central Scotland

Bright 106.4
The Market Place Shopping
Centre,
Burgess Hill,
West Sussex RH15 9NP
01444 248 127
reception@bright1064com
www.bright1064.com

Broadland 102
St George's Plain,
47–49 Colgate,
Norwich NR3 1DB
01603 630 621
www.musicradio.com

C

Capital Gold (1152)
30 Leicester Square,
London WC2H 7LA
020 7766 6000
info@capitalgold.co.uk
www.capitalgold.com
Birmingham

Capital Gold (1170 and 1557)

Capital Gold (1242 and 603)
Maidstone, Medway and
East Kent

Capital Gold (1305 and 1359)
Cardiff and Newport

Capital Gold (1323 and 945)
Brighton, Eastbourne and
Hastings

Capital Gold (1548)
London

Central FM
201 High Street,
Falkirk FK1 1DU
01324 6111 164
mail@centralfm.co.uk
www.centralfm.co.uk
Stirling and Falkirk

Centre FM
5–6 Aldergate,
Tamworth,
Staffordshire B79 7DJ
01827 318 000
studio@centrefm.com
www.centre.fm
South-east Staffordshire

Century 105
Laser House,
Waterfront Quay
Salford Quays
Manchester M50 3XW
0161 400 0105
info1054@centuryfm.co.uk
www.1054centuryfm.com
North West England

Century FM
Church Street,
Gateshead NE8 2YY
0191 477 6666
info@centuryfm.co.uk
www.100centuryfm.co.uk
North-east England

CFM (Carlisle)
PO Box 964,
Carlisle CA1 3NG

01228 818 964
reception@cfmradio.com
www.cfmradio.com
Carlisle

CFM (West Cumbria)
PO Box 964,
Carlisle CA1 3NG
01228 818 964
reception@cfmradio.com
www.cfmradio.com
West Cumbria

Champion FM
Llys y Dderwen Parc Menai,
Bangor LL57 4BN
01248 671 888
www.musicradio.com
Caenafon

Channel 103 FM
6 Tunnell Street,
St Helier,
Jersey JE2 4LU
01534 888 103
www.channel103.com

Choice 107.1 FM
291–299 Borough High Street,
London SE1 1JG
020 7378 3969
info@choicefm.com
www.choicefm.com

City Beat 96.7
PO Box 967,
Belfast BT9 5DF
028 9020 5967
music@citybeat.co.uk
www.citybeat.co.uk
Belfast

Clan FM
Radio House,
Rowantree Avenue,
Newhouse Industrial Estate,
Newhouses,
Lanarkshire ML1 5RX
01698 733 107

reception@clanfm.com
www.clanfm.com
North Lanarkshire

Classic Gold 666/954
Hawthorn House,
Exeter Business Park,
Exeter EX1 3QS
01392 444 444
www.musicradio.com
Exeter/Torbay

Classic Gold 774
Bridge Studios,
Eastgate Centre,
Gloucester GL1 1SS
01452 313 200
reception@musicradio.com
www.classicgolddigital.com
Gloucester/Cheltenham

Classic Gold 792/828
Chiltern Road,
Dunstable,
Beds LU6 1HQ
01582 676 200
www.classicgolddigital.
com
Luton/Bedford

Classic Gold 828
5 Southcote Road,
Bournemouth,
Dorset BH1 3LR
01202 259 259
newsbournemouth@
creation.com
www.classicgolddigital.com
Bournemouth

Classic Gold 936/1161 AM
Lime Kiln Studio,
Lime Kiln,
Wooton Bassett,
Swindon SN4 7EX
01793 842 600
reception@musicradio.com
www.musicradio.com
Swindon

Classic Gold 1152 AM
Earl's Acre,
Plymouth PL3 4HX
01752 275 600
www.classicgolddigital.com

Classic Gold 1260
One Passage Street,
Bristol BS99 7SN
0117 984 3200
admin@classicgolddigital.com
www.classicgolddigital.com

Classic Gold 1278/1530 AM
Pennine House,
Forster Square,
Bradford,
West Yorkshire BD1 5NE
01274 203 040
general@pulse.co.uk
www.pulse.co.uk
Bradford, Halifax and
Huddersfield

Classic Gold 1332 AM
PO Box 225,
Queensgate Centre,
Peterborough PEI IXJ
01733 460 460
www.classicgolddigital.com
Peterborough

Classic Gold 1359
Hertford Place,
Coventry CV1 3TT
02476 868 200
www.classicgolddigital.com
Coventry

Classic Gold 1431/1485
The Chase,
Calcot,
Reading RG31 7RB
0118 945 4400
enquiries@classicgolddigi-
tal.com
www.classicgolddigital.com
Reading, Basingstoke and
Andover

Classic Gold 1521
The Stanley Centre,
Kelvin Way,
Crawley,
West Sussex RH10 2SE
01293 519 161
studio@musicradio.com
www.musicradio.co.uk
Reigate and Crawley

Classic Gold 1557
19–21 St Edmunds Road,
Northampton NN1 5DY
01604 795 600
www.classicgolddigital.
com
Northampton

Classic Gold Amber
St George's Plain,
47–49 Colgate,
Norwich NR3 1DB
01603 630 621
www.classicgolddigital.com
Norwich

Classic Gold Amber
Alpha Business Park,
6–12 White House Road,
Ipswich IP1 5LT
01473 461 000
www.classicgolddigital.com
Ipswich and Bury
St Edmunds

Classic Gold Breeze
Radio House,
Clifftown Road,
Southend on Sea
Essex SS1 1SX
www.classicgolddigital.com
Southend and Chelmsford

Classic Gold GEM
29–31 Castle Gate,
Nottingham NG1 7AP
0115 952 7000
www.classicgolddigital.com
Nottingham/Derby

Classic Gold Marcher 1260 AM
The Studios,
Mold Road,
Wrexham L11 4AF
01978 752 202
www.classicgolddigital.
com
Wrexham and Chester

Classic Gold WABC
267 Tettenhall Road,
Wolverhampton WV6 0DE
01902 461 300
www.classicgolddigital.com
Wolverhampton, Shrewsbury
and Telford

Classic Hits
PO Box 262,
Worcester WR6 5ZE
01905 740 600/ 01432
360 246
info@classicgolddigital.fm
www.classichits.co.uk
Hereford and Worcester

Club Asia
Asia House,
227–247 Gascoigne Road,
Barking,
Essex IG11 7LN
020 8594 6662
info@clubasiaonline.com
www.clubasiaonline.com

Clyde 1 FM
Clydebank Business Park,
Glasgow G81 2RX
0141 565 2200
info@clyde1.com
www.clyde1.com
Glasgow

Clyde 2
Clydebank Business Park,
Glasgow G81 2RX
0141 565 2200
info@clyde2.com

www.clyde2.com
Glasgow

Coast FM
PO Box 963,
Bangor LL57 4ZR
01248 673 272
www.coastfm.co.uk
North Wales Coast

Compass FM
26a Wellowgate,
Grimsby DN32 0RA
01472 346 666
enquiries@compassfm.co.uk
www.compassfm.co.uk
Grimsby

Connect FM
Unit 1, Centre 2000,
Kettering,
Northants NN16 8PU
01536 412 413
info@connectfm.com
www.conectfm.com
Kettering, Corby,
Wellingborough

Cool FM
PO Box 974,
Belfast BT1 1RT
028 9181 7181
music@coolfm.co.uk
www.coolfm.co.uk
Northern Ireland

County Sound Radio 1566 AM
Dolphin House North Street,
Guildford GU1 4AA
01483 300 964
onair@countysound.co.uk
www.ukrd.com

Cross Rhythms City Radio
Stoke on Trent
0870 011 8008
admin@crossrhythms.co.uk
www.crossrhythms.co.uk

CTR 105.6 FM
6 Mill Street,
Maidstone ME15 6XH
01622 662 500
enq@ctrfm.com
www.ctrfm.com

D

Dearne FM
PO Box 458,
Barnsley S71 1YP
01226 321 733
enquiries@dearnefm.co.uk
www.dearnefm.co.uk
Barnsley

Dee 106.3
2 Chantry Court,
Chester CH1 4QN
01244 391 000
info@dee1063.com
www.dee1063.com
Chester

Delta FM
65 Weyhill,
Haslemere,
Surrey GU27 1HN
01428 651 971
studio@deltaradio.co.uk
www.deltaradio.co.uk

Desi Radio
30 Sussex Road,
Southall,
UB2 5 EG
020 8574 9591
info@desiradio.org.uk
www.desiradio.org.uk

Downtown Radio
Newtownards,
Co. Down,
Northern Ireland BT23 4ES
028 9181 5555
programmes@downtown.co.uk
www.downtown.co.uk
Northern Ireland

Dream 100 FM
Northgate House,
St Peter's Street,
Colchester,
Essex CO1 1HT
01206 764 466
info@dream100.com
www.dream100.com
North Essex/South Suffolk

Dream 107.7
Cater House,
High Street,
Chelmsford CM1 1AL
01245 259 400
www.dream107.com
Chelmsford

Dune FM
The Power Station,
Victoria Way,
Southport PR8 1RR
01704 502 500
studio@dunefm.co.uk
www.dunefm.co.uk
Southport

E

Easy Radio London
43–51 Wembley Hill Road,
London HA9 8AU
020 8795 1035
info@easy1035.com
www.easy1035.com

Essex FM
Radio House,
Clifftown Road,
Southend on Sea,
Essex SS1 1SX
01702 333 711
www.musicradio.com
Southend and Chelmsford

F

Fen Radio 107.5 FM
5 Church Mews,

Wisbech,
Cambs PE13 1HL
01945 467 107
studio@fenradio.co.uk
www.sound-wave.co.uk
Fenland

Fire 107.6FM
Quadrant Studios,
Old Christchurch Road,
Bournemouth BH1 2AD
01202 318 100
www.fire1076.com
Bournemouth and Poole

FM 102 – The Bear
The Guard House
Studios,
Banbury Road,
Stratford upon Avon CV37
7HX
01789 262 636
info@thebear.co.uk
www.thebear.co.uk
Stratford upon Avon

FM 103 Horizon
14 Vincent Avenue,
Crownhill,
Milton Keynes MK8 0ZP
01908 269 111
reception@horizon.
musicradio.com
www.musicradio.com

Forest of Dean Radio
Gloucester
01594 820 722
contactus@fodradio.org
www.fodradio.org

Forth AM
Forth House,
Forth Street,
Edinburgh EH1 3LE
0131 556 9255
info@forth2.com
www.forth2.com
Edinburgh

Forth FM
Forth House,
Forth Street,
Edinburgh EH1 3LE
0131 556 9255
info@forthone.com
www.forthone.com
Edinburgh

Fosseway Radio
PO Box 107,
Hinckley,
Leicestershire LE10 1WR
01455 614 151
enquiries@fossewayradio.
co.uk
www.fossewayradio.co.uk
Hinckley/Nuneaton

Fox FM
Brush House,
Pony Road,
Oxford OX4 2XR
01865 871 000
reception@foxfm.co.uk
www.foxfm.co.uk

Fresh Radio
Fresh Radio Ltd,
Firth Mill,
Firth Street,
Skipton,
North Yorkshire BD23 2PT
01756 799 991
info@freshradio.co.uk
www.freshradio.co.uk
Yorkshire Dales with
Skipton

G

Galaxy 102
5th Floor, The Triangle,
Hanging Ditch,
Manchester M4 3TR
0161 279 0300
mail@galaxy102.co.uk
www.galaxy102.co.uk
Manchester

Galaxy 102.2
1 The Square,
111 Broad Street,
Birmingham B15 1AS
0121 695 0000
galaxy1022@galaxy1022.co.uk
www.galaxy1022.co.uk
Birmingham

Galaxy 105
Joseph's Well,
Hannover Walk (off Park Lane),
Leeds LS3 1AB
0113 213 0105
mail@galaxy105.co.uk
www.galaxy105.co.uk
Yorkshire

Galaxy 105–106
Kingfisher Way,
Silverlink Business Park,
Tyne & Wear NE28 9NX
0191 206 8000
www.galaxy1056.co.uk
North-east England

Gemini FM
Hawthorn House,
Exeter Business Park,
Exeter EX1 3QS
01392 444 444
Gemini@geminifm.
musicradio.com
www.musicradio.com

GTFM
Pontypridd
01443 406 111
news@gtfm.fsnet.co.uk
www.gtfm.co.uk

GWR FM and Classic Gold Digital
PO Box 2000,
Woottonbassett SN4 7EX
01793 842 600
reception@musicradio.com
www.musicradio.com

GWR FM (Bristol and Bath)
PO Box 2000,
One Passage Street,
Bristol BS99 7SN
0117 984 3200
reception@gwrfm.
musicradio.com
www.musicradio.com

H

Hallam FM
Radio House,
900 Herries Road,
Sheffield S6 1RH
0114 209 1000
programmes@hallamfm.
co.uk
www.hallamfm.co.uk
South Yorkshire

Heart 106.2
The Chrysalis Building,
Bramley Road,
London W10 6SP
020 7468 1062
www.heart1062.co.uk

Heartland FM
Atholl Curling Rank,
Lower Oakfield Pitlochry,
Perthshire PH16 5HQ
01796 474 040
mailbox@heartlandfm.co.uk
Pitlochry and Aberfeldy

Hertbeat FM
The Pump House,
Knebworth Park,
Hertford SG3 6HQ
01438 810 900
info@hertbeat.com
www.hertbeat.com
Hertfordshire

Home 107.9
The Old Stableblock,
Lockwood Park,
Huddersfield HD1 3UR

01484 321 107
info@home1079.com
www.home1079.com
Huddersfield

I

Imagine FM
Regent House,
Heaton Lane,
Stockport SK4 1BX
0161 609 1400
info@imaginefm.com
www.imaginefm.co.uk
Stockport

Invicta FM
Radio House,
John Wilson Business Park,
Whitstable,
Kent CT5 3QX
01227 772 004
info@invictaradio.co.uk
www.invictafm.com

Isle of Wight Radio
Dodnor Park Newport,
Isle of Wight PO30 5XE
01983 822 557
admin@iwradio.co.uk
www.iwradio.co.uk

Isles FM
PO Box 333,
Stornoway,
Isle of Lewis HS1 2PU
01851 703 333
studio@isles.fm
www.isles.fm
Western Isles

Ivel FM
The Studios,
Middle Street,
Yeovil,
Somerset BA20 1DJ
01747 848 488
all@ivelfm.co.uk
www.ivelfm.co.uk

J

Jazz FM 100.4
8 Exchange Quay,
Manchester M5 3EJ
0161 877 1004
jazzinfo@jazzfm.com
www.jazzfm.com
North West England

Juice 107.2
170 North Street,
Brighton BN1 1FA
01273 386 107
info@juicebrighton.com
www.juicebrighton.com

Juice 107.6
27 Fleet Street,
Liverpool L1 4AR
0151 707 3107
mail@juiceliverpool.com
www.juice.fm
Liverpool

K

KCR FM
The Studios, Cables Retail
Park,
Prescot,
Knowsley L34 5NQ
0151 290 1501
kcrmusic@btconnect.com
www.kcr.fm
Knowsley

Key 103
Castle Quay,
Castlefield,
Manchester M15 4PR
0161 288 5000
www.key103.com
Manchester

Kick FM
The Studios,
42 Bone Lane,
Newbury,

Berkshire RG14 5SD
01635 841 600
mail@kickfm.com
www.kickfm.com

Kingdom FM
Haig House,
Haig Business Park,
Markinch,
Fife KY7 6AQ
01592 753 753
info@kingdomfm.co.uk
www.kingdomfm.co.uk
Fife

Kiss 100
Mappin House,
4 Winsley Street,
London W1W 8HF
020 7975 8100
www.kiss100.com

Kix 96
Watch Close,
Spon Street,
Coventry CV1 3LN
024 7652 5656
www.kix.fm
Coventry

KL.FM 96.7
18 Blackfriars Street,
Kings Lynn,
Norfolk PE30 1NN
01553 772 777
admin@klfm967.co.uk
www.klfm967.co.uk
Kings Lynn and West Norfolk

KMFM Canterbury
9 St George's Place,
Canterbury,
Kent CT1 1UU
01227 475 950
reception@kmfm.co.uk
www.kentonline.co.uk/kmfm

**KMFM for Folkestone and
Dover**

93–95 Sandgate Road,
Folkestone,
Kent CT20 2BQ
01303 220 303
scork@kmfm.co.uk
www.kentonline/kmfm

L

Lakeland Radio
Lakeland Food Park,
Plumgarths,
Crook Road,
Kendal,
Cumbria LA8 8QJ
01539 737 380
info@lakelandradio.co.uk
www.lakelandradio.co.uk
Kendal and Windermere

Lantern FM
2b Lauder Lane,
Roundswell Business Park,
Barnstable EX31 3TA
01271 340 340
www.musicradio.com

LBC 97.3 FM
The Chrysalis Building,
Bramley Road,
London W10 6SP
020 7314 7300
www.lbc.co.uk

LBC News 1152 AM
The Chrysalis Building,
Bramley Road,
London W10 6SP
020 7314 7309
newsroom@lbc.co.uk
www.lbc.co.uk

Leicester Sound
6 Dominus Way,
Meridian Business Park,
Leicester LE19 1RP
0116 256 1300
reception@leicesterfm.
musicradio.com

www.musicradio.com
Leicester

Lincs FM
Witham Park,
Waterside South,
Lincoln LN5 7JN
01522 549 900
enquiries@lincsfm.co.uk
www.lincsfm.co.uk
Lincoln

Lite FM
5 Church Street,
Peterborough PE1 1XB
01733 898 106
www.lite1068.co.uk
Peterborough

Lochbroom FM
Radio House,
Mill Street,
Ullapool,
Ross-shire IV26 2UN
01854 613 131
radio@lochbroomfm.co.uk
www.lochbroomfm.co.uk
Ullapool

London Greek Radio
437 High Road,
London N12 0AP
0871 288 1000
sales@lgr.co.uk
www.lgr.co.uk

London Turkish Radio LTR
185B High Road,
Wood Green,
London N22 6BA
020 8881 0606
info@londontv.org
www.londonturkishradio.org

M

Magic 105.4 FM
Mappin House,
4 Winsley Street,

London W1W 8HF
020 7955 1054
www.magic1054.co.uk

Magic 828
51 Burley Road,
Leeds LS3 1LR
0113 283 5500
www.radioaire.co.uk
Leeds

Magic 999
St Paul's Square,
Preston PR1 1YE
01772 477 700
www.magic999.co.uk
Preston and Blackpool

Magic 1152
Longrigg,
Swalwell,
Newcastle Upon Tyne NE99
1BB
0191 420 0971
www.magic1152.co.uk
Tyne and Wear

Magic 1161 AM
Commercial Road,
Hull HU1 2SG
01482 325 141
reception@magic1161.
co.uk
www.magic1161.co.uk
Humberside

Magic 1170
Radio House,
Yales Crescent,
Thornaby,
Stockton-on-Tees TS17 6AA
www.tfmradio.co.uk
Teesside

Magic 1548
St Johns Beacon,
1 Houghton Street,
Liverpool L1 1RL
0151 472 6800

www.radiocity.co.uk
Liverpool

Magic AM
Radio House,
900 Herries Road,
Sheffield S6 1RH
0114 209 1000
programmes@magicam.co.uk
www.magicam.co.uk
South Yorkshire

Manchester's Magic 1152
Castle Quay,
Castlefield,
Manchester M15 4PR
0161 288 5000
www.key103.co.uk
Manchester

Mansfield 103.2
The Media Suite,
Brunts Business Centre,
Samuel Brunts Way,
Mansfield,
Notts NG18 2AH
01623 646 666
info@mansfield103.co.uk
www.mansfield103.co.uk
Mansfield and District

Medway's KM–FM
Medway House,
Ginsbury Close,
Sir Thomas Longley Road,
Stroud ME2 4DU
01634 227 808
www.kentonline.co.uk/kmfm

Mercia FM
Hertford Place,
Coventry CV1 3TT
024 7686 8200
merciafm@musicradio.com
www.musicradio.com

Mercury FM
The Stanley Centre,
Kelvin Way,

Crawley,
West Sussex RH10 9SE
01293 519 161
studio@musicradio.
com
www.musicradio.com

Metro Radio
Longrigg,
Swalwell,
Newcastle Upon Tyne NE99
1BB
0191 420 0971
www.magic1152.co.uk
Tyne and Wear

MFM 103.4
The Studios,
Mold Road,
Gwersyllt,
Nr Wrexham LL11 4AF
01978 752 202
www.mfmradio.co.uk
Wrexham and Chester

Mid 106
2c Park Avenue,
Burn Road,
Cookstown BT80 8AH
028 8675 8696
www.mid106fm.co.uk
Mid-Ulster

Minister FM
PO Box 123,
Dunnington,
York YO19 5ZX
01904 488 888
general@ministerfm.com
www.ministerfm.com
York

Mix 96
Friars Square Studios,
11 Bourbon Street,
Aylesbury HP20 2PZ
01296 399 396
info@mix96.co.uk
www.mix96.co.uk

Moray Firth Radio (MFR)
Scorguie Place,
Inverness IV3 8UJ
01463 224 433
mfr@mfr.co.uk
www.mfr.co.uk
Inverness

N

NECR
The Shed,
School Road,
Kintore,
Aberdeenshire AB51 0UX
01467 632 909
necrradio102.1fmsales@sup
anet.com
Inverurie

Nevis Radio
Ben Nevis Estate,
Claggan,
Fort William PH33 6PR
01397 700 007
studio@nevisradio.co.uk
www.nevisradio.co.uk
Fort William and parts of
Lochbar

New Style Radio 98.7 FM
Birmingham
0121 456 3826
c_r_t@lineone.net
www.newstyleradio.co.uk

Northants 96
19–21 St Edmunds Road,
Northampton NN1 5DY
01604 795 600
www.musicradio.com
Northampton

North Norfolk Radio
PO Box 962,
The Studio,
Breck Farm,
Stody,
Norfolk NR24 2ER

01263 860 808
info@northnorfolkradio.com
www.northnorfolk.com
North Norfolk

Northsound One
Abbotswell Road,
West Tullos,
Aberdeen AB12 3AJ
01224 337 000
northsound@srh.co.uk
www.northsound1.co.uk
Aberdeen, northeast
Scotland

Northsound Two
Abbotswell Road,
West Tullos,
Aberdeen AB12 3AJ
01224 337 000
northsound@srh.co.uk
www.northsound2.co.uk
Aberdeen, northeast
Scotland

O

Oban FM
132 George Street,
Oban,
Argyll PA34 5NT
01631 570 057
obanfmradio@btconnect.com
www.obanfm.tk
Oban

Ocean FM
Radio House,
Whittle Avenue,
Segensworth,
West Fareham PO15 5SH
01489 589 911
info@oceanfm.co.uk
www.oceanfm.com

Orchard FM
Haygrove House,
Taunton,
Somerset TA3 7BT

01823 338 448
orchardfm@musicradio.com
www.musicradio.com

P

Passion 107.9
270 Woodstock Road,
Oxford OX2 7NW
01235 547 825
info@passion1079.com
www.passion1079.com

Peak 107 FM
Radio House,
Foxwood Road,
Chesterfield S41 9RF
01246 269 107
info@peak107.com
www.peak107.com
Chesterfield/north
Derbyshire/south
Sheffield/Peak District

Pirate FM102
Carn Brea Studios,
Wilson Way,
Redruth,
Cornwall TR15 3XX
01209 314 400
enquiries@piratefm102.co.uk
www.piratefm102.co.uk

Premier Christian Radio
22 Chapter Street,
London SW1P 4NP
020 7316 1300
premier@premier.org.uk
www.premier.org.uk

The Pulse
Pennine House,
Forster Square,
Bradford,
West Yorkshire BD15NE
01274 203 040
general@pulse.co.uk
www.pulse.co.uk

Bradford, Huddersfield
and Halifax

Q

Q97.2 Causeway Coast Radio
24 Cloyfin Road,
Coleraine,
Co. Londonderry BT52 2NU
028 7035 9100
manager@q972.fm
Coleraine

Q101.2 FM West
42A Market Street,
Omagh,
Co. Tyrone BT78 1EH
028 8224 5777
manager@q101west.fm
www.q101west.fm
Omagh and Enniskillen

Q102.9 FM
The Riverview Suite,
87 Rossdowney Road,
Waterside,
Londonderry BT47 5SU
028 7134 4449
manager@q102.fm
www.q102.fm
Londonderry

Q103 FM
Enterprise House,
The Vision Park,
Chivers Way,
Histon,
Cambridgeshire CB4 9WW
01223 235 255
www.musicradio.com

Quaywest FM
Quay West Road,
The Harbour Studios,
The Esplanade,
Watchet,
Somerset TA23 0AJ
01984 634 900

studio@quaywest.fm
www.quaywest.fm

R

Radio Borders
Tweedside Park,
Galashiels TD1 3TD
01896 759 444
programming@radioborders.com
www.radioborders.com
Borders

Radio Ceredigion
Yr Hen Ysgol Gymraeg
Ffordd,
Alexandra,
Aberystwyth,
Ceredigion SY23 1LF
01970 627 999
admin@ceredigionfmf9.co.uk
www.ceredigionradio.co.uk
Ceredigion

Radio City 96.7
St John's Beacon,
1 Houghton Street,
Liverpool L1 1RL
0151 472 6800
www.radiocity.co.uk
Liverpool

Radio Maldwyn
The Studios, The Park,
Newton,
Powys SY16 2NZ
01686 623 555
radio.maldwyn@ukonline.co.uk
www.magic756.net
Montgomeryshire

Radio Pembrokeshire
Unit 14, The Old School Estate,
Station Road,
Narbarth,
Pembrokeshire SA67 7DU
01834 869 384

enquiries@radiopem-
brokeshire.com
www.radiopembrokeshire.
com
Pembrokeshire/West
Carmarthenshire

Radio XL 1296 AM
KMS House,
Bradford Street,
Birmingham B12 OJD
0121 753 5353
arun@radioxl.net
www.radioxl.net

Reading 107 FM
Radio House,
Madejski Stadium,
Reading,
Berkshire RG2 OFN
0118 986 2555
www.reading107fm.com

Real Radio (Scotland)
PO Box 101,
Parkway Court,
Glasgow Business Park,
Glasgow G69 6GA
0141 781 1011
www.realradiofm.com
Central Station

Real Radio (South Wales)
PO Box 6105,
Ty-Nant Court,
Cardiff CF15 8YF
029 2031 5100
info@realradiofm.com
www.realradiofm.com
South Wales

Real Radio (Yorkshire)
Sterling Court,
Capitol Park,
Leeds WF3 1EL
0113 238 1114
info@realradiofm.com
www.realradiofm com
South and West Yorkshire

Red Dragon FM and Capital Gold
Atlantic Wharf,
Cardiff Bay CF10 4DJ
029 2066 2066
mail@reddragonfm.co.uk
www.reddragonfm.co.uk
Cardiff and Newport

Resonance 104.4FM
London
020 7836 3664
info@resonance.com
www.resonancefm.com

Ridings FM
PO Box 333,
Wakefield WF2 7YQ
01924 367 177
enquiries@ridingsfm.co.uk
www.ridingsfm.co.uk
Wakefield

River FM
Stadium House,
Alderstone Road,
Livingstone,
West Lothian EH54 7DN
01506 420 975
office@river-fm.com
www.river-fm.com
West Lothian

RNA FM
Radio North Angus Ltd,
Arbroath Infirmary,
Rosemount Road,
Arbroath,
Angus DD11 2AT
01241 879 660
info@radionorthangus.
co.uk
www.radionorthangus.
co.uk
Arbroath/Carnoustie

Rutland Radio
40 Melton Road,
Oakham,

Rutland LE15 6AY
01572 757 868
enquiries@rutlandradio.co.uk
www.rutlandraio.co.uk
Rutland and Stamford

S

Sabras Radio
Sabras Sound Ltd,
Radio House,
63 Melton Road,
Leicester LE4 6PN
0116 261 0666
enq@sabrasradio.com
www.sabrasradio.com
Leicester

Saga 105.7 FM
3rd Floor, Crown House,
Beaufort Court,
123 Hagley Road,
Edgbaston B16 8LD
0121 452 1057
onair@saga1057fm.co.uk
www.saga1057fm.co.uk
West Midlands

Saga 106.6 FM
Saga Radio House,
Alder Court,
Riverside Business Park,
Nottingham NG2 1RX
0115 986 1066
reception@saga1066fm.co.uk
www.saga1066fm.co.uk
East Midlands

Severn Sound
Bridge Studios,
Eastgate Centre,
Gloucester GL1 1SS
01452 313 200
reception@musicradio.com
www.musicradio.com

SGR Colchester
Abbey Gate Two,
9 Whitewell Road,

Colchester CO2 7DE
01206 575 859
sgrcolchester@musicradio.com
www.musicradio.com
Colchester

SGR FM
Alpha Business Park,
6–12 White House Road,
Ipswich,
Suffolk IP1 5LT
01473 461 000
www.musicradio.com
Suffolk

SIBC
Market Street,
Lerwick,
Shetland ZE1 0JN
01595 695 299
info@sibc.co.uk
www.sibc.co.uk
Shetland

Signal 1
Stoke Road,
Stoke on Trent ST4 2SR
01782 441 300
info@signalradio.com
www.signal1.co.uk
Stoke on Trent

Signal 2
Stoke Road,
Stoke on Trent ST4 2SR
01782 441 300
info@signalradio.com
www.signal1.co.uk
Stoke on Trent

Soul City 107.5
Lambourne House,
7 Western Road,
Romford,
Essex RM1 3LD
0870 607 1075
info@soulcity1075.com
www.soulcity1075.com

Sound Radio
Hackney,
East London
020 8533 8899
info@soundradio.info
www.svt.org.uk

Southern FM
Radio House,
PO Box 2000,
Brighton BN41 2SS
01273 430 111
news@southernfm.co.uk
www.southernfm.com

South Hams Radio
Unit 1G,
South Hams Business Park,
Churchstow,
Kingsbridge,
Devon TQ7 3QH
01548 854 595
southams@musicradio.com

South West Sound
Unit 40, The Loreburne
Centre,
High Street,
Dumfries DG1 2BD
01387 250 999
info@westsound.co.uk
www.westsound.co.uk
Dumfries and Galloway

Spectrum Radio
4 Ingate Place,
Battersea,
London SW8 3NS
020 7627 4433
www.spectrumradio.net

Spire FM
City Hall Studios,
Malthouse Lane,
Salisbury,
Wiltshire SP2 7QQ
01722 416 644
admin@spirefm.co.uk
www.spirefm.co.uk

Spirit FM
9–10 Dukes Court,
Bognor Road,
Chichester PO19 8FX
01243 773 600
info@spiritfm.net
www.spiritfm.net

Splash FM
Guildbourne Centre,
Worthing,
West Sussex BN11 1LZ
01903 233 005
mail@splashfm.com
www.splashfm.com

Star 106.6
The Observatory Shopping
Centre,
Slough SL1 1LH
01753 551 066
onair@star1066.co.uk
www.star1066.co.uk

Star 107
Unit 3, Brunel Mall,
London Road,
Stroud,
Gloucester GL5 2BP
01453 767 369
studio@star1079.co.uk
www.star1079.co.uk

Star 107.2
Bristol Evening Post
Building,
Temple Way,
Bristol BS99 7HD
0117 910 6600
dev@star1072.co.uk
www.star1072.co.uk
Bristol

Star 107.5
Cheltenham Film Studios,
1st Floor, West Suite Arle
Court,
Hatherly Lane,
Cheltenham GL51 6PN

01242 699 555
studio@star1075.co.uk
www.star1075.co.uk

Star 107.7 FM
11 Beaconsfield Road,
Weston-super-Mare BS23
1YE
01934 624 455
www.star1077.co.uk

Star 107.9
Radio House,
Sturton Street,
Cambridge CB1 2QF
01223 722 300
admin@star107.co.uk
www.star1079.co.uk
Cambridge, Ely, New Market

Sun FM
PO Box 1034,
Sunderland SR5 2YL
0191 548 1034
progs@sun-fm.com
www.sun-fm.com
Sunderland

Sunrise FM
Sunrise House,
30 Chapel Street,
Little Germany,
Bradford BD1 5DN
01274 735 043
www.sunriseradio.fm
Bradford

Sunrise Radio
Sunrise House,
Merrick Road,
Southall,
Middlesex UB2 4AU
020 8574 6666
reception@sunriseradio.com
www.sunriseradio.com

Sunshine 855
Unit 11, Burway Trading
Estate,

Ludlow,
Shropshire SY8 1EN
01584 873 795
sunshine855@ukonline.co.uk
www.sunshine855.com
Ludlow

Swan FM
PO Box 1107,
High Wycombe,
Buckinghamshire HP13 6WQ
01494 446 611
sales@swanfm.co.uk
www.swanfm.co.uk

Swansea Sound
PO Box 1170,
Swansea SA4 3AB
01792 511 170
info@swanseasound.co.uk
www.swanseasound.co.uk
Swansea

T

Takeover Radio
Leicester
0116 299 9600
office@takeoverradio.com
www.takeoverradio.com

Tay AM
6 North Isla Street,
Dundee DD3 7JQ
01382 200 800
tayam@radiotay.co.uk
www.radiotay.co.uk
Dundee/Perth

Tay FM
6 North Isla Street,
Dundee DD3 7JQ
01382 200 800
tayam@radiotay.co.uk
www.radiotay.co.uk
Dundee/Perth

Ten 17
Latton Bush Centre,

Southern Way,
Harlow,
Essex CM18 7BB
01279 431 017
www.musicradio.com
East Herts/West Essex

TFM
Radio House,
Yales Crescent,
Thornaby,
Stockton-on-Tees TS17 6AΛ
01642 888 222
www.tfmradio.co.uk
Teesside

Thanet's KM–FM
Imperial House,
2–14 High Street,
Margate,
Kent CT9 1DH
01843 220 222
www.kentonline.co.uk/
kmfm

Time FM
2–6 Basildon Road,
Abbey Wood,
London SE2 0EW
020 8311 3112
www.1068.com

Tower FM
The Mill,
Brownlow Way,
Bolton BL1 2RA
01204 387 000
info@towerfm.co.uk
www.towerfm.co.uk
Bolton and Bury

Trax FM
PO Box 444,
Worksop,
Notts S80 1HR
01909 500 611
enquiries@traxfm.co.uk
www.traxfm.co.uk
Bassetlaw

Trax FM
PO Box 44,
Doncaster DN4 5GW
01302 341 166
events@traxfm.co.uk
www.traxfm.co.uk
Doncaster

Two Lochs Radio
The Harbour Centre,
Pier Road,
Gairloch IV21 2BQ
01445 712 712
info@2ir.co.uk
www.2ir.co.uk
Gairloch and Loch Ewe

V

Valleys Radio
Festival Park Victoria,
Ebbw Vale NP23 8XW
01495 301 116
admin@valleysradio.co.uk
www.valleysradio.co.uk
Heads of South Wales
Valleys

Vibe 101
26 Baldwin Street,
Bristol BS1 1SE
0117 901 0101
info@vibe101.co.uk
www.vibe101.co.uk

Vibe FM
Reflection House,
The Anderson Centre,
Olding Road,
Bury St Edmunds IP33 3TA
01284 715 300
general@vibefm.co.uk
www.vibefm.co.uk
East of England

Virgin 105.8
1 Golden Square,
London W1F 9DJ
020 7434 1215

reception@virginradio.
co.uk
www.virginradio.co.uk

W

Watford's Mercury 96.6
Unit 5, The Metro Centre,
Dwight Road,
Watford WD18 9UP
01923 205 470
www.musicradio.com
St Albans and Watford

Wave 96.5
965 Mowbray Drive,
Blackpool,
Lancashire FY3 7JR
01253 304 965
wave@thewavefm.co.uk
www.wave965.com
Blackpool

Wave 102
8 South Tay Street,
Dundee DD1 1PA
01382 901 102
studio@wave102.co.uk
www.wave102.co.uk
Dundee

Wave 105 FM
5 Manor Court,
Barnes Wallis Road,
Segensworth,
East Fareham,
Hampshire PO15 5TH
01489 481 057
www.wave105.com

Waves Radio Peterhead
7 Blackhouse Circle,
Peterhead AB42
1BW
01779 491 012
waves@radiophd.freeserve.
co.uk
www.wavesfm.co.uk
Peterhead

Wessex FM
Radio House,
Trinity Street,
Dorchester DT1 1DJ
01305 250 333
admin@wessexfm.co.uk
www.wessexfm.co.uk

West FM
Radio House,
54a Holmston Road,
Ayr KA7 3BE
01292 283 662
info@westfm.co.uk
www.westfmonline.com
Ayr

West Kent's KM–FM
1 East Street,
Tonbridge,
Kent TN9 1AR
01732 369 200
tonbridgestudio@kmfm.
co.uk
www.kentonline.co.uk/radio

West Sound AM
Radio House,
54a Holmston Road,
Ayr KA7 3BE
01292 283 662
info@westsound.co.uk
www.west-sound.co.uk
Ayr

Win 107.2
PO Box 107,
The Brooks Shopping
Centre,
Winchester,
Hants SO23 8FT
01962 841 071
www.winfm.co.uk

Wirral's Buzz 97.1
Media House,
Claughton Road,
Birkenhead CH41 6EY
0151 650 1700

www.musicradio.com
Wirral

Wythenshawe FM
Manchester
0161 499 7982
info@wfmradio.org
www.wfmradio.org

Wyvern FM
5–6 Barbourne Terrace,
Worcester WR1 3JZ
01905 612 212
www.musicradio.com
Hereford and Worcester

X

XFM
30 Leicester Square,

London WC2H 7LA
020 7766 6600
info@xfm.co.uk
www.xfm.co.uk

Y

Yorkshire Coast Radio
PO Box 962,
Scarborough,
North Yorkshire YO11 3ZP
01723 581 700
studio@yorkshirecoastradio.
com
www.yorkshirecoastradio.com
Bridlington, Scarborough,
Whitby

Yorkshire Coast Radio
Bridlington's Best,

PO Box 1024,
Bridlington,
East Yorkshire YO15 2YW
01262 404 400
info@yorkshirecoastradio.
com
www.yorkshirecoastradio.
com
Bridlington

Your Radio
Unit 1–3, Pioneer Park
Studios,
80 Castlegreen Street,
Dumbarton
G82 1JB
01389 734 422
info@yourradio.com
www.yourradio.com
Dumbarton

NEWS, SPORT AND PICTURE AGENCIES

Major news, sport and picture agencies

The Press Association
Covers the UK, providing news, sport, business, entertainment, weather, pictures and other services.

292 Vauxhall Bridge Road,
London SW1V 1AE
0870 1203200
http://www.thepagroup.com/

Reuters
Covers the world, providing multi-media services in news, business, sport and financial services.

The Reuters Building,
30 South Colonnade,
Canary Wharf,
London E14 5EP
020 7250 1122
http://about.reuters.com/careers/

Sportsbeat
Covers the world, providing sports news, features and picture coverage.

Runs Europe's largest network of football reporters, covering 300 matches a week.

News Associates
LLP/Sportsbeat,
Tuition House, 2nd Floor, St George's Road, London SW19 4DS 0870 445 0156 Newsdesk@sportsbeat. co.uk
www.newsassociates. co.uk

Regional news, sport and picture agencies

Many regional agencies are members of the Association of Press Agencies (NAPA). NAPA's contact} details are:
0870 609 1935
members@napa.org.uk
http://www.napa.org.uk/html/napalist.asp

Anglia press agency
Covers Essex, Suffolk, and Norfolk.
01284 702421
news@angliapressagency.co.uk
http://www.angliapressagency.co.uk

Bellis news agency
Covers North Wales
0149 254 9503
bellis@aol.com

Bournemouth News and Picture Service
Covers Dorset, and Wiltshire
0120 255 8833
news@bnps.co.uk

Calyx Multimedia
Covers Wiltshire, mid-west England, Oxfordshire and west Berkshire.
0179 352 0131

richard@calyxpix.com
http://www.calyxpix.com

Capital Press Agency
Covers Edinburgh, Lothians and Borders.
0131 652 3999
capitalnews@hemedia.co.uk
http://www.hemedia.co.uk

Cassidy and Leigh
Covers Surrey, Sussex, Hampshire and Kent.
0142 860 7330
denis@cassidyandleigh.com

Caters News Agency
Covers West Midlands and surrounding counties.
0121 616 1100
news@catersnews.com
http://www.catersnews.com

Cavendish Press
Covers Greater Manchester and the North West.
0161 237 1066
newsdesk@cavendish-press.co.uk
http://www.cavendish-press.co.uk

Centre Press Agency
Covers central and southern Scotland.
0141 774 6969
centrenews@hemedia.co.uk
http://www.hemedia.co.uk

CopyLine Scotland
Covers the Highlands of Scotland.
0146 371 0695
copylinescotland@aol.com

Deadline Press and Picture Agency
Covers Scotland.
0131 561 2233
info@deadlinescotland.co.uk

Dragon News and Picture Agency
Covers South and West Wales.
0179 246 4800
mall@dragon-pictures.com
http://www.dragon-pictures.com

Ferrari Press Agency
Covers Kent, South London, Essex and East Sussex.
0132 262 8444
news@ferraripress.com
http://www.ferraripress.com

Hayters Teamwork
Covers London, the South East the North East and Yorkshire.
0208 808 3300
sport@haytersteamwork.com
http://www.haytersteamwork.com

IPS Photo Agency
Agents cover Japan, Italy, Germany, Spain, France and Scandinavia.
0208 855 1008
info@ips-net.co.uk

John Connor Press Associates
Covers East and West Sussex.
0127 348 6851
news@jcpa.co.uk

KNS News
Covers East Anglia.
01603 765188
info@knsnews.co.uk
http://www.knsnews.co.uk

Lappas of Exeter
Covers Devon, Cornwall and Somerset.
0139 244 6670
lappas@freeuk.com
http://www.richardlappas.com

London Media Press
Covers London.
0207 613 2548
news@london-media.co.uk
http://www.london-media.co.uk

M & Y News Agency
Covers Hampshire, West Sussex and the Isle of Wight.
0239 282 0311
mynews@dircon.co.uk

Mason's News Service
Covers Cambridgeshire, Suffolk, Northamptonshire, south Lincolnshire, Bedfordshire and Hertfordshire.
01480 302302
newsdesk@masons-news.co.uk

Mercury Press Agency
Covers Merseyside, Lancashire and parts of North Wales.
0151 709 6707
reporters@mercurypress.co.uk
http://www.mercurypress.co.uk

National News Press Agency
Covers London and the surrounding counties.
0207 684 3000
news@nationalnews.co.uk
http://www.pressnet.co.uk

Newscast
London and New York, with affiliates in Dublin, Sydney, Paris and Hong Kong, and a global network of photographers.
020 8886 5895
contact@newscast.co.uk
www.newscast.co.uk

Newsflash Press Agency
Covers Central Scotland, Perthshire, Fife, Edinburgh and the Borders.
0131 226 5858
news@nflash.co.uk
http://www.newsflashscotland.com

North News and Pictures
Covers the North East of England, Cumbria and the Borders.
0191 233 0223
news@northnews.co.uk

Northscot Press Agency
Covers Grampian and the Highlands.
0122 421 2141
northnews@hemedia.co.uk
http://www.hemedia.co.uk

Pacemaker Press International
Covers Northern Ireland.
0289 066 3191
david@pacemakerpressintl.com
http://www.pacemakerpressintl.com

Press Team Scotland
Covers Lanarkshire, and Glasgow
0123 644 0077
mail@presseye.com
http://www.presseye.com

Raymonds Press Agency
Covers the East Midlands, Derby, Nottingham, Lincoln, Leicester and the surrounding areas.
0133 234 0404
news@raymondspress.com

Ross Parry Picture Agency
Covers Yorkshire and Humberside.
0113 236 1842
picturedesk@rossparry.co.uk

Solent News and Photo Agency
Covers Hampshire, the Isle of Wight and Wiltshire.
0238 045 8800
news@solentnews.biz

Somerset Photo News
Covers Somerset, the South West, the UK and abroad.
0182 328 2053
somersetphotonews@bolt-blue.com

South Beds News Agency
Covers Hertfordshire, Bedfordshire and Buckinghamshire, Northamptonshire.
0158 257 2222
southbedsnews@btconnect.com

South West News Service
Covers the South West of England.
0117 906 6500

news@swns.com
http://www.swns.com

Space Press News and Pictures
Covers Alderley Edge, Wilmslow, Knutsford, Macclesfield, Nantwich, Cheshire and the surrounding areas.
0147 533403
scoop2001@aol.com

Specialist News Service
Covers the UK.
020 7831 3267
desk@snsnews.co.uk
http://www.specialistnews.co.uk

Sports Photo / Allstar Picture Library
Covers the world.
0172 336 7264
stewart@sportsphoto.co.uk
http://www.allstarpl.com

The 24/7 Media
Covers Birmingham and the West Midlands.
0121 753 1329

Tim Wood Agency
Covers London. Law courts and other courts
0207 248 6858

Tony Scase News Service
Covers East Anglia.
0148 560 0650
news@scase.co.uk
http://www.scase.co.uk

Wales News and Picture Service
Covers Wales.
0292 066 6366

news@walesnews.com
http://www.walesnews com

Warwickshire News and Picture Agency
Covers Warwickshire, the West Midlands, and the Midlands.
0192 642 4181

btracey@wnpa.freeserve.co.uk
barrie@traceynews.co.uk

Westcoast News
Covers Devon, Cornwall and west Somerset.
0159 876 3296
westcoast.news@dial.pipex.com

WireImage UK
Covers London, and worldwide coverage of entertainment, news and sport.
0207 659 2811
jc@wireimage.com
http://www.wireimage.com

ONLINE PUBLISHERS

This list is of major online publishers. These publishers all have websites, and often have their own teams of journalists. Many are members of the UK Association of Online Publishers (http://www.ukaop.org.uk/).

The vast majority of online publishers are predominantly involved in other media; that is they also have newspaper, magazine or broadcast outlets, and you will find them listed under the category that is most relevant to them. If you can't find a publisher or broadcaster listed here, look for them in the section that relates to their main media interest.

Major online publishers

Ananova
(part of the Orange network)
Ananova Ltd,
PO Box 36,
Leeds LS11 9YJ
www.ananova.com

AOL (UK) Limited
80 Hammersmith Road,
London W14 8UD
020 7348 8000
http://www.aol.co.uk/
(Note: This web address is
to the publicly accessible
service; AOL subscribers can
access www.aol.com.)

**Associated Northcliffe
Digital**
Northcliffe House,
2 Derry Street,
London, W8 5TT

020 7938 6000
Operates the following
websites:
Daily Mail:
www.dailymail.co.uk
Mail on Sunday:
www.mailonsunday.co.uk
This is London
www.thisislondon.
co.uk
This is Money:
www.thisismoney.co.uk
This is Travel:
www.thisistravel.co.uk

BBC
Main BBC addresses:

Television Centre,
Wood Lane,
London,
W12 7RJ

BBC White City,
201 Wood Lane,
London W12 7TS

Broadcasting House,
Portland Place,
London
W1A 1AA
www.bbc.co.uk
020 8743 8000

BBC Television
Television Centre
020 8743 8000
General enquiries:
info@bbc.co.uk
www.bbc.co.uk/television

BBC Recruitment
PO Box 48305,
London W12 6YE
recruitment@bbc.co.uk

Jobs web area:
http://www.bbc.co.uk/jobs/
gettingintobbc/index.shtml
Work experience web area:
http://www.bbc.co.uk/jobs/
workexperience/journalism.
shtml

BSkyB
Athena Court
Grant Way,
Isleworth
Middlesex TW7 5QD
Recruitment team at
queries@bskyb.com
http://jobs.sky.com/

Channel 4
Channel 4 Television
124 Horseferry Road.
London SW1P 2TX
020 7396 4444
http://www.channel4.com
Jobs microsite:
http://www.channel4.com/le
arning/microsites/W/wtc4/

Condé Nast Interactive
Vogue House,
Hanover Square,
London W1S 1JU
020 7499 9080
http://www.condenast.co.uk

**Operates the following
websites;**
Vogue: www.Vogue.com
Glamour: www.Glamour.com
GQ: www.GQ media pack
GQ Style: www.GQStyle.com
CN Traveller:
www.CNTraveller.com
Easy Living:
www.EasyLivingMagazine.com
Brides Magazine:
www.BridesMagazine.co.uk

Dennis Interactive
Dennis Publishing Ltd,

30 Cleveland Street,
London W1T 4JD
020 7907 6000
Fax: 020 7907 6020

**Operates the following
websites:**
www.inside-edge-mag.co.uk/
www.pokerplayermagazine.
co.uk/
www.totalgambler.com/
www.bizarremag.com/
http://www.forteantimes.
com/
www.maxim-magazine.co.uk/
www.mensfitnessmagazine.
co.uk
www.viz.co.uk/
www.autoexpress.co.uk/
www.evo.co.uk
www.computerbuyer.co.uk
www.computershopper.co.uk
www.custompc.co.uk
www.itpro.co.uk
www.macuser.co.uk
www.micromart.co.
www.pcpro.co.uk

The Economist Group
Human Resources
Executive,
26 Red Lion Square,
London WC1R 4HQ
020 7576 8112
Fax: 020 7576 8482
Publishes
www.economist.com/Email:
recruitmentfive@economist.
com
www.economistgroup.com

Emap
Emap has many websites
associated with its maga-
zines. For contact details for
particular websltes, go to:
www.emap.com/Contact_
Brand.asp
Websites include

www.zooweekly.co.uk
www.graziamagazine.co.uk
www.fhm.com
www.closermag.co.uk
www.empireonline.com
www.maxpower.co.uk
www.anglingtimes.co.uk
www.todaysgolfer.co.uk

Financial Times
1 Southward Bridge,
London SE1 9H2
0207 873 3000
www.ft.com

The Future Network
Beauford Court,
30 Monmouth Street,
Bath BA1 2BW
01225 442244

London office:
2 Balcombe Street,
London NW1 6NW
020 7042 4000
The group has over 40
websites that accompany its
magazines. These include:
www.mbuk.com
www.netmag.co.uk/
www.pcanswers.co.uk/
www.classicrockmagazine.com/

Guardian Unlimited
The online version of *The
Guardian* newspaper.
3–7 Ray Street,
London EC1R 3DR
0207 278 2332
www.guardian.co.uk

Haymarket Publishing
Haymarket is principally a
magazine publisher, but has a
wide range of websites to
support those magazines,
and others that aggregate
content from more than one
magazine.

Haymarket Business
Publications Ltd,
174 Hammersmith Road,
London W6 7JP
020 8267 5000

Websites include:
Autosport:
www.autosport.com
Brand Republic:
www.brandrepublic.com
Classic & Sports Car:
www.classicandsportingcar.
com
Horticulture Week:
www.hortweek.com
Management Today:
www.clickmt.com
Practical Caravan:
www.practicalcaravan.com
PrintWeek:
www.printweek.com
Regeneration & Renewal:
www.regen.net
Revolution:
www.revolutionmagazine.
com
Stuff:
www.stuffmag.co.uk
WhatCar?:
www.whatcar.com
Young People Now:
www.ypnmagazine.com

IPC Media
King's Reach Tower,
Stamford Street,
London SE1 9LS
0870 4445000

IPC has a range of over 70
websites that support its
magazines. These include:
Country Life:
www.countrylife.co.uk

Decanter:
www.decanter.com
Horse and Hound:
www.horseandhound.com
NME:
www.nme.com
Web User:
www.webuser.co.uk

**The National Magazine
Company**
National Magazine House,
72 Broadwick Street,
London W1F 9EP
020 7439 5000
www.natmags.co.uk

Websites include:
Cosmopolitan:
www.cosmipolitan.co.uk
Company:
www.company.co.uk
Country Living:
www.countryliving.co.uk
Esquire:
www.esquire.co.uk
Good Housekeeping:
www.goodhousekeeping.
co.uk
Men's Health:
www.menshealth.co.uk
Prima:
www.primamagazine.co.uk
She:
www.shemagazine.co.uk

News International
1 Virginia Street,
London E98 1SN
020 7782 4000

News International newspapers – the *Sun*, the *News of
the World,* and *The Times*
and *The Sunday Times*

combined – have their own
websites:
www.thesun.co.uk
www.newsoftheworld.co.uk
www.timesonline.co.uk

Reuters
The Reuters Building,
30 South Colonnade,
Canary Wharf,
London E14 5EP
020 7250 1122
http://about.reuters.com/
careers/

TEAMtalk
TEAMtalk, based in Leeds,
runs sports websites,
including www.sportinglife.
com (the companion
site to the *Sporting Life*
newspaper),

Websites include:
teamtalk.com
sportal.com
bettingzone.co.uk
football365.com
golf365.com.

3rd Floor, Apsley House,
78 Wellington Street,
Leeds LS1 2EQ
0113 399 2277
www.teamtalk.com

Telegraph.co.uk
The online version of the
Daily Telegraph.
Telegraph Group Limited,
1 Canada Square,
Canary Wharf,
London E14 5DT
0207 538 5000
www.telegraph.co.uk

USEFUL REFERENCE SOURCES

These reference books, magazines and websites will help you get to know more about journalism, and will help in finding potential sources of work experience, training and jobs.

BENNS Media
Comprehensive media reference book.
Miller Freeman UK Ltd,
Riverbank House,
Angel Lane,
Tonbridge,
Kent TN9 1SE
01732 362666
Fax: 01732 367301

Broadcast
Weekly trade magazine for TV and radio.

www.broadcastnow.co.uk

Holdthefrontpage
Website serving the provincial press.

www.holdthefrontpage.co.uk

Media Guardian
The Guardian newspaper's online media coverage.

http://media.guardian.co.uk/

Media Week
Weekly magazine serving the media.

www.mediaweek.co.uk

New Media Age
Magazine serving the online media industry.

www.nma.co.uk/

UK Press Gazette
Weekly magazine serving national and local newspapers.

www.pressgazette.co.uk

Willings Press Guide
Waymaker Ltd,
Chess House,
34 Germain Street,
Chesham HP5 1SJ
0870 7360010
Fax: 0870 7360011

GLOSSARY

Journalism has its jargon, like any other trade. Here are translations for the bits of jargon and technical terms I've felt it necessary to include in this book.

Back bench – the area in the newspaper newsroom where the editor and senior journalistic sit when working on the edition, the newspaper that is to be printed within a few hours.

Banner ads – the majority of advertisements which appear on websites are banner ads. They are a standard size and so can be slotted into standard-sized spaces built into any website. Adverts online are usually clickable, which means the surfer can click on them with the cursor, and bring up further information.

Bi-media – the practice, especially at the BBC, of requiring reporters and specialists to report on both radio and TV. Previously, staffs on radio and TV would mirror reach other.

Block release – the practice of allowing trainees to attend college for periods in order to gain their qualifications in government, law and shorthand. (See the Courses section of this book for full details of different training arrangements.)

Blog – short for web log. An online diary or series of pieces of news or comment, regularly updated.

Business-to-business magazines – magazines aimed at particular trades, professions or interest groups, such as general practitioners, mortgage brokers and nursery school teachers. Often referred to as B2B Magazines.

By-line – the author's name on a published article.

Channel – on a website, a section covering a particular subject. So named to indicate online journalism's affinity with broadcast media.

Citizen journalist – the unqualified, amateur writer of comment or news pieces, often in a blog or on a website. Some citizen journalists are very good but most are unreadable and unreliable.

Consumer magazines – magazines which are directed at the general reader and sold on newsstands and through subscription, as opposed to trade titles, which are aimed at a particular trade, business or profession and are often only sold via subscription and other non-newsstand methods.

Contacts book – a record of all those individuals who may be able to help a journalist on a story. This will include official spokesmen and women, experts in particular fields, the famous or prominent, and those who are friendly to the press. Once a paper record, often now held on an electronic organiser or in a file on a computer. Many journalists record the names and contact details of everyone they speak to in case they can be of help in the future, cross-referencing these entries with others on the contact's interests, expertise, and where they live.

Content management system – a system used to manage the content of a website. It allows a content creator, who may not know Hypertext Mark-up Language (HTML), to manage the creation, modification and removal of content from a website.

Content providers – organisations which provide material which is published on a website. Providers can range from news agencies, who supply news and other information for a fee, and commercial partners, who may supply content for free as part of a commercial contract.

Convergence – the tendency for media companies formerly strong in just one medium to use techniques from a range of media – e.g. a television station having a website, a local newspaper group starting a radio station. Most noticeable on the web, where methods of story telling from different media – print reports, audio reports and video coverage – are all used.

Copytakers – essentially typists who take down a report over the phone from a journalist at an event where time is of the essence, typically a sports game or a court case.

Correspondent – a correspondent is one up from a reporter and one down from an editor. So, for instance, the hierachy in a political team might run: Political Reporter, Political Correspondent, Political Editor.

Credit – an acknowledgement of the name of the reporter who originated a story or article. Often, copy filed by agencies has the original by-line removed in favour of that of a staff reporter on the newspaper that receives it and who may add information to it.

Customer magazines – magazines given to customers by a company as a marketing device and as a reward for loyalty to the brand.

Cuttings – copies of items a newspaper or magazine journalist has had published. In a cuttings book they can be used to give a representative sample of a person's best work.

When working to pass the NCTJ's National Certificate Examination, cuttings representing work carried out in a range of categories are put in a binder for marking by examiners.

Direct entry – a direct entry trainee obtains a job before taking NCTJ training. Their employer pays them while they undertake their training.

Distance learning – studying through a correspondence course, and hence avoiding attending a college or university.

Down table – on a sub-editor's desk, there has traditionally been one end where the chief sub and his or her deputy sits. Close to them sit the senior subs. More junior sub and freelances will sit at the far end. Today the rigid seating structure is often not maintained, but the distinction between up and down table subs is. Every young sub's ambition is to move up the table.

Feature – an article in a newspaper or magazine that is not concerned with breaking news, but rather covers areas of interest where the news imperative is not so strong. Interviews are features, so are items about interests such as travel or fashion.

Flat plans – the plans drawn up once the number of pages is known and the advertisements have been placed. The flat plan is a sort of map of the publication, and is referred to throughout the production process.

Fleet Street – Once, almost all national newspapers had offices in London's Fleet Street, or in the narrow streets leading off it. In the 1980s and 1990s newspapers relocated, and are now based in Canary Wharf, Kensington, Victoria, Wapping and various other locations.

Forums – online debating chambers. Some are monitored, which means a person reads comments submitted for posting on the site. Others are unmoderated, which means anything submitted immediately appears on screen.

HTML – stands for Hypertext Mark-up Language, the code which is added to text in order for it to appear as intended on a website with, among other things, the correct type styles and sizes. HTML is the electronic equivalent of the pencilled instructions to printers which sub-editors put on copy in the days when type had to be set in metal to create a page which could be printed.

ISPs – Internet Service Providers. To go online you need a contract with a company that will allow you access to the internet. Companies such as Orange, AOL and Tiscali charge a monthly fee to provide this access.

Lobby – as in lobby correspondent. The lobby is the body of political reporters based in Westminster who have passes to the Houses of Parliament and, usually, an office within its walls. As a member of the lobby they are entitled to attend official briefings by the prime minister's official spokesman and others.

Night editor – in charge of the newspaper once the overall editor has left, usually after agreeing content for the first edition. Responsible for ensuring the paper is updated for subsequent editions, that any necessary improvements and essential corrections are made as they come to light.

Off diary – if a story is known about in advance, such as a court appearance or an annual general meeting, it can be added to a forward-planning diary, so that a publication, broadcaster or website can make sure it is covered. An off-diary story is something that cannot be predicted. One benchmark by which reporters are measured is how many off-diary stories they bring in. Ideally, such stories should be exclusive – things which no one else knows about. By running as many exclusives as possible, a news operation hopes to show that it offers a unique, and uniquely informative, service.

PA – The Press Association, a British-based news agency which supplies reports to a wide range of newspapers, magazines, TV, radio and online customers.

Package – on TV and radio, news and feature items may, if time allows, be enhanced with interviews, case studies and appropriate pictures (on TV) and sounds (on radio). Bringing all these elements together and crafting them into a report is known as developing a package.

Photo-op (or **photo-opportunity**) – a pre-arranged opportunity for a famous or otherwise newsworthy person, or an event, to be photographed.

Photoshop – a computer software programme which enables the manipulation of pictures and other graphical elements.

Podcasts – a word created by combining iPod and broadcast. A method of publishing audio files to the internet, allowing users to subscribe to a feed and receive new files automatically by subscription, usually for free.

Postgraduates – in journalistic terms, those who have completed a degree, which might or might not be in journalism, and who have gone on to obtain a postgraduate qualification in journalism prior to entering the profession.

Pre-entry – pre-entry students complete their NCTJ preliminary certificate examinations at a university or other institution before finding a job in the industry. Once they have a job, have passed their shorthand examination and completed between 18 months and two years at work, they are likely to be ready to take the NCTJ's National Certificate Examination.

Production editor – a person who is responsible for the collation of a publication ready for printing. He or she must see that all pages are ready on time, and are supplied to the printer in a state that means they can be printed. He or she also liaises with printers to ensure that the publication is printed at the required standard and in the agreed time frame.

Repro house – a company (or department within a large publisher's operation) to which pages are sent and made ready for printing.

Re-purposed – material that was created originally for one medium but which is later converted – re-purposed – for use in another. So, a newspaper's print edition content can be re-used on its website. This process may be performed automatically, by computer, or human intervention may be needed. For instance, html coding may need to be added so that it can be re-used online. Web material can also be re-purposed for use in mobile phone alerts.

RSS feeds – standing for either Rich Site Summary or Really Simple Syndication. A method of syndicating website content. A website can allow other sites to publish some of its content by creating an RSS document. A web publisher can post a link to the RSS feed so users can read the distributed content on his or her site. Individuals can subscribe to RSS feeds, enabling them to receive content without visiting the website that originated it.

Slide show – one of the methods of telling a picture-led story effectively online is to create a series of screens, with typically one picture and a caption on each screen. To move from one to the next chronologically, a reader clicks on a link at the bottom of each page.

Standfirst – display text that acts as an additional opportunity to 'sell' an article after the headline and **strap lines** (*see below*). The standfirst tells the reader more about the article, and often includes the by-line of the writer. It stands first, before the body of the copy.

Strap line – type that is smaller than a main headline but larger than body type and which offers an additional opportunity to 'sell' an article to the reader. Strap lines often run right across a page.

Style – the rules and conventions a publication has put in place which should be followed when copy is subbed and presented in the publication. The style guide will cover alternative spellings, rules on when to use initial capital letters, how to present dates and figures, and many other rules. Several publications, including *The Guardian*, the *Economist* and *The Times*, have either published their style guides or make them available on their websites. On publications which do not have their own style guides, the *Oxford Dictionary for Writers and Editors*, is often followed.

Subbing – the checking of material prior to publication. Sub-editors check for accuracy, spelling, grammar, sense and legality. They cut material to fit an allotted space, and write headlines, captions and any other items designed to enhance the display of the material.

Sub-editor – sub-editors do the **subbing**, which involves taking material and preparing it for publication. Sub-editors check for accuracy, spelling, grammar, sense and legality. They cut material to fit an allotted space, and write headlines, captions and any other items designed to enhance the display of the material.

Trade magazines – magazines aimed at the members of a trade, profession or craft. They are often sold through subscription, or given to members of a professional organisation, rather than being available at newsstands.

Vodcasts – a video podcast (*see also* **podcast**). Vodcasts are sound and moving image packages that can be watched on a computer or mobile application. They can be delivered via **RSS** feeds.

INDEX

Entries in *italics* denote publications, broadcast programmes and websites.